1-2 PETER
1-3 JOHN, JUDE

1–2 PETER
1–3 JOHN, JUDE

A Commentary for Bible Students

DAVID A. CASE AND DAVID W. HOLDREN

© 2006 by Wesleyan Publishing House. All rights reserved.
Published by Wesleyan Publishing House
Indianapolis, Indiana 46250
Printed in the United States of America

ISBN-10: 0-89827-306-4
ISBN-13: 978-0-89827-306-9

WESLEYAN BIBLE COMMENTARY SERIES

GENERAL PUBLISHER
Donald D. Cady

EXECUTIVE EDITOR
David W. Holdren, D.D., S.T.D.

EDITORIAL ADVISORY COMMITTEE

Joseph D. Allison, M.Div.
Publishing Manager
Evangel Publishing House

Ray E. Barnwell
District Superintendent, Illinois
The Wesleyan Church

Barry L. Callen, M.Div., M.Th., D.Rel.
University Professor of Christian
Studies
Anderson University

Ray Easley, M.Div., Ed.D.
Vice President of Academic Affairs
Wesley Biblical Seminary

Maj. Dorothy Hitzka
National Consultant for Christian
Education
The Salvation Army

Arthur Kelly
Coordinator of Christian Education and
Congregational Life
Church of God Ministries

Stephen J. Lennox, Ph.D.
Professor of Bible and Chair, Division
of Religion and Philosophy
Indiana Wesleyan University

Bonnie J. Perry
Director
Beacon Hill Press of Kansas City

Dan Tipton, D.Min.
General Superintendent (Retired)
Churches of Christ in Christian Union

John Van Valin
Free Methodist Pastor
Indianapolis, Indiana

EDITORS
Lawrence W. Wilson, M.Div.
Managing Editor

Stephen J. Lennox, Ph.D.
Theological Editor

Darlene Teague, M.Div.
Senior Editor

CONTENTS

EXECUTIVE EDITOR'S PREFACE

Life change. That, we believe, is the goal of God's written revelation. God has given His written Word so that we might know Him and become like Him—holy, as He is holy.

Life change is also the goal of this book, a volume in the Wesleyan Bible Commentary Series. This series has been created with the primary aim of promoting life change in believers by applying God's authoritative truth in relevant, practical ways. This commentary will impact Bible students with fresh insight into God's unchanging Word. Read it with your Bible in hand.

A second purpose of this series is to assist laypersons and pastors in their teaching ministries. Anyone called to assist others in Christian growth and service will appreciate the practical nature of these commentaries. Writers were selected based on their ability to soundly interpret God's Word and apply that unchanging truth in fresh, practical ways. Each biblical book is explained paragraph by paragraph, giving the reader both the big picture and sufficient detail to understand the meaning of significant words and phrases. Their results of scholarly research are presented in enough detail to clarify, for example, the meaning of important Greek or Hebrew words, but not in such a way that readers are overwhelmed. This series will be an invaluable tool for preaching, lesson preparation, and personal or group Bible study.

The third aim of this series is to present a Wesleyan-Arminian interpretation of Scripture in a clear and compelling fashion. Toward that end, the series has been developed with the cooperative effort of scholars, pastors, and church leaders in the Wesleyan, Nazarene, Free Methodist, Salvation Army, Church of God (Anderson), Churches of Christ in Christian Union, Brethren in Christ, and United Methodist denominations. These volumes present reliable interpretation of biblical texts in the

11

tradition of John Wesley, Adam Clarke, and other renowned interpreters.

Throughout the production of this series, authors and editors have approached each Bible passage with this question in mind: How will my life change when I fully understand and apply this scripture?

Let that question be foremost in your mind also, as God speaks again through His Word.

DAVID W. HOLDREN

1 PETER

INTRODUCTION TO 1 PETER

We could begin our study of Peter's first letter immediately with the exposition of 1:1. On the other hand, there are several items of interest under the heading of "introductory matters" that should be examined at the outset of our study. First, there are general introduction issues. General issues deal with matters that apply to every study of the Bible: the concept of divine inspiration, the issue of inspiration, questions of biblical geography, a chronology of biblical times, archaeology, and different versions and texts of the Bible, just to name a few examples. We examine these issues and arrive at conclusions that continue in our thinking throughout any biblical study. Once these issues have been carefully examined, the results of that investigation continue with every study of God's Word.[1]

There is a second type of introduction that is our primary concern: special introduction. Every book of the Bible has its own peculiar number of specific issues that should be examined prior to the actual study of the text. Some of the issues, like authorship, will be included for every book. In addition, a book has its own set of issues that apply only to that book. For our study of 1 Peter, we will include authorship, recipients of the letter, date and purpose of writing, major themes (including holiness), and several other items of interest.

AUTHORSHIP

The question of authorship is not a significant issue for some New Testament books. Many of Paul's epistles, for instance, have received nearly unanimous recognition by scholars as having been written by the apostle. On the other hand, some New Testament books have occasioned considerable debate as to who wrote the material. First Peter falls into this second category. There are three possibilities concerning the authorship of 1 Peter.

The first is that it was written by Peter, the disciple of Jesus and leader of the early Church mentioned in the book of Acts. The second possibility is that 1 Peter was composed by Silas, writing on behalf of Peter or in memory of Peter's teaching. The third option is that the book was written by an unknown individual who attached Peter's name to the writing in hopes of gaining apostolic authority.

The first view is the traditional one, held by the early Church and by most conservative scholars: Peter is the author, and there is considerable evidence for that view. The author explicitly identifies himself as Peter (1:1). Further, he identifies himself as "a witness of Christ's sufferings" (5:1), which is consistent with what is said of Peter elsewhere in the New Testament (Luke 24:33–34). The author exhibits knowledge of and consistently appeals to the Old Testament and Old Testament characters (Abraham, Sarah, Noah and his family). The theology of 1 Peter reflects early Christian thought. The ideas and images are associated with Peter in the Gospels and the book of Acts. The basic character of church order presupposed in this letter (5:1–5a) and its concept of spiritual gifts (4:10–11) point to an early date of composition, which would be true if Peter is the author.

It is also known that Peter had early contact with Jewish pilgrims from Pontus, Cappadocia, and Asia at the Pentecost festival in Jerusalem (Acts 2:9–11). Post-New Testament tradition unanimously attests Peter's presence and death in Rome, the likely location to which "Babylon" (5:13) refers. The reference to "my son Mark" (5:13) indicates an intimate relationship (Acts 12:1–17). Finally, the early acceptance of the letter as written by Peter[2]—from the Church Father Irenaeus onward—and its early and unchallenged reception into the Canon testify to the assumption of its apostolic authenticity.[3]

The second view, proposing that Silas is the author of 1 Peter, is based on an interpretation of 1 Peter 5:12, "with the help of Silas . . . I have written to you." This view interprets the phrase **with the help of** to mean that Silas did the actual writing. Two possible reasons for Silas actually writing the letter are offered. Peter may have been unable to compose the letter because of his imprisonment in Rome. That seems improbable because it would require a different understanding of imprisonment than that experienced by Paul, for instance.

A second reason offered for Silas composing the letter is that Peter may have been incapable of writing, so Silas undertook the task of recording the thoughts and teaching of Peter.[4]

So the question is what does "with the help of Silas" mean? Reference is often made to Acts 4:13, where Peter and John are described as "unschooled, ordinary men" as proof that Peter could not have written this letter. The implication is that the term *unschooled* means nearly illiterate. Yet another interpretation of the Acts reference is that these two men were unschooled compared to the standard education for those who were to become the "rulers, elders and teachers of the law" (Acts 4:5). Surely this does not mean that Peter was incapable of writing.

The third view of authorship proposes that the epistle was written by an unknown writer who attached Peter's name to the letter to give it apostolic authority.[5] The main argument for this view is based on the notion that the quality of writing contained in the letter is too elegant for a Galilean fisherman. The polished style, the classical vocabulary, and quality composition in the Greek language make this epistle one of the most refined writings in the New Testament. Support for this theory of authorship is taken from the reference in Acts 4:13 to Peter being "unschooled." As additional evidence, it is noted that the numerous Old Testament quotations in 1 Peter are cited from the Greek Septuagint, not the Hebrew version of the Old Testament with which Peter would have been acquainted. Also, this letter contains little mention of Jesus' teaching and virtually nothing of Jesus' life and ministry, a fact difficult to reconcile with authorship by one of Jesus' closest disciples. Some who deny that Peter is the author of this letter would propose that there is no historical evidence that Peter himself evangelized in Asia Minor; 1 Peter contains no mention of any personal contact between Peter and those addressed in this letter. Finally, the author of this letter presents himself as "a fellow elder" (5:1), a unique designation never used by or attributed to Peter elsewhere in the New Testament.

The arguments against Peter as the author do not appear to be of sufficient strength to cause the rejection of the traditional view, which is the position taken in this commentary.

RECIPIENTS OF THE LETTER

Peter wrote his letter to a specific group of individuals. He identifies them geographically, but not by name. We are left to piece together fragments of evidence to further identify them. There are three possibilities. First, the recipients might have been converts to the Christian faith from Judaism. This was the view of the early Church Fathers. Second, the recipients might have been Gentile converts to Christianity. Third, the recipients might have included both Jews and Gentiles who had become Christians.

We do know that the recipients were living in a wide geographical area identified as "Pontus, Galatia, Cappadocia, Asia and Bithynia" (1:1). This area corresponds to modern-day Turkey. The recipients are further identified by two key terms: *strangers* and *scattered*. Those terms might be applied to any Christian living on earth but having citizenship in heaven. Yet it could be that the Christians who received this letter were not originally from Asia Minor, but were from Jerusalem and had been dispersed there to avoid persecution. With that in mind, some have referred to 1 Peter as a "dispersion letter." The prophet Jeremiah wrote such a letter to the exiles in Babylon (Jer. 29:1–23). The book of James is a New Testament example of a dispersion letter, written to "the twelve tribes scattered among the nations" (1:1). It is possible that Peter addressed Jewish converts who were forced to leave their homeland, and at the time of his letter, were living in Asia Minor. The letter's references to various Old Testament characters, the Flood, and disobedient angels lend support to this view.

Other internal evidence supports the idea that the letter was addressed to Gentile converts to Christianity. Their former way of life is referred to as living in ignorance (1:14), exhibiting pagan characteristics (4:3), and "the empty way of life handed down to you from your forefathers" (1:18). It is difficult to envision Peter referring to the Jewish people in this manner.

The best conclusion is that the audience was mixed, including both believers who had Jewish roots and those who had Gentile backgrounds. "They formed a dispersed alien minority within a larger, generally hostile society. They were presumed to have been exposed to hostility, verbal abuse, and degrading shaming from ignorant (2:15) native outsiders, a harassment that had led to their innocent suffering."[6]

DATE

Peter's authorship of this letter demands a date of composition in the early A.D. 60s. Church tradition holds that both Peter and Paul died as martyrs in Rome around A.D. 64. In 2 Peter we note the statement, "This is now my second letter to you" (3:1). If Peter died in A.D. 64 and if he wrote both 1 and 2 Peter, then a date of about A.D. 62 is most likely.

SOURCES

God's Word is the direct revelation from God to His people. Yet the biblical authors were inspired to include material from various sources in their writing. In 1 Peter we note at least three kinds of material. The first are quotations from the Old Testament, of which there are 13 in 1 Peter. Peter was knowledgeable of, and quoted from, all major sections of the Old Testament: the Law (Exodus and Leviticus), the Prophets (Isaiah), and the Writings (Psalms and Proverbs).

By making use of Exodus 19:5–6 (1 Pet. 2:9), Peter draws from the Mosaic Covenant, the Scriptures that establish a covenant relationship

KEY IDEAS • PETER'S USE OF THE OLD TESTAMENT

1 Peter	Old Testament Source
1:16	Lev. 11:44
1:24–25	Isa. 40:6–8
2:6	Isa. 28:16
2:7	Ps. 118:22
2:8	Isa. 8:14
2:9a	Isa. 43:20
2:9b	Isa. 61:6
2:9c	Exod. 19:6
2:9d	Exod. 19:5
2:22	Isa. 53:9
3:10–12	Ps. 34:12–16
4:18	Prov. 11:31
5:5	Prov. 3:34

between God and the Israelites. By doing so, Peter reminds his audience that they are continuing participants in this covenant.

The prophecy of Isaiah was of particular importance for Peter. All of the quotations from the Prophets are drawn from this book, accounting for six of Peter's thirteen Old Testament quotations. Of the six quotations from Isaiah, four are from that special section of Isaiah's prophecy that predicts the coming Messiah and His redemptive work (Isaiah 40–66).

The second kind of material Peter used in this letter is the teachings of Jesus. This includes allusions to the thought and teachings of the Master, not merely quotations. For example, compare 1 Peter 2:12, "that . . . they may see your good deeds and glorify God," to Matthew 5:16, "that they may see your good deeds and praise your Father in heaven."

KEY IDEAS • JESUS' TEACHINGS IN 1 PETER

1 Peter	Teaching of Jesus
1:5	John 10:29
1:7	Luke 17:30
1:8	John 20:29
1:10	Matt. 13:17
1:11	Matt. 26:24
1:17	Matt. 16:27
1:20	Matt. 25:34
1:21	John 17:5, 24
1:22	John 13:34
1:23	John 3:3, 13

The third source for Peter is his own speeches and sermons as recorded in the book of Acts. These speeches from Acts are important because they connect Peter's words from the days of the early Church with the content of 1 Peter. As Edward Selwyn observed, "The connection is not literary but historical: the common ground lies in the mind of St. Peter who gave, and was known to have given, teaching along these lines and to a great extent in these terms."[7]

FORM OF THE WRITING

The New Testament is a rich collection of writing in a variety of styles. The books of the New Testament contain historical narratives, parables, miracle accounts, sermons, prophetic literature, and other forms of writing. First Peter is an epistle, or letter.

The standard form of a New Testament letter includes a salutation, prayer or words of thanks, the body of the letter containing both doctrine and ethical instruction, and a conclusion. First Peter exhibits the same basic structure. The salutation is contained in 1:1–2 and includes three important items: identification of the sender (Peter), identification of the recipients (to God's elect), and a greeting (grace and peace). First Peter is a general epistle in that it is addressed not to an individual or to a single congregation but to a general audience.

The body of the letter is the material between 1:3 and 5:11. The body of a typical New Testament epistle addresses two distinct topics: doctrine and ethical instruction. Both elements are present in 1 Peter. To make a transition from one topic to another, Peter uses the phrase **dear friends**, found in 2:11 and 4:12.

So in 1 Peter, the body of the epistle is divided into three segments: 1:3–2:10, 2:11–4:11, and 4:12–5:11. Each of these three sections begin or conclude with a doxology. The first section (1:3–2:10) begins with a note of praise, the second section (2:11–4:11) concludes with a doxology, and the third section (4:12–5:11) concludes with a similar doxology.

The conclusion is 5:12–14, which fits the standard form of a conclusion. It conveys final greetings to the reader, names others who are helpful to Peter or are known to the audience, and summarizes the content of the letter.

While 1 Peter is a letter written to a group of people, it was most likely read aloud to its original audience. This means that it also has the qualities of a speech. As the audience members listened, they had to follow the rhetorical style of the author in order to understand his message.[8]

THEMES

One way to identify the key themes of this letter is to note the special vocabulary used by Peter. Three Greek words predominate these five chapters and indicate the key themes.

The first word is *anastrophe*, meaning way of life, conduct, or behavior. This word appears in the New Testament thirteen times with six of these occurrences in 1 Peter. The NIV translates this word variously as "in all you do" (1:15), "live your lives" (1:17), "live such good lives" (2:12), "behavior" (3:1), "reverence of your lives" (3:2), and "good behavior" (3:16).

The second word is *pascho,* which means to suffer or to be acted upon. This word is found forty times in the New Testament with twelve uses in 1 Peter. Peter divides his use of this word between describing the suffering an individual may be called upon to bear and contrasting that suffering with the sufferings of Christ. The NIV renders *pascho* with a form of the word *suffer* in 1 Peter. When the suffering endured by Christ is meant, the verb is translated in the past tense (*suffered*). An interesting use of *pascho* is found in 4:1, where the suffering of Christ and the sufferings a Christian may experience are addressed in the same verse.

A third key theme is introduced by the word *hypotasso*, which means subject or subordinate. This word is found thirty-nine times in the New Testament with six occurrences in 1 Peter. In five of the occurrences, the word refers to submission to an individual or individuals on earth (1 Pet. 2:13, 18; 3:1, 5; 5:5). There is one usage of the word that refers to the heavenly world in submission to Christ (3:22).

These are the key themes of 1 Peter: there is an ethical lifestyle that is to be lived among unbelievers; the Christian life may involve suffering, even as Christ experienced suffering; and the Christian lifestyle is one of willing subjection to another.

HERMENEUTICAL ISSUES

It is tempting to assume that epistles should be easy to understand and interpret. Yet several issues are important to consider when interpreting a New Testament epistle.[9]

The first is that they are *occasional documents*, meaning that they were written for a specific occasion in the first century. To interpret the letter, a reader must reconstruct as much of this first-century occasion as possible, as this introduction has done by identifying the author, date, form, and themes of the letter.

The occasional nature of the epistles means that they are not primarily theological treatises. There is theology in 1 Peter, but it is always *task theology*, theology written for or brought to bear on the task at hand. As Gordon Fee and Douglas Stuart remind us, "It is always theology at the service of a particular need."[10]

A final consideration for interpretation of epistles is that they must be read in context. Each paragraph is not simply a natural unit of thought, but is a necessary key to understanding the argument of 1 Peter as a whole.

THE THEOLOGY OF 1 PETER

First Peter addresses the doctrines of God, the Son, the Holy Spirit, the people of God, and eschatology.

When Peter reminds his audience of their Heavenly Father, he mentions certain divine qualities of God. God is known by His divine foreknowledge (1:1), His relationship with a particular people (1:1), and as one who is worthy of our praise (1:3). God is the author of the new birth (1:3) and an eternal inheritance (1:4). God is a holy God (1:15), the one who judges each person's work (1:17), and who raised Christ from the dead and glorified Him (1:21).

The doctrine of the Son is divided into two categories: the person of Christ and the work of Christ. Christ's preexistence and His being revealed in these last days (1:5). The Son is a living Stone (2:4), the Shepherd and Overseer of your souls (2:25), and the Chief Shepherd (5:4).

The work of the Son includes that He sprinkled us with His blood (1:2), redeemed us with precious blood (1:19), suffered for us (2:21), and bore our sins (2:24). The Son has gone into heaven where all are in submission to Him (3:22) and from there He will return to earth.

Peter's mention of the Holy Spirit includes the sanctifying work of the Spirit (1:2). He is the one who prompted Old Testament prophets to speak concerning the sufferings and glories of Christ (1:11), and the gospel was preached to Peter's audience by the Holy Spirit (1:12).

In 1 Peter, a significant theological concern is the description of the people of God. They are identified as elect, strangers, and scattered (1:1) who are to rejoice over what God has provided (1:6). They are to endure present suffering (1:7). They are called to be holy (1:15), to remember they are the people of God (2:10), and to follow Christ's example (2:21). The people of God are like living stones following Christ, the living Stone (2:5). They are a chosen people, a royal priesthood, a holy nation, and God's special possession (2:9). They are called to suffer (2:21) and participate in the suffering of Christ (4:13) as members of God's flock (5:2).

Theological references to the last days, or eschatology, are found in phrases like **the coming of the salvation that is ready to be revealed** (1:5) as well as the statements that Jesus is soon to be revealed (1:7, 13) and that the end is near (4:7).

HOLINESS AND 1 PETER

One of Peter's prime objectives was to remind his audience that a holy God demands holiness among His people (1:15). This call to pursue the holy life resonated with John Wesley eighteen centuries later. However, only two of Wesley's 52 standard sermons are drawn from this epistle.[11]

Greater influence of 1 Peter on John Wesley is seen in the Wesley hymns. These are found in the collection *Hymns for the Use of the People Called Methodist*. A review of these hymns reveals that the songs sung by early Methodist congregations were steeped in scriptural truth. There are 104 references to the text of 1 Peter in this collection of hymns.[12]

▣ WHAT OTHERS SAY

PETER IN THE BOOK OF ACTS

Hymn 38

Ps. 45:4	O Jesus, ride on till all are subdued;
1 Pet. 1:2	Thy mercy make known, and sprinkle thy blood
Rev. 5:9	Display thy salvation, And teach the new song
Rev. 14:3	To every nation, And people, and tongue!

In addition to Wesley's references to the text of 1 Peter in sermons and hymns, writers within the Holiness Movement have shown considerable interest in 1 Peter. T. Crichton Mitchell, working specifically with the writings of Wesley and his close associates, John Fletcher and Adam Clarke, has noted several references to 1 Peter in their writings.[13]

The first volume of *Exploring Christian Holiness* is devoted to the biblical foundation of the doctrine of holiness. In it, the Nazarene writer W. T. Purkiser[14] demonstrates the importance of 1 Peter for understanding the doctrine of holiness in a chapter entitled "Holiness in the Letters of Peter." In his outline of 1 Peter in the *Beacon Bible Commentary*, Roy S. Nicholson illustrates the manner in which many within the holiness movement interpret this book.[15]

GREAT THEMES

HOLINESS IN 1 PETER

1. Holiness Purposes—1:2–12
2. Holiness Commanded—1:13–16
3. Holiness Provided—1:17–21
4. Holiness Experienced—1:22–25
5. Holiness Exemplified—2:1–3:17
6. Holiness Triumphant—3:18–22
7. Holiness Superior—4:1–19
8. Holiness in Action—5:1–9
9. Holiness and Eternal Glory—5:10–11

—Outline by Roy S. Nicholson

We are now ready to begin the exposition of the letter.

ENDNOTES

1. The interested reader can consult a number of texts that deal with general introductory issues, including Norman Geisler and William E. Nix, *General Introduction to the Bible* (Chicago: Moody Press, 1968).

2. Note for example the comments by Gerald Bray in *James, 1–2 Peter, 1–3 John, Jude*, Ancient Christian Commentary on Scripture, vol. XI (Downers Grove: InterVarsity Press, 2000), p. 65. "With few exceptions, the Fathers believed that this letter was written by the apostle Peter and sent to Jewish Christians in the Diaspora (Eusebius of Caesarea, Didymus, Andreas, Oecumenius). They recognized that the letter had close resemblances to James and accounted for this by saying that both men were apostles to the Jews, though Peter seems to have concentrated more on those who lived outside Palestine (Andreas). Peter explains his calling from God with a Trinitarian promise, and

the Fathers were quick to pick this up (Andreas, Bede). They recognized him as the chief of the apostles and believed that this letter had been sent from Rome."

3. The following commentaries, listed in the bibliography, support the traditional view of authorship: Clowney (1988), Grudem (2002), Lenski (1966 printing), McNight (1966), Marshall (1991), and Selwyn (1981 reprint).

4. The following commentaries, listed in the bibliography, support the second view of authorship: Bigg (1975 reprint) and Michaels (1988).

5. The following commentaries, listed in the bibliography, support the third view of authorship: Achtemeier (1996), Best (1971), Elliott (2000), and Perkins (1995).

6. John H. Elliott, *I Peter*, The Anchor Bible (New York: Doubleday, 2000), p. 97.

7. Edward Gordon Selwyn, *The First Epistle of St. Peter* (Grand Rapids: Baker Book House, reprinted 1981), p. 36. Selwyn underscores the importance of examining the speeches in Acts with the text of 1 Peter as a valuable source of establishing Peter as the author of this epistle. Selwyn states, "The internal evidence for St. Peter's authorship of the Epistle is borne out and amplified when we compare it with the speeches attributed to the Apostle in Acts" (p. 33).

8. Note for example J. R. Michaels's comment in "1 Peter," *Dictionary of the Later New Testament*, Ralph P. Martin and Peter H. Davids, Eds. (Downers Grove: InterVarsity Press, 1997), 918: "Rhetorically 1 Peter is best described as an appeal, or persuasive discourse. In his postscript (1 Pet. 5:12–14), Peter seems to describe the letter as a combination of appeal and testimony, but the two terms are not to be separated."

9. For what follows I am indebted to Gordon D. Fee and Douglas Stuart, *How to Read the Bible for All Its Worth*, 2nd ed. (Grand Rapids: Zondervan Publishing House, 1993), pp. 48–49; 54–55.

10. Ibid., p. 49.

11. Albert C. Outler, ed., *The Works of John Wesley*, Volume 1 (Sermons 1–33 [1984]), Volume 2 (Sermons 34–70 [1985]), Volume 3 (Sermons 71–114 [1985]), and Volume 4 (Sermons 115–151 [1987]) (Nashville: Abingdon Press).

12. Franz Hildebrandt and Oliver Beckerlegge, eds., *The Works of John Wesley*. Volume 7 (Nashville: Abingdon Press, 1983), p. 128.

13. A. F. Harper, Executive Editor. *Great Holiness Classics,* Vol. 2, *The Wesley Century*, T. Crichton Mitchell, ed. (Kansas City: Beacon Hill Press, 1984).

14. W. T. Purkiser, *Exploring Christian Holiness: The Biblical Foundations*. Volume 1 (Kansas City: Beacon Hill Press, 1983), pp. 214–220.

15. Roy S. Nicholson, *First Peter*, Beacon Bible Commentary, vol. 10, A. F. Harper, ed. (Kansas City: Beacon Hill Press, 1967), pp. 255–309.

OUTLINE OF 1 PETER

I. The Plan of God and the Work of Christ (1:1–2:10)

   A. Salutation (1:1–2)

   B. Praise to God for Great Salvation (1:3–12)

   C. Hope and Holiness (1:13–21)

   D. Purity and Love (1:22–25)

   E. Addition by Subtraction (2:1–3)

   F. The Living Stone and a Chosen People (2:4–10)

II. Accepting Submission and Living for God (2:11–4:11)

   A. Living among the Pagans (2:11–12)

   B. The Life of Submission (2:13–3:22)

      1. Submission to Authority (2:13–17)

      2. Submission to Masters (2:18–25)

      3. Submission to Spouse (3:1–7)

      4. Living in Harmony (3:8–22)

   C. Living for God (4:1–11)

III. Three Things That Bind Us Together (4:12–5:11)

   A. Suffering as a Christian (4:12–19)

   B. Unity among Elders and Younger Men (5:1–5a)

   C. Trust with Humility (5:5b–11)

IV. Conclusion (5:12–14)

Part One

The Plan of God
and the Work of Christ

1 PETER 1:1—2:10

SUCH A GREAT SALVATION

1 Peter 1:1–12

1. SALUTATION 1:1–2

First Peter begins in the usual style for a first-century letter. The first element is the salutation, which serves three purposes.

First, it identifies the relationship between the writer and the audience. Peter accomplishes this by identifying himself as **an apostle of Jesus Christ** (1:1).

Second, it introduces the major themes of the letter. Peter does this by identifying the audience by three images: **God's elect**, **strangers**, and **scattered** (1:1). Some writers have suggested that these three terms provide the structure for the entire letter. "The interrelationship of the three words describing the readers reveals the author's underlying conviction about the nature of the Christian community and its relationship to its surrounding world."[1]

Third, the salutation conveys a greeting. A writer might express a desire for the good health of the recipient. New Testament writers infused their letters with Christian content, so the words **grace and peace be yours in abundance** (1:2) are more than a wish that all is well.

THE WRITER

The text begins with the identification of the author, **Peter** (1:1). This is the same individual who was called Simon and was introduced to Jesus by Andrew (John 1:42). Jesus changed Simon's name to Cephas, which is translated Peter and means rock or stone. Peter became one of the original twelve disciples (Mark 1:17) and soon joined John and James as one of Jesus' three closest associates (Luke 9:28). Although Peter denied Jesus on the night of His arrest (Luke 22:61), Jesus reinstated him. Peter rose as a leader among the believers (Acts 1:15), and on the Day of Pentecost, he became the spokesman for the infant Church (Acts 2:14).[2]

Peter is identified as **an apostle of Jesus Christ** (1:1). The word *apostle* occurs in the New Testament seventy-nine times,[3] including one reference each in Matthew, Mark, and John. There are six occurrences in Luke and twenty-eight in Acts. Paul used this word twenty-nine times. The word denotes a person who is sent with full authority; in the New Testament, the person is sent with Christ's authority. The phrase **apostle of Jesus Christ** indicates "the unique relationship in which it stood to the historic Christ."[4]

Peter received his apostleship when "He [Jesus] called his twelve disciples to him and gave them authority to drive out evil spirits and to heal every disease and sickness . . ." (Matt. 10:2). Matthew, Mark, and Luke make a distinction between a disciple—a follower of Jesus—and an apostle—one sent forth with full authority (Matt. 10:1–4; Mark 3:13–19; Luke 6:12–16). All three Gospel writers name Peter first.

Peter's authority was enhanced by his having seen the resurrected Christ. John Elliott writes in reference to 1 Corinthians 15:3–8 that "Peter was the first such privileged witness of Christ's resurrection (see also Luke 24:34), and it was this privilege that established his priority and leading role among the first followers of Jesus."[5] By the time of writing 1 Peter, the sense of being an apostle had grown in Peter's consciousness to the point that it became a driving force. This is what motivated Peter, and this is how the epistle's audience identified him.

THE AUDIENCE

Peter has written to God's people. They are known as the elect and thus have a significant relationship with God. They have a unique relationship with the world also. Though they inhabit a particular region of the earth, they are citizens of heaven. This will create tension for them as they live out their faith among unbelievers.

A Relational Description. God's people are first all **God's elect** (1:1).[6] The word *elect* is derived from a verb meaning to pick out or select. This term is applied to individuals who have responded in faith to the gospel offer. Those who believe become known as *the elect*. This term thus identifies individuals who have a special relationship with God.

A Temporal Description. The recipients are also identified as **strangers in the world** (1:1). *Strangers* indicate a relationship with the world. The word identifies one who lives alongside others, a sojourner. Is *strangers* used literally or figuratively? If it is applied literally, the audience is composed of individuals who have been dispersed from their homeland. If the term is a figure of speech, then it may describe the people of God as they live here on earth. This figurative sense of the term *strangers* better fits the role of the expanding Church in an unbelieving world. They are strangers in society yet chosen by God.

The third description of the recipients of this letter is found in the phrase **scattered throughout** (1:1). The Greek word here translated means dispersed or scattered and is the root of the term *diaspora*. First Peter is often called a *dispersion letter* because it is written to those who have been dispersed abroad. If the audience for this letter is a mixture of both Jewish and Gentile converts to Christianity, then **scattered throughout** may refer to Christian people inhabiting a wide territory rather than to a displaced people. This term, when used of Christians, "describes the fact that because of their unwillingness to adopt the mores of their surrounding society, they can expect the disdainful treatment often accorded exiles."[7] Again, the figurative sense of *scattered* makes proper sense. Peter wrote to Christians living in a secular, pagan society.

This epistle was sent to believers in **Pontus, Galatia, Cappadocia, Asia and Bithynia** (1:1).[8] This area encompasses a wide circle of churches on the frontier of the Roman Empire in five provinces of Asia Minor. It is possible that the order in which Peter named the provinces indicated the route of the messenger who would deliver the letter.

A Theological Description. Having described his readers in terms of their relation to God and location in the world, Peter describes them in theological terms. Though they may be suffering, there are some positive things to say about these Christians. To do this, Peter invokes a Trinitarian formula, touching on the work of God the Father, the Spirit, and Jesus Christ.

Peter's readers have been **chosen according to the foreknowledge of God the Father** (1:2). The word *foreknowledge* is a compound word meaning to know beforehand. One of the attributes of God is His omniscience, His complete knowledge of the world and time. Those who believe in God are known as the elect and are said to be chosen by God. It is God's purpose to have for himself a particular people. This does not imply, however, the choice of particular individuals. Because God is omniscient, He does know who will ultimately be saved. Yet it is His desire that all people might be included in that number (2 Pet. 3:9).

Human freedom complicates the matter. God is a gracious and will never coerce one to become a believer. God knows all things because He is God. Yet His divine foreknowledge does not impede one's free will. Peter is written to those who had accepted God's gracious work on their behalf. By doing so, they became part of the elect. God knew they would make this choice.

The second theological expression Peter uses to describe his audience is **through the sanctifying work of the Spirit** (1:2). The word *sanctifying* has a rich Old Testament background. There, the word indicates separation for a specific task. The tribe of Levi was sanctified in that it was separated for specific work in connection with the tabernacle. Priests were sanctified in that they were separated for the work of offering sacrifices. Certain holy things were separated for use in worship. In the New Testament, the notion of being made holy by separation is continued with an emphasis on moral purity. The preposition *through* indicates that this is accomplished by the Holy Sprit. It is the Holy Spirit who sets us apart and purifies us.

The third part of the Trinitarian formula Peter uses to describe his audience is found in the words **for obedience to Jesus Christ**, which is connected with **sprinkling by His blood** (1:2). It is interesting that Peter refers to the practice of sprinkling with blood (see Heb. 9:11–14). The Old Testament refers to sprinkling blood: "In only three cases was blood ceremonially sprinkled on the people themselves: in the covenant initiation ceremony at Mt. Sinai (Exod. 24:8); in the ceremony of ordination for Aaron and his sons as priests (Exod. 29:20); and in the purification ceremony for a leper who had been healed from leprosy (Lev. 14)."[9]

A clue to the way the three theological references are connected is found in the preposi-

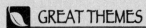

GREAT THEMES
A PLAN FOR ALL AGES

The Origin of the Plan:
  "Chosen according to the foreknowledge of God."

Instrument of the Plan:
  "Through the sanctifying work of the Holy Spirit."

The Purpose of the Plan:
  "For obedience to Jesus Christ and sprinkling by his blood."

tions associated with them. The plan of salvation was formed **according to** the God's foreknowledge. This plan was affected **through** the sanctifying actions of the Holy Spirit. The preposition **for** in the third part of the Trinitarian formula can be interpreted to mean because of the obedience of Christ and His blood sprinkled. That rendering of the clause would mean that it identifies the result—not the purpose—of Christ's work. "The end result is they will be the people of a new covenant characterized by obedience and sacrifice."[10]

A GREETING

The salutation concludes with a greeting: **grace and peace** (1:2). Similar greetings were common in first-century letters, but this one has more significance than a casual wish for the reader's well being. This greeting combines *grace*, the usual Christian welcome, with *peace*, the typical Hebrew greeting. This reflects the priestly blessing of Num. 6:25–26, "The LORD . . . be gracious to you . . . and give you peace." It sounds almost frightening to express the wish that these two blessings might **be yours in abundance** (1:2). Peter prays for the multiplication of grace and peace as if he knows that his readers will have great need of them. Even in the salutation of this letter, we get the feeling that its recipients may be facing trying circumstances. It will come as no surprise that the body of the letter addresses suffering and the trials through which the Asiatic Christians were about to pass.

2. PRAISE TO GOD FOR GREAT SALVATION 1:3–12

This first major section in 1 Peter begins at 1:3 and extends through 2:10. This begins the body of the letter with a doctrinal section discussing the plan of God and the work of Christ. It follows the typical pattern of a New Testament letter: the first major section contains a theological discussion and an explanation of the ethical implications of that particular teaching.

The opening paragraph of this first major section provides a stunning review of God's work on our behalf.

BLESSED BE GOD

The NIV renders 1 Peter 1:3–9 in seven sentences. But in the original language, this paragraph is a single, complex sentence. The first statement speaks to what God has accomplished, **Blessed be the God and Father of our Lord Jesus Christ** . . . (1:3, KJV). This term *blessed* is applied only to God in the New Testament. In 2 Corinthians 1:3 (KJV), the word *blessed* is used in the same way and replaces Paul's typical prayer of thanks to God. The NIV interprets *blessed* as *praise*. The usual Pauline prayer is found in Romans 1:8; 1 Corinthians 1:4; Philippians 1:3; 1 Thessalonians 1:2. Why does Peter call God blessed? Because God **has given us** (1:3) something of great value.

What prompted this gift is two-fold; one reason is mentioned in the text and the other one is implied. The one mentioned in the text is God's **great mercy**. The concept of the mercy of God will become a prime aspect of God's plan for humankind. The early Church found it to be true, as illustrated by the Church Father Hilary who said, "His mercy is great enough to be able to forgive every sin which has been committed in thought, word and deed, from the beginning to the end of the world."[11] The word *mercy* can also be translated *pity* or *compassion*. When Jesus saw the multitude (Matt. 9:36), He was moved with compassion. This is how God and Jesus Christ respond to human need.

The implied factor of God's gift comes from the greeting aspect of Peter's salutation. It is there we find "grace and peace be yours in abundance." Not only does God have mercy, but He is a gracious God. Mercy and grace go together. In this context, the grace of God is known as prevenient grace, the grace that goes before conversion. As Wesley frequently noted, the grace of God is "free to all and free in all." Another way to express this concept is in the words of the old hymn, "Mercy there was great and grace was free." Mercy and grace motivate God's gift, the **new birth**, to us. The word Peter uses here is a rare word that appears only twice in the New Testament, both in 1 Peter.[12] From this word comes the idea of regeneration, or the cause to be born again. This new birth concept goes back to the conversation between Jesus and Nicodemus (John 3:7) and the familiar refrain "You must be born again." Peter has made use of a dramatic metaphor to describe the new life brought by God's mercy.[13]

THE RESULTS OF THE NEW BIRTH

The gift of the new birth leads to three spiritual realities.

First, it leads into **a living hope** (1:3). To live life hopefully is a characteristic of the people of God. Rather than allowing circumstances or conditions to determine our direction, we follow a living hope that transcends the everyday affairs of life and is focused on the eternal. It is as easy to extinguish a living hope as it is to stop spring of water; it continually grows and increases. But what makes this hope more than just wishful thinking? It is the fact of **the resurrection of Jesus Christ**. This is why the early Christians were so insistent that Jesus Christ did in fact arise from the dead. The teaching of Paul in 1 Corinthians 15 on the resurrection reflects the belief and teaching of the early Church: If Christ has not been raised from the dead, the entire Christian faith is centered on a falsehood. And as Paul wrote the church at Corinth, "If only for this life we have hope in Christ, we are to be pitied" (1 Cor. 15:19).[14]

The second spiritual reality Christians enter into is **an inheritance** (1:4). The word for inheritance is an interesting term. It can mean property already received, as well as one that is expected to be received. Another way to understand this word is to contrast earth and heaven. "The New

Testament regularly uses inheritance to refer not only to an earthly inheritance but also to a believer's share in the heavenly kingdom, his or her future heavenly reward, as in Gal. 3:18; Eph. 1:14, 18; 5:5; Col. 3:24; and Heb. 9:15."[15] When the term inheritance is used in its "heavenly" aspect, it is underscoring an inheritance God has for us at the end of time. This inheritance is **kept in heaven for you**. The fact of the new birth provides a "spiritual deposit" (Eph. 1:14) now that guarantees our inheritance in the future. Christians have a foretaste of glory divine. This inheritance kept in heaven can never **perish, spoil, or fade**. The first term, *perish*, indicates something that is not corruptible or not liable to pass away. The second term, *spoil*, means unstained or undefiled. The third term, *fade*, means unfading, where it is used in reference to flowers. It could be said that this inheritance is marked by immortality, purity, and beauty. Peter Davids explains that "this inheritance is described using three adjectives: (1) incorruptible—it is permanent. (2) undefiled—it is morally and religiously pure. (3) unfading—it is eternal. Thus it is better than any earthly reward."[16] This reward is **kept** in heaven, meaning to guard or to take care of. The tense of this verb indicates a completed action in past time that carries the benefits into the present time. The inheritance is already in place. The full benefits of the inheritance are being kept for individuals who are now **shielded by God's power** (1:5).

The word **shielded** implies guarded or kept watch over. The term has military connotations and is in the present tense, indicating that Christians continually need and have this type of protection. There is a constant battle over the souls of every believer. God is on our side and is protecting us; our part is to live **through faith**. Faith in the keeping power of our Heavenly Father becomes the guarantee of our final victory.

Peter refers to this day as **the coming of salvation**, which introduces the third spiritual reality. While we are correct in testifying to our present salvation, it will only be final at the Day of Judgment. That salvation is now **ready**. All that is required to be accomplished has already been done. It is ready **to be revealed**; God will do the action. The coming of salvation is an eschatological event. Peter speaks of events **in the last time**. This term *time* means appointed time or proper time, and the term *last* in this sense means last of all.

PRESENT SUFFERING ONLY FOR A LITTLE WHILE

Peter is not telling his readers something they do not already know. They understand the reality of the new birth and the implications of their spiritual inheritance. In fact, as they consider their present spiritual status, they **greatly rejoice** (1:6). However, "the rejoicing is not a continual feeling of hilarity, nor a denial of the reality of pain and suffering, but an anticipatory joy experienced even now, despite the outward circumstances."[17] In their present circumstance, there is great joy.[18] Alongside this joy is the reality of the suffering they experience **now for a little while**. But suffering that is for a little while implies two things: suffering is not a normal part of life, and suffering is under the control of God.[19] Peter's readers are experiencing something that must be endured a short while or briefly. Their future is bright, though Christians **may have had to suffer grief** (1:6). With this phrase, Peter continues to contrast the present with what will come to pass. This phrase speaks to two distinct periods of time: the present, characterized by grief, and the future, characterized by joy. Peter is not speaking of joy in suffering but rather in an eschatological sense of joy after suffering.[20] The present grief is a necessity. The question remains whether this is physical pain and injury or mental pain and suffering. The next several paragraphs will explain this point.

We do know that what they had to suffer came in **all kinds of trials**; it was varied and diversified. The trials here refer to a period or process of testing one's faith. Later in 1 Peter, the same word will be used for painful trial (4:12) or fiery ordeal (NASB).

But why must the Christian suffer? What purpose could it possibly serve? And, in fact, can one even provide an answer to this question?[21] A partial answer begins with the recognition that this topic of various trials is followed by a purpose clause, **so that your faith may be proved genuine** (1:7). The word *genuine* is interesting; it means approved after trial or tried. The process of proving faith to be genuine is one similar to the process whereby gold is **refined by fire**. The refining fire literally destroys any impurities in the gold. If gold is put through this process because of its supposed value, your faith **is of greater worth**. To demonstrate that faith is genuine faith, it must be tested, and must be understood as coming from the hand of loving Heavenly Father, as the "Three Qualifications of Christian Suffering" chart illustrates.[22]

The testing process results in **praise, glory, and honor** (1:7). These three results may not be exhibited while in the refining process, but they will be evident **when Jesus Christ is revealed**. Once again, Peter draws the contrast between the here-and-now with the yet-to-come aspect of Christian life. The future results of God's merciful plan of begetting a new people (hope, inheritance, salvation) is contrasted with the present (suffering and testing). Peter concludes verse 5 with a reference to "salvation that is ready to be revealed in the last time," a clear reference to the second coming of Christ.

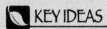

KEY IDEAS

THREE QUALIFICATIONS OF
CHRISTIAN SUFFERING

1. Suffering is a potentiality of Christian experience, but suffering is not a necessity.
2. Suffering is only a temporary situation; it is not permanent.
3. Suffering should be regarded as "various testings" from God, the purpose of which is the testing of one's faith.

Here in verse 7 is Peter's second reference to that great event: the revelation of Jesus Christ. The coming of Jesus Christ into our world the first time, known as the incarnation, made God visible to humanity. This was the first advent. Christians live in the now of earthly existence waiting for the yet-to-come of eternal life which will be accomplished by Christ's return for His Church at the Second Advent. At the Advent, or revelation of Jesus Christ, the now of the present will pass away, and the then of actually gaining our inheritance will become a reality.[23]

Peter continues the contrast between the here-and-now and the yet-to-come aspects of the Christian faith. Although at the present time **you have not seen him** (1:8), faith is not hampered. **Seen** indicates physical eyesight. But not seeing Jesus with the physical eye does not diminish affection for Him. While not seeing Him, **you love him**. The present tense of this verb indicates continual action in the present time. **Even though** Peter's readers do not see Jesus, Peter concludes, **you believe in him**. The combination of love and belief produces **an inexpressible and glorious joy**. The type of joy Peter is describing is twofold: unspeakable, because it contains a sense of divine mystery, and glorious, because it is glory from above.

The believer experiences this "inexpressible and glorious joy" for a specific reason. They **are receiving the goal** (1:9). *Receiving* means obtaining or paying back. Faith has an eternal goal in mind. There is a finish line to which the Christian presses toward. Peter describes it as **the salvation of your souls**. This covers humanity as a whole.

THE PROPHETS SPOKE OF SALVATION

The teaching about the salvation of your souls is not a new teaching. Peter traces this message back to the Old Testament **prophets** (1:10) and their ministry among the Jewish people. The prophets had a twofold function. First, he was one who spoke to his people; he was a forth-teller. Secondly, he was a fore-teller; he predicted the sufferings and glories of Christ.

The prophets **searched intently and with the greatest care**, trying to understand the message of grace. To search intently means to seek with diligence; greatest care signifies making a careful search. These two ideas stated together intensify the action. Taken together, they indicate a careful and minute search for truth. The prophets were earnest in their investigation.

Why were the prophets so earnest in their search for truth? They were **trying to find out** (1:11) something. The term used here is the same as **greatest care** in the previous verse without the higher degree of intensity. The goal of their quest was to discover **the time and circumstances** that would fulfill the Spirit's prompting within them concerning Christ. As readers of the New Testament, we now understand what the prophets were seeking. What was guiding their search? The Spirit of Christ **was pointing** to something. The word *point* means to make clear or to show. The tense indicates continuous action in past time. This message was not a one-time, causal message. This was the heart of the prophets. It burned within them, and they spoke of it over and over again. The substance of these predictions was the **sufferings . . . and the glories** of Christ. Commentator Peter Davids states, "The order is critical: the glories follow the sufferings. Neither Christ nor his people receive the crown of glory without the crown of thorns."[24] This combination of terms forms an

41

outline of the life of Christ. The sufferings refer to the humiliation of Christ that began with His incarnation and concluded with His passion. The glories of Christ refer to His resurrection and ultimate exaltation. Paul, in Philippians 2:5–11, gives the clearest account of the suffering/glories theme. In the Old Testament, the greatest commentary on the suffering and glories of the Messiah is found in Psalm 22.

In the process of trying to discover the time and circumstances of these things, something else was **revealed to them** (1:12). The truth unveiled to the prophets was that they were **serving . . . you** in this entire process. To serve means to minister to; the tense indicates continual action in past time. Foretelling the things that **have now been told you** was the prophets' service. The message is the same as the message foretold by the prophets. There are more details, but the basic content is the same. How was this message delivered to Peter's readers? Individuals **have preached the gospel to you.** The content of the preaching was the work of Christ; the plan of God has been fulfilled within human history by that work.

The voice of those who preached the good news was heard, but behind the voice was the person of **the Holy Spirit sent from heaven** (1:12). It was the power of the Holy Spirit, working through the messengers, which energized the message and made it effective. Human beings are privileged to hear while angels **long to look into these things**. "The purpose of verses 10–12 is to show Peter's readers that the spiritual blessings they now have are greater than anything that was envisaged by prophets or even angels. Thus Peter seeks to increase his readers' appreciation for their great salvation in Christ."[25]

ENDNOTES

1. Paul J. Achtemeier, *1 Peter* (Minneapolis: Fortress Press, 1996), p. 80. See T. W. Martin, "Metaphor and Composition in 1 Peter" *Society of Biblical Literature Dissertation Series: Dissertation 131* (Atlanta: Scholars Press, 1992) pp. 160–161.

2. It is possible to outline the book of Acts under two personalities: Peter (chapters 1–12) and Paul (chapters 13–28).

3. The numerical information following the word *apostle* is an example of the study known as linguistic frequency, providing helpful information about the

number of times a particular word is used in the New Testament and how many times it appears in a particular book. At times this information will be provided for key terms in 1 Peter.

4.   Edward Gordon Selwyn, *The First Epistle of St. Peter,* second edition (Grand Rapids: Baker Book House, reprinted 1981), p. 117.

5.   John H. Elliott, *1 Peter* (New York: Doubleday, 2000), p. 310.

6.   The word *elect* occurs twenty-two times in the New Testament, four times in 1 Peter.

7.   Achtemeier, *1 Peter,* p. 82. He continues to clarify the point: "It refers for that reason less to the notion of Christians disdaining the temporal because of their longing for their eternal, heavenly home, with the implications of withdrawal from secular society, than to the notion that despite such treatment, they must nevertheless continue to practice their faith in the midst of those who abuse them."

8.   For a helpful summary of the area addressed, see Achtemeier, *1 Peter,* pp. 83–85.

9.   Wayne Grudem, *1 Peter* (Grand Rapids: William B. Eerdmans, reprinted 2002), p. 52.

10.   Achtemeier, *1 Peter,* pp. 87–88.

11.   Gerald Bray, ed., *James, 1–2 Peter, 1–3 John, Jude,* (Downers Grove: InterVarsity Press, 2000), p. 68.

12.   Achtemeier, *1 Peter,* p. 94. Achtemeier states that "the use of the rare word puts emphasis rather on re-begetting or begetting anew than on being born anew." He explains the word "reflects the totally changed and hence new situation in which the rebegotten persons find themselves." (Footnote 17, p. 94.)

13.   Elliott, in *1 Peter,* p. 331, says the born again metaphor illustrates "the decisive transformation of life that believers have experienced through God's mercy." Elliott continues the "Father" metaphor when he comments that "God has honored the readers by 'rebirthing' them as his children (1:14), and newborn babies (2:2), and incorporating them into his family (2:4–10)."

14.   Grudem, *1 Peter,* p. 56. For "the resurrection of Christ from the dead secures for his people both new resurrection bodies and new spiritual life. Christians do not in this age receive new bodies but God does grant, on the basis of Jesus' resurrection, renewed spirits."

15.   Ibid., p. 56.

16.   Peter Davids, *The First Epistle of Peter* (Grand Rapids: William B. Eerdmans, 1996), p. 53.

17.   Ibid., p. 55.

18.   In Elliott's note, *1 Peter* (New York: Doubleday, 2000), p. 339, he stresses this paradox. He writes, "the jubilation of believers, however, is tempered

by the fact that they are currently with the reality of suffering for the commitment to Jesus Christ. Once again the letter notes at the outset a further and paradoxical feature of Christian existence; namely, rejoicing despite, or even because of, suffering."

19. Note Davids' discussion on these two points beginning on page 56.

20. Note J. Ramsey Michaels, *1 Peter* (Waco: Word Books Publishers, 1998), p. 29, for a further discussion of this point.

21. For instance, Davids reminds his readers that "God's purposes in present grief may not be fully known in a week, in a year, or even in this lifetime. Some of God's purposes will only be discovered at the day of final judgment when the Lord reveals the secrets of all hearts and commends with special honor those who trusted him in hardship even though they could not see the reason for it. They trusted him simply because he was their God and they knew him to be worthy of trust" (p. 65).

22. Elliott, *1 Peter*, pp. 339–340.

23. Note Michaels' comment: "Suffering and sorrow belong to the present while vindication and joy, although very near, belong to the future. Peter's vision transcends the limitations of the present, yet he never denies the hard reality of present suffering or calls it something it is not." *1 Peter*, p. 37.

24. Davids, pp. 63–64.

25. Grudem, *1 Peter*, p. 67.

CHRISTIAN QUALITIES

1 Peter 1:13–2:3

This second section of doctrinal teaching switches from the plan of God and the work of Christ to practical doctrinal implications for Peter's readers. "The emphasis on 'hope' in verse 13b and verse 21c forms an inclusion marking the opening and closing of the unit. Two internal subunits have 'holiness' as their unifying theme."[1]

1. HOPE AND HOLINESS 1:13–21

The passage begins with **therefore.** This inferential conjunction is used to draw a conclusion from a truth just stated or to indicate a result from what has preceded. In this context, what are Peter's readers to conclude from the preceding section? (1:3–12). They are to **prepare** [their] **minds for action** (1:13). A call to prepare means to make one's mind ready and to be on the alert. "Such spiritual alertness is appropriate to life in a new covenant age characterized by God's powerful working in people's hearts."[2] Preparation of the mind refers to more than mental activity. This concept communicates the idea of understanding, intention, and purpose. It goes to the very thought and attitude of the heart. This amounts to a call for the readers to be alert in their total being. This is not just a New Testament concept but is also found in the Old Testament (Job 38:3; 40:7; Prov. 31:17; Nah. 2:1). To gird the loins (KJV; **prepare your minds** in the NIV) was to get ready for action.[3] In addition to the call to action is the call to be **self-controlled**. "This word forbids letting the mind wander into any other kind of mental intoxication or addition which inhibits spiritual alertness, or any laziness of mind which lulls Christians into sin through carelessness."[4] The NIV variously translates this word as keep your head (2 Tim. 4:5) or self-controlled (1 Thess. 5:6, 8). The twin ideas of self-control and clarity of mind seem to catch the importance of this word.

But the preceding section (1:3–12) could also point to another conclusion: to **set your hope fully on the grace** (1:13) that will be given when Christ is revealed. The adverb *fully* is best taken with the main verb *hope*. To hope fully means to hope in grace completely and without reserve. Notice that "this phrase does not mean to compare qualities of hope but compare objects of hope."[5] The object of hope is on the grace **to be given** at some point in the future. Where the NIV renders given, the NASB translates the idea "to be brought to you." Thus, grace is connected with the time **when Jesus Christ is revealed** and, once again, Peter has reminded his readers of the Second Advent and the part this final revelation of Christ has in his theology.

THE HOLINESS OF THE BELIEVER

In light of this fast approaching revelation, the Christian community is characterized as **obedient children** (1:14). One way to understand the metaphor "children" is as sounding "the theme of newness (newly begotten, 1:3, 23; or newly born, 2:2)."[6] Obedience is seen in a very practical manner. Those who are obedient **do not conform**. The challenge is for Christians to be distinctive in their lifestyle in contrast to the unbelieving world around them. "Obedience to God and holiness of life (see v. 15) are radically different from a life that follows 'natural' desires wherever they lead."[7] This word *conform* is also found in Romans 12:2, where the idea is be conformed to or be shaped by.

Peter's readers are being warned against conforming **to the evil desires of their former life** (1:14). What exactly does Peter have in mind? The term *evil desire* represents the longing or lust of their former life. The word means "cravings, a vice universally decried in the Greco-Roman, Israelite, and Christian circles. It is variously rendered as insatiable craving, sexual lust, and uncontrolled passion."[8] Peter acknowledges that this former life was lived in **ignorance** or unawareness. But what was done in ignorance, and perhaps implying here a Gentile audience, does not mean Christians can continue to live with these evil desires. Peter is drawing a sharp contrast between the life lived formerly, with its sinful lifestyle, and the lifestyle they are now being commanded to follow. The command is to live a holy life.

The command to holiness is not given without adequate background. The call to holiness is predicated on the fact **he who called you is holy** (1:15). God is identified as a holy God. The concept of the holiness of God is a primary concept in Christian theology. "The moral quality that best points to God's incomparably good character, as one incomparable in power, is holiness, for holiness implies that every excellence fitting to the Supreme Being is found in God without blemish or limit."[9] It is this holy display of the character of God that separates Him from His created world. The word *holy* carries the idea of being separated or marked off. The holiness of God has certain implications for Peter's audience and for us today. Some of the implications refer to God only. As Thomas Oden remarks, "Holiness implies the perfect goodness of God's character, that God is good without defect." He continues by noting, "The divine holiness does not, however, apply only to God's essential or inner being, but also to God's works—everything God does, the entirety of God's activity."[10]

But the concept of God's holiness does not stop with descriptions of His character and nature. In light of God's holiness, Peter commands his audience to **be holy in all you do** (1:15). The phrase *in all you do* brings us back to one of the key words for this epistle. It is the word rendered elsewhere as *conduct*. This word covers all manner of life and conduct. It appears in the New Testament thirteen times, with six of the occurrences in 1 Peter. The word is used of public activity and relationships with others. Thus, it is evident that the call to holiness is not a theoretical concept. Holiness is to characterize the actions of a holy people in all their dealings with other people. This brings us to Oden's third implication of the holiness of God. He writes that "God's holiness is finally the criterion for human moral activity, even though our finitude is such that we can reflect perfect goodness only inadequately."[11]

47

The conclusion of this call to holiness is introduced by the phrase **for it is written** (1:16). The word *for* is rendered *since* in some translations. This is a causal clause and introduces the reason or ground for such a call. The NASB renders the phrase "because it is written." The call to holiness is grounded in the unchanging Word of God. Peter quotes Leviticus 19:2, "a favorite passage for early Christian ethical teaching,"[12] to clarify this call. The phrase *it is written* carries the force of "it stands written" and was used of legal documents whose validity continued.

"Be holy, because I am holy" was God's command to the Israelites and is His command to us today.

THE HOLINESS OF CHRIST

The fact that a holy God commands His people to be holy should make us live our life here on earth with great care. The fact that Christians **call on a Father** (1:17), in reference to God, points to at least one potential problem; if Christians "call God Father, they should remember His character and not allow familiarity to be an excuse for evil."[13] Familiarity will not produce special favors because God **judges impartially**, without showing respect of favoritism. This emphasis on an impartial God is a common theme in both the Old and New Testaments.[14]

In light of the fact that God is an impartial judge, Peter's audience is commanded to **live as strangers here** (1:17), which takes them back to the salutation (1:1). While on earth, Christians are to live as strangers among the unbelieving population. This day-by-day life is to be characterized by a **reverent fear**. Why does Peter introduce the element of fear? Perhaps it goes back to the call to be alert and sober (1:13). Perhaps fear is simply the consequence of being in intimate relationship with a God, who is the impartial judge of the world.[15] Or "another motivation for a life of holiness is fear of God's fatherly discipline."[16]

Authentic reverent fear is based on what one knows. In this particular context, a reverent fear is based on what is known of the work of Christ that makes redemption possible. There are three aspects of this knowledge that Peter develops for his audience.

First, the work of Christ is contrasted in a negative manner. He begins this discussion by pointing out that it was **not with perishable things ... that you were redeemed** (1:18). Perishable items include things that are subject to decay and corruption. Things of this nature cannot provide redemption, which carries the idea of free by paying, ransom, or set free. Peter Davids has provided helpful insight into ransom as a major theme of the Old Testament. He states that ransom refers to "the redemption of ancestral property that had been sold because of poverty or because a person had had to sell himself into slavery (Lev. 25:25; 48–49), which redemption in context is linked to the great redemption of slaves that God accomplished in the Exodus (Exod. 6:6; 15:13) and that was symbolized in the worship of Israel (Exod. 30:12; Num. 18:15)."[17] Redemption cannot come through things that perish **but** (with strong contrast) **with the precious blood of Christ** (1:19).

This is the second aspect of knowledge we have.

Stated in positive terms, redemption is made possible by

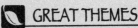

GREAT THEMES

THE BLOOD OF CHRIST

- Provides the removal of our judicial guilt before God (Rom. 3:25–26)

- Cleanses our consciences (Heb. 9:14)

- Allows us to gain bold access to God in worship and prayer (Heb. 10:19)

- Purifies us from all sin (1 John 1:7)

- Enables us to conquer the accuser of the believers (Rev. 12:11)

- Rescues us out of a sinful way of life (1 Pet. 1:19)

the passion of Jesus Christ. It was on Calvary that the Son of God shed His blood for lost humankind. In His role as the Lamb of God, He was **without blemish** (blameless) or **defect** (spotless, without stain). "These two terms indicate the total perfection of Christ as a sacrifice (Heb. 9:14)."[18]

The third thing we know concerning our redemption is that the work of Christ transcends time. As Peter reminds his readers, **He was chosen before the creation of the world** (1:20) but also **was revealed in these last times.** Peter would have his audience to know that "it was not an accident that this price was paid: God paid it deliberately; that is, it was a plan chosen in advance, before the foundation of the world."[19] To put what we know about this plan in New Testament terms, the preexistent Son of God became incarnate in our world (John 1:1, 14). But He died.

Peter ultimately seeks to confirm knowledge of redemption in the fact of the resurrection of Jesus Christ, for God **raised him from the dead** (1:21). The end result of this knowledge is that **your faith and hope are in God**. Thus, Christians stand on the brink. "The last age of the world has already dawned and God's chosen ones expect its close in the imminent future with the final manifestation of the King and Christ."[20]

2. PURITY AND LOVE 1:22–25

The plan of God and the work of Christ have produced a response in the lives of Peter's readers. The paragraph begins with the phrase **now that you have purified yourselves** (1:22), which indicates a present reality based on a past action. The phrase, however, can be understood in two different ways. It could refer to their time of conversion, or it could refer to their post-conversion growth in moral purity. Wayne Grudem suggests several reasons for interpreting this as a reference to their post-conversion experiences.[21] He mentions the following: the word *obedience* never clearly means initial saving faith; (2) Peter uses *obedience* in verses 1:2 and 1:14 in reference to obedience in conduct; the word *purify* when used figuratively elsewhere in the New Testament is used in reference to moral cleansing subsequent to conversion; and the context of the apostle's call to holiness in 1:15 suggests that the purifying obedience Peter has in view results from an active response to that call.

THE POWER OF THE TRUTH

The means by which one obtains moral purity is by obeying the truth. This word *truth* contains the gospel message in its entirety, for "truth, like grace, summarizes in a single term that to which Christian believers have been introduced as a result of their rebirth and that reality by which their actions are controlled."[22] The phrase **obeying the truth** contains two ideas.

First, there is the action noun, which in this case is *obeying*. Connected with this noun is the object or recipient of that action, which in this example is *truth*. "The truth here carries a sense of the true way pleasing to God, including not merely the gospel message but the whole of Christian teaching in doctrine and life."[23] To underscore this point, notice how often the term *truth* is used in the New Testament as a synonym for the gospel.[24]

The result of such action is **you have a sincere love for your brothers.** The word *sincere* indicates genuine, unhypocritical conduct. It "marks a brotherly love that is genuine, authentic, without dissimulation (see Rom. 12:9; 2 Cor. 6:6), and in accord with the truth."[25] And Peter is careful to limit this term to the Christian community; brothers is understood as those in the Christian faith.[26]

Since Peter's audience has experienced the above—**now that you have purified**—an imperative command follows. The command is to **love one another deeply.** To love deeply means to do so earnestly, fervently, or constantly. To put the same idea in the negative, we are not to love lightly or perfunctorily. The command to love deeply goes further than having a **sincere love for your brothers**, which is stated in the previous phrase. The idea here is that this term is "used elsewhere of strong, deeply felt, even fervent, emotions or desires."[27] The source of this love is **from the heart.** Notice that the NIV, in a footnote for this verse, indicates that some early manuscripts read *from a pure heart*. This early reading would fit the context of a paragraph treating purity and love. Also, note that with this early reading, this command is placed in a strongly theological context.

THE IMPERISHABLE SEED

Peter continues his argument with another reference to being born again. Peter reminds his readers, **you have been born again** (1:23), which is another example of his frequent use of a verb tense that refers to a past action that has benefits that carry over into the present time. The idea is "you have been and continue to be" born again. This entire phrase is introduced with *for,* which carries the idea of "in light of the fact." Their present circumstance is due to the fact of **seed** at work in their lives. The word Peter selects for *seed* is a rare word and it appears to have been chosen because it focuses more on the process of sowing than on the seed as such.[28] Peter is drawing the contrast between human seed which produces mortal human life and divine seed which produces eternal life. This is not a new idea that Peter develops. He is echoing the apostle John in his gospel prologue where the contrast is between "children born of natural descent" and those "born of God" (John 1:13). The word that pinpoints the contrast is **imperishable**, which means immortal and incorruptible. Peter's point is that seed sown bears characteristics;

> this relegating comes from seed. The idea of human reproduction is in view. Such rebegetting, in contrast to their original begetting, comes from imperishable seed, with the result that the ensuing life shares the characteristics of the divine and imperishable rather than the human and this perishable world.[29]

THE LIVING AND ENDURING WORD

The source of this imperishable seed is **through the living and enduring word of God** (1:23). Previously, in verse 3, Peter drew his readers' attention to "a living hope." Here, it is the word that lives. This living word can refer to the spoken word of God, the written Word of God, or both, since the quotation from Isaiah 40:6–8 refers to the words of God spoken and/or written through Old Testament prophets.[30] The quote Peter uses to support his idea here is important as one reflects on the place this quote is found in Isaiah's prophecy. Isaiah 40–66 are the messages of hope and renewal for a people who must first endure captivity. Many writers have commented on these chapters as being the New Testament gospel message in the Old Testament. From Isaiah's perspective, even in the face of captivity there is hope of a rebirth. The gospel seed will produce its intended result. There are three contrasts in regard to the living and enduring seed: (1) human seed is contrasted with divine seed, (2) perishable is contrasted with imperishable, and (3) the temporary quality of humanity is contrasted with the eternal Word.

The third contrast between the temporal and the eternal is described in terms reminiscent of James 1:10. Humanity is like grass and flowers of the field. Their temporary quality is described as it **withers** and **falls** (1:24). The verb tense indicates the rapid blooming and sudden fading of the flower. In contrast, **the word of the Lord** (1:25) stands forever.

"Peter's assumption is that what Isaiah knew as the word of the Lord lives on as the message of Jesus, and that for himself and his readers the message of Jesus 'endures forever.'"[31]

3. ADDITION BY SUBTRACTION 2:1–3

The doctrinal section of this epistle is quickly moving to a conclusion. Peter has already drawn his readers' attention to the plan of God, the work of Christ, a call to holiness, and the enduring Word of God. Now, Peter takes up the issue of spiritual growth with the intriguing use of basic mathematics. He tells his readers that spiritual growth—the addition of good qualities—can only come about by radical removal—the subtraction of negative traits. This short paragraph contains two commands: the first in the negative (**rid yourself**) and the second, which is stated in the positive (**crave**). The truth of this paragraph is supported by a quote from Psalm 34.

PUT OFF WRONG PRACTICES

The paragraph begins with a link to previous material. **Therefore, rid yourselves** (2:1) begins the first verse. The word *therefore* resumes the line of argument that was interrupted by verses 1:23–25.[32] The word *rid* carries the literal idea of throwing off a piece of clothing. Here, the word is being used as a metaphor to exhort Christians to put off wrong practices.[33]

What exactly are Peter's readers to put off? The answer is in the form of a vice list:[34] **all malice and all deceit, hypocrisy, envy, and slander of every kind** (2:1). The use of a vice and virtue list is a common form within the New Testament Epistles. These lists consist of qualities or actions that typify morality or immorality from a Christian perspective. Examples from the New Testament include Romans 1:29–31; 1 Corinthians 6:9–10; Galatians 5:19–23; James 3:17–18; and 2 Peter 1:5–7.

Before looking at Peter's list in some detail, a couple of remarks seem pertinent. First, "the threefold use of 'all' modifying evil, guile, and slander, conveys the sense of totality and inclusiveness (no exceptions!) and frames this list."[35] Also, it is interesting what Peter instructs his readers to put off. Peter does not mention the grosser vices of paganism, as one might expect. Rather, Peter addresses the "community-destroying vices that are often tolerated by the modern church."[36] We are now ready for a closer look at Peter's vice list.

LIFE CHANGE

IDENTIFYING AND REJECTING VICES

Specific Vice	Broader Implication
all malice	evil, wickedness, ill will, depravity
all deceit	guile, treachery, deceitfulness that harms others through trickery or falsehood
hypocrisy (a plural) as noted in NASB	pretense, insincerity, the masking of inward evil by an outward show of righteousness
envy (a plural) as noted in NASB	jealousy, spite, the opposite of thankfulness for good that comes to others
slander of every kind	evil speech, saying bad things about someone, any speech that harms or is intended to harm another person's status, reputation

As can be seen, all these sins aim at harming other people, whereas love seeks the good of others. There can be no spiritual growth as long as these sins are tolerated. They must be put off.

CRAVE PURE SPIRITUAL MILK

Peter now turns to a positive exhortation. That command is to **crave pure spiritual milk** (2:2). By the use of the imagery milk, Peter makes use of a bold analogy. He states that growing Christians are **like new born babies**. The word *like* has two uses: it may be a particle of comparison or it may be a temporal and consequential particle. The first use is intended here with *as* or *like* introducing verse 2. In a literal context, the phrase *newborn babies* would refer to a baby or an infant. This word would be appropriate as long as the child nurses at its mother's breast. Some writers have taken this to mean that Peter's readers were new in the Christian faith. It is true that new Christians are referred to as babes in Christ. It is also important to remember that this term is not always used in a positive manner. Paul refers to the church at Corinth (1 Cor. 3:1–3) as mere infants and identifies traits that identify them as spiritually immature, like jealous and quarrelsome.

This sounds similar to the vice list that Peter identified. But does this mean that Peter's readers were spiritual infants themselves? "The phrase 'like new born babes' does not imply that Peter thought of his readers as young or immature Christians. The point of comparison is merely the intensity of the longing."[37] New babies crave food. In similar fashion, Christians are to **crave pure spiritual milk** (2:2). The word *crave* implies longing for, or even yearning over. The identical word is used in the Greek translation of Psalm 42:1: "As the deer pants for streams of water, so my soul pants for you, O God." The intense craving of the Christian is directed toward pure milk. The word *pure* means to be without admixture, to be without deceit, or uncontaminated. But this is a special kind of milk. Peter refers to it as spiritual milk. What exactly does Peter have in mind? There is the tradition of the early Church, as the quote from Hilary[38] indicates, that spiritual milk refers to the Word of God. There is strong contextual evidence in 1 Peter to support this understanding of the term milk.[39] Those who favor the identification of milk with the Word of God point to the following evidence:

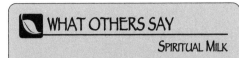

WHAT OTHERS SAY

SPIRITUAL MILK

The pure spiritual milk you long for is found in the Scripture taken in its literal, moral, and spiritual sense.

—Hilary of Arles

- The phrase *Word of God* has just been mentioned in the previous verses (1:23–25).

- The Word of God is said to be living which suggests it is life-giving (1:23) and capable of nourishing and sustaining life, enabling Christians to "grow up in [their] salvation" (2:2).

- The Word of God as spiritually nourishing is consistent with statements elsewhere in Scripture (Deut. 8:3; Matt. 4:4).

- The purity of God's Word is an Old Testament concept (Ps. 12:6;

18:30; 119:96) and would fit the imagery of pure milk.

- The idea of longing for God's Word is an Old Testament concept (Ps. 119:20, 131).

- Reading or listening to God's Word involves a process of taking information into oneself, a process readily represented by a metaphor of drinking milk.

OUR GOAL IS TO GROW

The activity of craving spiritual milk is a healthy response. It produces a desired ultimate goal: **by it you may grow** (2:2). The phrase *so that* introduces a purpose clause. The intended meaning is that the result of "the entire action of craving the guileless milk of the Word"[40] is spiritual growth. The verb *grow* carries with it the idea of spreading, or reaching full growth. The identical idea is found in Ephesians 4:15–16. This full growth is defined as **in your salvation.** In one sense of the word, believers know salvation now; they are saved from their sins. In another sense, Christians are moving towards their salvation. In the current context, "salvation is not spoken of as something that they have already but, as in 1:5, 9, they will receive the reward at the revelation of Christ."[41]

What accounts for this intense desire for spiritual milk? The readers of this epistle have experienced something they cannot escape; they have experienced the reality of God in their lives. While it may not be the entire reality of God's final salvation, they have **tasted** (2:3) enough to give them a craving for more of God. The word *taste* implies to eat or to experience. Peter is using a quote from Psalm 34, which has as its theme the rescue of the faithful by God from danger. "The psalm's metaphor of 'tasting the goodness of the Lord' admirably suits Peter's context, where nursing on milk is the image."[42] Peter assumes they have indeed experienced the work of God in their lives, for he uses the phrase **now that you have** (2:3), which is used for conditional sentences that accept the reality of the condition. The NASB expresses the identical point by introducing the clause with "if you have tasted." What exactly have they experienced? They have tasted that **the Lord is good.** This is not the usual Greek word for *good*, which carries the idea of character or quality. Here, Peter uses a seldom-used word that is interpreted as kind, merciful, or upright. The NASB renders the phrase "tasted the kindness of the Lord."

ENDNOTES

Sidebar: Hilary of Arles, Introductory Commentary on 1 Peter (PL Supp 3:88).

1. John H. Elliott, *1 Peter* (New York: Doubleday, 2000), p. 355. Elliott further divides the theme of holiness into two parts: the holiness of believers, which models that of the holy God who called them (vv. 14–16) and the holiness of Christ through whom their redemption was secured (vv. 17–21b).

2. Wayne Grudem. *1 Peter* (Downers Grove: InterVarsity Press, 2002 reprint) p. 76.

3. Elliott, *1 Peter*, p. 348.

4. Grudem, *1 Peter*, p. 76.

5. Peter Davids, *The First Epistle of Peter* (Grand Rapids: William B. Eerdmans, 1990), p. 65.

6. Paul J. Achtemeier, *1 Peter* (Minneapolis: Fortress Press, 1996), p. 119. He further develops the power of this metaphor by stating, "This points to their need to be as obedient to God, who has newly begotten them, as children normally are to be obedient to the father who begot them," p. 120.

7. Grudem, *1 Peter*, p. 78.

8. Elliott, *1 Peter*, p. 358.

9. Thomas C. Oden, *The Living God*, Systematic Theology: Volume One. (San Francisco: Harper, 1992), p. 99.

10. Ibid., p. 101.

11. Ibid., p. 102. "This is not to say that God requires what is impossible. For it is not impossible for creatures to reflect proportionally the goodness of God as their gifts and capacities allow it. It is in this sense that God calls men and women to be holy and provides them with the means of grace in order to reflect God's holiness in a partial, yet real, vital, and individual way." p. 102.

12. Davids, *The First Epistle of Peter*, p. 69.

13. Ibid., p. 70.

14. See Deut. 10:17; Lev. 19:15; Ps. 82:2; Rom. 2:11; Gal. 2:6; Eph. 6:9; Col. 3:25.

15. Achtemeier, *1 Peter*, p. 125.

16. Grudem, *1 Peter*, p. 80.

17. Davids, *The First Epistle of Peter*, p. 71.

18. Ibid., p. 73.

19. Ibid., pp. 73–74.

20. Ibid., p. 74.

21. Grudem, *1 Peter*, pp. 87–88.

22. Elliott, *1 Peter*, p. 383.

23. Grudem, *1 Peter*, p. 88.

24. Attention is directed to the following: John 8:32; Rom. 2:8; 3:7; 9:1; 2 Cor. 6:7; Gal. 2:5; Eph. 1:13; Col. 1:5; 1 Tim. 2:4; 2 Tim. 2:25; Heb. 10:26; James 1:9; 2 Pet. 2:2; 1 John 2:21.

25. Elliott, *1 Peter*, p. 386.

26. See Achtemeier's comments on this concept in *1 Peter* (Minneapolis: Fortress Press, 1996), p. 137.

27. Grudem, *1 Peter*, p. 89. He calls attention to Acts 12:5 and 26:7 as support.

28. See J. Ramsey Michaels on this point in *1 Peter* (Waco: Word Books Publishers, 1988), p. 76.

29. Achtemeier, *1 Peter*, p. 139.

30. Note Grudem's comments in his commentary on this point, p. 90.

31. Michaels, *1 Peter*, p. 79.

32. Grudem, *1 Peter*, states, "The word 'so' or 'therefore' refers back to the command 'love one another' in verse 22," p. 97.

33. Other illustrations of the metaphorical use of rid can be found at Rom. 13:12; Eph. 4:22, 25; Col. 3:8; Heb. 12:1; James 1:12.

34. See the vice and virtue list in William W. Klein, Craig L. Blomberg, and Robert L. Hubbard *Introduction to Biblical Interpretation* revised and expanded (Nashville: Thomas Nelson Publishers, 1993), p. 438. The authors point to interesting issues for understanding these lists. For instance, the ancient Greek world regularly condoned homosexual acts. Paul's uniform condemnation of them (compare Rom. 1:24–32; 1 Cor. 6:9; 1 Tim 1:10) would have stood out and caused offense. Also, the first and last items on a list often prove the most important, but the subsequent order of items probably indicates no particular hierarchy.

35. Elliott, *1 Peter*, p. 396.

36. Davids, *The First Epistle of Peter*, p. 80.

37. Grudem, *1 Peter*, p. 94.

38. Quotation found in Gerald Bray, ed., *James, 1–2 Peter, 1–3 John, Jude* Ancient Christian Commentary on Scripture (Downers Grove: InterVarsity Press, 2000), p. 82.

39. Wayne Grudem is an example of those who see Peter's context identifying milk with the Word of God. See pp. 95–96.

40. Elliott, *1 Peter*, p. 401.

41. Davids, *The First Epistle of Peter*, p. 82.

42. Elliott, *1 Peter*, p. 403.

3

THE LIVING STONE AND A CHOSEN PEOPLE

1 Peter 2:4–10

With this paragraph we come to the conclusion of the first division in Peter's epistle. This division is the doctrinal section of the letter, with the theme being the plan of God and the work of Christ. As this is brought to a conclusion, one is struck by the use of Old Testament quotes to conclude this section. This passage is notable as representing one of the largest collections of Old Testament images in the New Testament, supported by either direct quotes or allusions from the Old Testament text. Note the chart:

GREAT THEMES

OLD TESTAMENT REFERENCES IN 1 PETER 2:6–10

2:6b	Isa. 28:16
2:7b	Ps. 118:22
2:8a	Isa. 8:14
2:9a, c–d	Deut. 10:15
2:9a–b	Isa. 62:12
2:10:a–b	Hos. 1:6, 9; 2:23

As the title for this chapter suggests, there are two themes that are developed in the passage. The first half of the passage is dominated by the stone metaphor (vv. 4–8) announced in verse 4. The second half is dominated by the idea of the people of God (vv. 9–10) announced in verse 5.[1]

1. CHRIST, THE LIVING STONE 2:4

The paragraph begins with a figure of speech in reference to Christ: **As you come to him**, which is a present tense action, **the living Stone** (2:4). The phrase *come to him* employs a verb frequently used in the Old Testament for drawing near to God, either to hear Him speak (Lev. 9:5; Deut. 4:11; 5:27) or to come into His presence in the Tabernacle to offer sacrifices (Exod. 16:9; Lev. 9:7–8; 10:4–5).[2] The term *come to him* also has a New Testament context in the book of Hebrews as a specialized term for drawing near to God in worship (Heb. 4:16; 7:25; 10:1, 22; 11:6; 12:18, 22). The phrase *living stone* applies a word to Christ (stone), which is often applied to God in the Old Testament (Deut. 32:4; 2 Sam. 23:3; Ps. 18:31; 19:14; 62:2, 7; Isa. 26:4; 30:29).[3] The concept of Christ as a living stone "introduces the stone imagery and designates Christ not as a monument or dead principle, but as the living, resurrected, and therefore life-giving one."[4]

The irony of this statement has not been lost on the Church. Here is Peter, the rock, referring to Christ, as a living Stone. But Peter has precedent for this reference, as Jesus made this application of Psalm 118:22 to himself (Matt. 21:42; Mark 12:10; Luke 20:17).[5] This stone has been **rejected by men** (2:4). The term means rejection after testing. Paul Achtemeier is probably correct when he suggests that "it is the contemporaries of the author who reject the gospel, rather than the rejection Christ suffered at the time of his crucifixion" that is being referred to by this phrase.[6] When Peter introduces the idea of rejection, he is making the contrast of the world's estimate of Christ with God's estimate. He warns the readers that while coming to Christ is to side with God, it will mean human opposition.[7] Peter would have his readers understand the gravity of the situation. When people rejected Christ it was not a causal decision. They examined Him carefully and deemed Him useless. He was rejected after being tested.

But God knew better. This living Stone was **chosen by God**—a phrase that indicates choice or selection on God's part. Christ, the living Stone, was chosen to be by the side of God. What made the difference between being chosen and being rejected? God examined the living Stone, and, in contrast to human assessment, considered Christ to be **precious to him**. The word *precious* implies that He is valuable, honored, esteemed, or distinguished. It was the work of Christ that made Him precious to God.

2. THE CHRISTIAN AS A SPIRITUAL HOUSE 2:5–8

This work now becomes evident in the lives of believers. **You also**, where the intensified use of the personal pronoun is used, **are being built into a spiritual house** (2:5). The word *built* implies erect, build up, or to raise a building. The apostle Paul frequently used the metaphor of a building to indicate the life of the Christian, as in 1 Corinthians 3:9 and 1 Timothy 3:15. The term *spiritual house* is a reference to the nonphysical Church replacing the material Temple in Jerusalem. There is widespread New Testament use for this metaphor.[8] How shall the inhabitants of this house be identified? The New Testament believer will be identified by terms associated with a select group of Old Testament individuals. Notice the terminology in the chart.

GREAT THEMES

THE CHRISTIAN AS
A SPIRITUAL HOUSE

Built into a Spiritual House:
The place where the Spirit is to be found

Being a Holy Priesthood:
The purpose of God in building Christians into a spiritual house

Offering Spiritual Sacrifices through Christ:
Even the worship and praise of the Christian is dependent on the work of Christ for its acceptability

What are we to make of Peter's imagery? Peter hints "that all believers now enjoy the great privilege, reserved only for priests in the Old Testament, of 'drawing near' to God in worship."[9] In light of this great concept, the Protestant Church has always believed in the priesthood of all believers. Thus, Christians are made a spiritual house to the end that they are a body of priests whose purpose is to offer acceptable sacrifices to God. For Peter's message to be fully understood, one must appreciate two significant shifts of thought that occur at verse 5.

The first shift is Christ as the cornerstone and human beings as the builders. The second shift is Christians as stones and part of the building to Christians as priests serving in the building.[10]

Jesus as the Stone is supported by various Old Testament quotations. As mentioned in the opening paragraph of this section, this is where we find a great concentration of quotes. Verse 6 begins with **for**, or *therefore*, or in some translations *hence*. This is the identical word used to introduce the quotation in 1 Peter 1:16 and 1:24. In the present context, its use shows that the intention is to begin the explication of the themes in verses 4 and 5. The phrase **in Scripture it says** (2:6) is an impersonal verb meaning it stands or it says. The actual quote begins with **see,** or *behold,* and carries the implied command look or listen. The theme of this quote from Isaiah is **I lay a stone in Zion**. What does Isaiah say about this stone? It is **chosen**, a concept mentioned in verse 4. Both Christ and the people of God (1:1) are said to be chosen. This stone is **precious**, which is again mentioned in verse 4. This stone is **the cornerstone**, by which is meant the keystone, or "chief cornerstone" as in Ephesians 2:20.

Why is this stone so important? "One's fate is determined by one's relation to Christ. Either one builds on him as a precious cornerstone and thus belongs to God's people, or one stumbles over him and rejects him and is not a member of that people."[11] One's relationship to Christ is determined by one's faith response to Christ, or in Peter's terms, **one who trusts in him**. The verb action is present tense, so it literally means the one who is trusting or believing. This trusting individual **will never** be put to shame. The Greek language has five different ways to express the negative. The usage here is the strongest possible in the Greek language. In Greek, it is a double negative. While in English a double negative becomes a positive statement, in Greek the double negative serves to intensify the negation. It carries the thought of "Don't you even dare." The NIV translation "will never" carries the same intensity. The one who is believing will never **be put to shame**. This verb carries the basic idea of dishonor or disgrace.

At this juncture in the paragraph, many writers draw attention to another contrast Peter has used in making his point to his readers. This contrast is between honor and shame. "Honor, which means one's worth, good name, fame, social rating, and esteem as recognized by others, was a pivotal value of ancient Mediterranean culture."[12] The one who trusts will be honored; the one who rejects will be put to shame.

Verse 7 in this paragraph is admittedly a difficult verse to interpret. The various English translations provide a number of possibilities. One way to gain an understanding of this verse would be to review several English versions. The NASB, for instance, begins verse 7 with the phrase *this precious value*, which is the rendering of the basic Greek word for *honor*. Honor, as mentioned previously, carries the idea of respect, price, or value. The basic idea the NIV would have us understand is that of a contrast between those who believe and those who do not believe. The ones who believe have made their commitment based on the idea of the stone being precious. Those who do not believe have examined the stone and have determined there is no value to the stone. Both situations imply an examination of the stone, but each has different results. The ones who believe found the value; the unbelievers did not see the worth of the stone and **rejected** the Stone (2:4).

Verse 8 is a quote from Isaiah 8:14: **A stone that causes men to stumble** . . . The word *stumble* points to that which causes stumbling or offense. The stone imagery is now **a rock that makes them fall**. The term *fall* implies that which causes sin or gives occasion for sin. This quote from Isaiah 8:14 identifies a tragic mistake that humankind is prone to make: to examine the stone and then reject the stone because it is considered to be of no value. This mistake will produce eternal results.

The stone has become the capstone of the building. If rejected, this stone causes people to stumble. This stone ultimately makes people fall. Why? They ultimately fall because they **disobey the message** (2:8). When Peter uses the word disobey, he points to the root cause of their fall. To disobey means to be an unbeliever, or to refuse to believe. It is actually their own fault. They refused to believe and obey.

 GREAT THEMES

JESUS AS THE STONE

- Some believe the Stone and commit to Him.

- Others reject the Stone and do not believe.

- Those who reject the Stone are destined to stumble and fall.

- Those who believe in the Stone will never be put to shame.

- Christians are living stones because they are in Christ.

As people move toward the future, Jesus encounters them. This encounter can have two results. The "stone" in their way is either a "foundation stone" to which they can commit themselves without any concern over being let down, or it is the "stone" which, due to their rejection and God's eventual exaltation, leads to their fall. They must, however, encounter the stone; it lies in their way.[13]

Their tragic end, to stumble and fall, is **what they were destined for**. In referring to the phrase *they were destined for*, Peter Davids observes that "the deliberate control of God in this process and His forcing this division by this encounter with 'the stone' is indicated."[14] The text is referring more to corporate destiny than to individual destiny, to the irony that a group formerly estranged from God is now elect, is in, while a group that would seem to have a good or better chance of being in is now out.

Their eternal destiny is the appointed end of all those who deliberately refuse to believe. It is not an inability to understand, but rather it is a deliberate refusal to do what one knows they should do. For such an individual, there is only one end.

3. THE SPIRITUAL STATUS OF BELIEVERS 2:9–10

Peter is determined to end this doctrinal section on a positive note. He concludes with a review of the status of the believer. Verses 9–10 "return to the topic of their privileged position in God's temple, using the emphatic 'but you' to make the transition and contrast clear."[15] As we note when we read 1 Peter 2:9–10, this privileged position is described by transferring to the Church the titles of Israel in the Old Testament.

Why this special status? Those who believe have a special assignment while here on earth. Their status is so that they may become a witness of the good things of God. They are to **declare the praises of him** (2:9). The purpose of their special position is that they might announce the glorious deeds of God.[16] The content of their praise is noted in the contrast of God's call on them **out of darkness into his wonderful light.** The connotation of darkness is sin and evil. In contrast, light has theological meaning: a deliverance from sin and evil. This is further clarified by this light being described as **wonderful.**

The entire paragraph concludes with allusions to the book of Hosea. Peter makes these points:

- Once you were not a people, but now you are the people of God.

- Once you had not received mercy, but now you have received mercy.

These allusions are to the life of Hosea and how children not his own have become his own children (Hos. 2:23). In the sense of the New Testament, Gentiles, who formerly were not the people of God, have now become the people of God through His great mercy.

ENDNOTES

1. For further study of the structure of this paragraph, refer to Paul J. Achtemeier, *1 Peter* (Minneapolis: Fortress Press, 1996), p. 150. Here and in the surrounding paragraphs, the writer analyzes the structure for this last paragraph.

2. Wayne Grudem, *1 Peter* (Grand Rapids: William B. Eerdmans Publishing Company, 2002 reprint), p. 97.

3. See Achtemeier, *1 Peter,* p. 154.

4. Peter Davids, *The First Epistle of Peter* (Grand Rapids: William B. Eerdmans Publishing Company, 1990), p. 85.

5. Note Grudem's discussion of this in *1 Peter*, p. 97.

6. Achtemeier, *1 Peter*, p. 154.

7. See Grudem, *1 Peter*, p. 98, for a full discussion of the implications of this contrast.

8. Davids, *The First Epistle of Peter,* p. 87, draws attention to the following texts: Mark 14:58; 15:29; John 2:19; 4:21, 23–24; Acts 7:48; 17:24.

9. Grudem, *1 Peter*, p. 97.

10. See Davids, *The First Epistle of Peter,* p. 86, for a complete discussion of this important point.

11. Achtemeier, *1 Peter*, p. 163.

12. John Elliott, *1 Peter* (Minneapolis: Fortress Press, 2000), p. 411. Elliott continues to show the importance of Peter's contrast when he writes, "Such honor was connected to and contrasted with 'shame' (the actual loss, or sensitivity regarding the loss of honor)." Elliott's summary is important: "The honor that is conferred by God upon both Jesus Christ (vv. 4d, 6b, 7c) and his believers (vv. 5,

regarding the loss of honor)." Elliott's summary is important: "The honor that is conferred by God upon both Jesus Christ (vv. 4d, 6b, 7c) and his believers (vv. 5, 7a, 9–10) is contrasted to the divine shaming (vv. 6c, 7bc, 8ab) of those who have shamed and rejected both Jesus (v. 4c) and his followers (4:14–16)." p. 411.

13. Davids, *The First Epistle of Peter*, p. 89 and following.

14. Ibid., p. 90.

15. Ibid.

16. See Davids, *The First Epistle of Peter*, p. 92, for further development of this concept.

Part Two

Accepting Submission and Living for God

1 PETER 2:11–4:11

4

LIVING AMONG THE PAGANS

1 Peter 2:11–12

How would one know that a new section begins at verse 2:11? A couple of factors aid one's understanding of the structure of 1 Peter. For instance, the descriptive adjective with which 2:11 begins, "Dear friends," repeated in 4:12, indicates the boundaries of this passage. Another key would be the benediction found in 4:11b. Taken together, one feels assured that Peter intends 2:11–4:11 to be recognized as the next major section in his epistle. "The organization of this material is determined by shifts in groups addressed rather than by repeated linguistic patters."[1] The chart identifies the groups that are addressed in this passage.

If Peter is following the

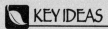

KEY IDEAS

INTENDED AUDIENCE FOR INSTRUCTIONS

Readers in general (2:11–12)

Specific groups (2:13–3:7)

- to those subject to authorities (2:13–17)
- to those subject to masters (2:18–25)
- to wives and husbands (3:1–7)

Readers in general (4:1–7)

structure of an epistle as found in other New Testament letters, we would expect a change in content and writing style beginning in this section. The usual structure of the body of a New Testament letter is doctrine first and then ethical instruction on how the theological truths impact one's daily life. One can discern this structure in the Pauline letters. The book of Romans, for example, has an extensive theological section (1:18–11:36) that is followed by the ethical instruction (12:1–15:33). Another example from the book of Galatians shows the theological section (3:1–4:31) followed by the ethical teaching (5:1–6:10). The identical structure is found in 1 Peter.

In addition to a shift from doctrine to ethical instruction, there is a shift in the style of writing. Doctrinal instruction is presented with straightforward declarative sentences. Theology is presented in this manner to convince, instruct, or correct. Theological writing performs a task. It offers instruction to specific issues either raised by the readers of the epistle or correction to wrong theology. But ethical instruction is different. This type of writing clarifies the implications of doctrine for daily life. The key in the detection of when one turns from doctrine to ethics is to pick up on the commands that accompany ethical writing. Thus we are not surprised when we turn to 1 Peter 2:11 and read that Peter urges his readers to take a particular action. Likewise, we are not surprised to find that Peter commands readers to submit to a particular course of conduct (2:13). This is the terminology of ethical instruction.

Throughout 2:11–4:11, Peter continually makes the point that a specific code of conduct is demanded of Christian believers. The believers reading Peter's letter find themselves in a paradox. The readers have identified themselves with Christ, the Savior of the world. For God, this Christ is chosen and precious. But the unbelievers have rejected this Christ. The issue identifies the tension of "appropriate conduct for Christians whom their contemporary culture looks upon as they do other exiles and aliens who are members of a foreign people and who follow strange and often unacceptable customs."[2]

Also, it is clear from the tone of this section that Peter fully expects Christians to continue in the life of their societies. He does not present a message of escapism or resignation. Even in the face of opposition, Christians are to continue to live in their world and seek to be the salt and light of their world as their Savior commanded them. By continuing to participate in their world, Christians may have the opportunity to witness to their faith (3:15b) and may win some nonbelievers to the faith (3:1–2). Whether this happens or not, participation in their world is to continue, even when that participation results in rejection and suffering, as it inevitably will (2:20b; 3:17).

1. THEOLOGY AND PRACTICE 2:11

This small paragraph forms the transition between Peter's articulation of doctrine and his practical exhortations in regards to ethical conduct. "The subject under consideration is Peter's readers' engagement with outsider 'Gentiles' (that is, nonbelievers) and the manner in which their honor as the elect and holy people of God can be maintained in the face of slander, insult, and suffering—issues taken up throughout the remainder of the letter."[3] Peter addresses his readers as **dear friends** (2:11), a form of greeting which will be found later in 4:12 and 2 Peter 3:14. The term *beloved* or *dear friend* is frequently used in the New Testament when the readers are reminded of tradition, a force it may also carry here.[4] The phrase *dear friends* carries the idea of loved one, beloved, or dearest.

We recognize that we are in the ethical section of 1 Peter when he writes **I urge you** where the term means urge or beseech. When the word *urge* is connected with the word *beloved*, it serves as a way of introducing detailed instructions on Christian behavior (Rom. 12:1; Eph. 4:1; 1 Thess. 2:8).[5]

The twofold manner in which Peter addresses his readers reminds us of the salutation (1:1). Here, they are **aliens and strangers** (2:11). The basic understanding of the term *alien* is of one who lives in a foreign country. The term *stranger* implies a temporary sojourner. But Peter has more than just a secular understanding of these two terms. This combination continues Peter's practice of applying to Christians the terms originally applied to Israel in the Old Testament. Abraham is the prime example of an "alien" or "stranger."[6] Peter is not drawing from the secular vocabulary used to indicate classes of residents in lands other than their own.

2. ABSTAIN FROM THE NEGATIVES 2:11

Peter's readers are **to abstain from sinful desires**. The word *abstain* carries with it the idea of avoiding or keeping free from something. The phrase conveys the sense of continually keeping away from sinful desires. The object of the verb will indicate what one is to avoid. In this context, the object is sinful desires. The word rendered *sinful* is used to convey the idea of belonging to this world and not being under the control of God's Spirit. It also has the connotation of fleshy, that which pertains to human bodies. It is used to identify those impulses that belong to the selfish and lower side of humankind's nature. "In 1 Peter the adjective refers to the human beings apart from God. This is the only place where 'flesh' carries the Pauline ethical sense. The contrast here is not with 'spirit' as is usual in Paul, but with 'life' or 'soul,' the only place that contrast appears in the New Testament."[7]

Why must the Christian abstain from sinful desires? As Peter reminds his readers, sinful desires **war against your soul** (2:11). The imagery of one's natural impulses waging war against one's ultimate best interests is paralleled in Romans 7:23 and James 4:1. On the other hand, Paul describes the counter-warfare necessary against such inward rebellion in 2 Corinthians 10:3–6.[8] The word *war* is an unusual word with seven different connotations, all within a military context. This particular verb means to serve as a soldier, wage war, or battle. A commentary on this verse would be Galatians 5:17, where the same thought is given by Paul with his flesh/Spirit imagery and his reminder that "they are in conflict with each other." The tense of the verb *war* is the present tense, which carries the idea of continuous action in the present time. The point of Peter's exhortation is that the inward sinful desire continually wages a spiritual battle against the spiritual soul of the believer.

3. GOOD LIVES AMONG THE PAGANS 2:12

The compliment of the negative "abstain from sinful desires" is the positive exhortation to **live such good lives among the pagans** (2:12). The emphasis is "on conduct that can be seen and appreciated as 'good' even by fellow citizens who are not believers in Christ."[9] The phrase *good lives* is one of the key theological themes for this letter as was noted in the Introduction. It was first introduced to the readers at 1:15 and Peter returns to the same thought here. The word *lives* carries with it a manner of life, conduct, or behavior. Underlying this call to live good lives is the conviction that both Christians and pagans recognize good behavior, yet without the idea that the good is identical for both.[10] The call to live good lives refers to one's general conduct, public and private. Of the six times it is used in 1 Peter, four are connected to witness to the unbelievers: 2:12; 3:1–2, 16 (the other two are 1:15, 18). This good life is to be lived among the pagans. When *pagan* is in the singular, it implies nation. In the plural, as here, it indicates heathens, those who have no knowledge of the true God.

It should be apparent to all that living the good life is preferable just because it is the good life. No further reason is needed. But, Peter does remind his readers that living the good life has residual benefits even for the unbeliever. Peter exhorts his readers to live the good life that "in the circumstances when" or "in the case where" something will occur. What is the circumstance that Peter foresees? People will **accuse you of doing wrong.** The word *accuse* means to speak evil of, say bad things against, or slander. The terminology of this circumstance covers verbal abuse.[11] Other terms used by Peter include *insult* (2:23; 3:9), *retaliate* (2:23), *malign* (4:4 NASB); *revile* (3:16 NASB), and *reproach* (4:14 KJV). Peter forewarned his readers about the potential of verbal abuse back in verse 2:1. The accusation is one of doing wrong where the term refers to an evildoer, a wrongdoer, or even a criminal.

But this accusation cannot be sustained. The very ones who make the accusations prove themselves wrong by what they actually see. They **see your good deeds** (2:12).[12] The word *see* carries the idea of looking upon, observing, being eyewitnesses to, or carefully watching over a period of time. The idea Peter presents is that the unbeliever is an observer who carefully watches the conduct of the Christian over a period of time. The entire phrase *see your good deeds* suggests an act of observing that leads to a change of mind or outlook, like having one's eyes opened to something not seen before.[13] The end result is that the unbeliever will **glorify God.** There is a difference of interpretation of this phrase among biblical scholars. Some, like Elliott[14] understand this phrase to mean that the positive impact of living good lives is not only the refutation of slander as baseless but the moving of erstwhile detractors to glorify God. On the other hand, writers like Michaels[15] say the circumstance was not that

Christians would proclaim to the unbeliever the gospel of Christ, but that simply by observing the good conduct of those who believe in Christ, the accusers would see that their charges were false. If, as seems apparent, that Peter is drawing from the teaching of Jesus in Matthew 5:16, then Elliot's view seems to be the correct one.

4. UNBELIEVERS WILL SOMEDAY GLORIFY GOD 2:12

Four observations can be made in comparing and contrasting the teaching of Jesus and that of Peter.

GREAT THEMES

JESUS' TEACHINGS IN PETER

Jesus (Matt. 5:16)	Peter (1 Pet. 2:12)
1. "Let your light shine"	1. "Keep you behavior excellent"
2. "before men"	2. "among the Gentiles"
3. "that they may see"	3. "as they observe"
4. "your Father in heaven"	4. "God in the day of visitation"

The basic concept is the same, but there are four subtle differences. Peter's instructions are more specific than the teachings from the Sermon on the Mount. For instance, Jesus speaks of letting one's "light shine" whereas Peter specifically mentions "your excellent behavior." Jesus speaks of the light shining before "men," and Peter specifically directs excellent behavior before "the Gentiles." Also, Jesus speaks of people "seeing good works," and He uses a rather basic word for seeing. Peter, on the other hand, uses a word that means to look upon, to observe, or to view carefully. Finally, Peter speaks of individuals glorifying God "in the day of visitation." This day is to be understood as the final Day of Judgment.

The unbeliever will glorify God. When will this praise be given? It will be made **on the day he visits us** (2:12). The visitations of God may be positive, as when He visited His people to liberate them from Egyptian bondage (Gen. 50:21–25; Exod. 3:16; 4:31; 13:19) and from

Babylonian Exile (Jer. 27:22; 29:10; 32:5). On the other hand, the day of God's visitation has a negative, judgmental connotation (Zeph. 1:7, 14–15; 2:2–3; Zech. 14:1–20).

How is it being used in the present context? The marginal reading of the NASB suggests "Christ's coming again in judgment." Paul Achtemeier supports the NASB when he states this visitation "points to the time of the final judgment."[16] Wayne Grudem states that this refers to "the final judgment when the unbelievers who are currently slandering Christians will glorify God."[17] On the other hand, John Elliott believes that "it is more likely that this phrase refers to God's visitation of individual nonbelievers as an occasion of testing when they are confronted with the winsome behavior of the believers and are thereby motivated to join the Christians in their glorification of God."[18]

ENDNOTES

1. Paul J. Achtemeier, *1 Peter* (Minneapolis: Fortress Press, 1996), p. 169.

2. Ibid., p. 170.

3. John Elliott, *1 Peter* (New York: Doubleday, 2000), p. 456.

4. The interested reader can pursue this concept by reading Achtemeier, *1 Peter*, p. 173.

5. Elliott draws attention to the fact that the word *exhort* occurs frequently in the New Testament, often with the overlapping sense of appeal, urge, or exhort. He also notes that "often it is used to introduce traditional hortatory [or strong encouragement] material (Rom. 12:1; Eph. 4:1; 1 Thess. 4:1,10; 5:14; 2 Thess. 3:12; 1 Tim 6:2; Titus 2:6, 15)." See his discussion in *1 Peter*, beginning on p. 462.

6. Achtemeier, *1 Peter*, p. 174.

7. Ibid., p. 176.

8. See J. Ramsey Michaels, *1 Peter* (Waco: Word Books Publishers, 1988), p. 116, for a detailed discussion of the imagery of waging war.

9. Ibid., p. 117.

10. Turn to Achtemeier, *1 Peter*, p. 176, for a discussion of this topic.

11. Elliott, *1 Peter*, pp. 466–467.

12. The stress on good deeds is found frequently in the New Testament. Note 1 Timothy 5:10, 25; 6:18; Titus 2:7, 14; 3:8, 14.

13. See Michaels, *1 Peter*, p. 118, for a continuation of this idea.

14. Elliott, *1 Peter,* p. 469.

15. *Michaels, 1 Peter,* p. 118.

16. Achtemeier, *1 Peter,* p. 178.

17. Wayne Grudem, *1 Peter* (Grand Rapids: William B. Eerdmans, 2002 reprint), p. 117.

18. Elliott, *1 Peter,* p. 471.

5

LEARNING SUBMISSION

1 Peter 2:13–3:7

1. SUBMISSION TO AUTHORITY 2:13–17

With this paragraph we find in 1 Peter a series of exhortations that apply to the general ethical principle that was stated in 2:11–12. This principle is applied to specific social behaviors, civil and domestic, involving the interaction of believers with nonbelievers. Peter's basic concern is the life of submission in its varied relationships. While the content of Peter's instruction is similar to Paul's teaching in Romans 13 in regard to civil authority, there are subtle differences between them to indicate that Peter is not simply restating Paul's position.[1]

DO WHAT IS RIGHT

The text begins with the command "submit yourselves," which is the clue that we are in the ethical section of the letter. Each of the following paragraphs (2:13–17; 2:18–25; and 3:1–7) has the common feature of a command to be in subordination. This common feature is noted at 2:13, 18; and 3:1, 5. But "subordination is an illustration of the larger theme that dominates 2:13–4:19, namely the necessity of doing what is right rather than doing what is wrong."[2] The word **submit** (2:13) implies to be subject to, to be under the authority of, or to take a subordinate place. The question as to the extent of this subjection, and what to do when the call to subjection goes against Christian duty, becomes the immediate issue when this topic is presented. "The principle to be drawn is 'obey except when commanded to sin.' This is the Christian's responsibility toward all forms of rightful human authority, whether the individual Christian agrees with all the policies of that authority or not."[3]

WHAT OTHERS SAY

SUBMITTING TO AUTHORITIES

By "every human authority" Peter means those which have been ordained by rulers. We are called to submit to them for the Lord's sake, because he himself said: "Render unto Caesar the things that are Caesar's," but if they command something which is not God's will we must not obey them.

—Andreas, Catena CEC 55

Paul Achtemeier introduces the idea that perhaps the Christian reader has the wrong idea of what subordination actually implies. He suggests that Peter's purpose in using this term is to help individuals "find their proper place and act accordingly, rather than calling upon one to give unquestioning obedience to whatever anyone, including governing authorities, may command."[4] As the quote from the Church Father Andreas illustrates, the early Church also struggled with the issue of submission.[5] This is the first of six occurrences of the word *submit* in 1 Peter. The other uses are found in verses 2:18; 3:1, 5, 22; 5:5. The word occurs 38 times in the New Testament. It is frequently found in contexts of moral instruction (Rom. 13:1, 5; 1 Cor. 14:32; 16:16; Eph. 5:21,22; Col. 3:18; Titus 2:5,9; 3:1; James 4:7).

The motivation for the command to submit is action done **for the Lord's sake** (2:13) or literally *because of the Lord*. When this kind of phrase is used, it gives the theological basis for this submission.[6] The extent of this command is as wide as possible. Submission is to **every authority instituted among men** or as the NASB renders it, "to every human institution." The civil authority described here is authority that is characteristic of humankind, that which is made by human beings, or that which proceeds from humankind.

The civil official with the authority is now described. Authority is introduced with the "whether . . . or . . ." construction.[7] In this context, the contrast is between the king, as one in authority or to governors, who represent the king. **Governors** could be appointed by the emperor or appointed by the Roman senate. Civil authorities have two basic sanctions. The first is negative: they are **to punish those who do wrong** (2:14). The second is a positive act when they **commend those who do right**. *Punish* implies rendering justice or retribution. The word *wrong* implies an action that is evil, harmful, or injures someone else. The positive side of civil authority is to praise right actions. The one who does what is right is said to be one who does good. The root for this word *do good/right* appears six times in 1 Peter. These are found in verses 3:6 and 4:19 to describe Christian behavior generally; in verses 2:14, 15 to describe Christian behavior in the pagan world; and in verses 2:20 and 3:17, to describe Christian behavior that may cause suffering at the hands of society.[8]

THEOLOGY BEHIND RIGHT CONDUCT

Right conduct is not only conduct that pleases the king, but more importantly, right conduct is **God's will** (2:15). The idea of God's will is introduced by the phrase *for it is the will of God,* where the preposition *for* becomes the causal explanation for the preceding exhortation. There are eleven such occurrences in 1 Peter.

In each of these instances, the causal explanation provides the theological foundation for the exhortation. This understanding of the will of God removes it from the purely theoretical domain and makes theological discussion a very practical issue. Doing what is right and thus accomplishing the will of God is positive obedience. It will **silence ignorant talk of foolish men** (2:15). "In their rebellion against God they are ignorant of his ways and thus perceive the behavior of Christians in a warped manner."[9] The verb *to silence* means to muzzle, put to silence, gag, or restrain. Ignorant talk is not simply talk based on the wrong facts. Ignorant talk implies a disregard for something. It becomes a sin in ignorance, as Hebrews 5:2 illustrates.

Verse 16 implies a command for free men, but we must supply the verb. The NIV uses live, while the NASB uses act. To **live as free men** (2:16) indicates a man or woman who is free as opposed to being a slave. But from what are Peter's readers specifically free? Freedom is usually understood as Christian freedom in a theological sense.[10] As Christians, Peter's readers are to live as free men and women and to act accordingly. However, they are not to live this ethical lifestyle as a **cover-up for evil**. The word cover-up implies a concealment or a pretext. Rather, they are to live and act as free men and women because they are **servants of God**. The last part of this verse is introduced with a strong contrast (*but*), and it is clear that the contrast is not between free people and servants of God, but between those who regard freedom as a cover for evil and those who are such servants.

THE "PROBLEM" OF RIGHT CONDUCT

This paragraph concludes with four commands. This occurrence of the command is so vital for ethical writing that a brief comment on the verb tense of commands is required. Command statements are of two types. The first type of command implies the simple action. Its meaning is do this, or do that. The second type of command implies a continual or habitual action. The meaning then would be do this—and keep on doing it. The four commands in verse 17 are (1) **show proper respect**, (2) **love your Christian brothers and sisters** (NLT), (3) **fear God**, and (4) **honor the king**. There is a certain order implied in these four commands. Peter has "established a hierarchy of values and allegiances: all people, including the emperor, are to be shown due honor and respect; fellow Christians are to be regarded as members of one's own family and shown appropriate love; God alone is to be shown reverence."[11] Another way of looking at these four commands is by seeing them as a well-structured piece of poetry.

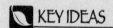 KEY IDEAS

HOW TO RELATE TO OTHERS

A. Honor everyone (external relations)
B Love the brotherhood
(internal relations)
B¹ Revere God (internal relations)
A¹ Honor the emperor
(external relations)

John Elliott[12] sees here a distinction being drawn between the respect due to outsiders and the loyalty due within the community to fellow members and God. The first command, "Show proper respect," is a simple command. The act of showing respect is the point of this command. The

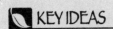

KEY IDEAS

WHOM TO OBEY

Where civic and Christian good intersect, the Christian is to perform it; where they diverge, the Christian is to follow God's will, not the emperor's decrees. The former will keep the Christian from unnecessary difficulty with civil authorities; the latter virtually guarantees such difficulty.

other three commands imply ongoing activity. They are to love their Christian brothers and sisters and keep on loving them; they are to fear (or reverence, hallow) God and continually or habitually fear God; and to honor and keep on honoring the king. The will of God is seen in active obedience, and, in this paragraph, obedience is to civil authority.

With this first paragraph in the ethical section of 1 Peter, we come face-to-face with the "problem" of 1 Peter: Christians must obey God.[13]

2. SUBMISSION TO MASTERS 2:18–25

This last paragraph of chapter 2 continues the theme of submission. Previously, Peter outlined the believer's responsibility of submission to civil authorities. Now, he turns his attention to relationships between servants and their masters. The admonitions Peter uses to address the relationship between servant and master are a part of New Testament household codes, a form widely used in the first-century secular literature as well.[14] Comparing the secular codes with the New Testament examples, it is interesting that the proper response of a servant to his master is even mentioned. As Paul Achtemeier states: "Lack of advice to slaves in secular codes reflects their legal status in the Roman Empire, where, according to classical theory, they were defined as chattel [or property] who, lacking citizenship, lacked the essential qualifications of humanity."[15]

THE CHRISTIAN AND SUBMISSION

The paragraph begins with **submit yourselves**, with the subject to be discovered by the context. The NASB begins the paragraph with "Servants, be submissive." It is interesting to note that the NASB identified the servants as household servants. This type of servant might be well-educated and would perhaps hold a responsible position in the household. While this description may seem to differ from Achtemeier's definition of a slave as mere chattel, it remains a correct point that Jewish and Stoic duty codes put no such moral demands on slaves, only on masters.[16]

Servants are to be characterized by two traits: submission to their masters and an attitude of **respect** (2:18). The word *respect* can be used as reverence for God or respect for people. When used of relationships to human authorities the word translated *respect* has the implication of a healthy desire to avoid their displeasure as in Romans 13:7; 1 Peter 3:2, 16; and the related verb in Ephesians 5:33. The word *respect* is the nearest English equivalent. On the other hand, "subordination is to be carried out with all reverence and fear, [and it] does not refer to the slaves' attitude to their owners but to God."[17] It is the spirit of reverence towards God that induces respect and faithfulness to duty in the sphere of human relations.

Peter does not allow for partial submission. One cannot choose to whom he or she will submit. Nor can submission be based on the kind conduct of a master. The admonition is to be submissive **not only** to good and considerate masters, **but** also to those who are **harsh**. A considerate master is gentle and forbearing. Submission to this type of individual does not require much Christian ethic. However, in as strong as contrast as possible, submission to a harsh, unreasonable, perverse, crooked, and dishonest individual requires real Christian faith and ethics. Regardless of which kind of master, the servant is admonished to be in submission to either one.

Why would Peter make such strong demands of a servant when his master is perverse and harsh? There is no earthly reason to justify such commands, and so the answer must be found in the spiritual realm. It is there that Peter reminds his readers that such action is **commendable** (2:19). The word translated *commendable* is that which is frequently translated *grace*. It also can mean thanks or excellence. In the present context, the word means "patiently bearing unjust suffering. It does not here have its usual meaning of divine grace; rather, it is used in the sense of something pleasing to God."[18]

What is commendable? Peter raises the possibility that if a person **bears up** under **pain**, that is commendable. To *bear up* implies endurance, or bearing up under. But mere endurance is no cause for pride. If the beating is deserved, there is no glory in bearing it. On the other hand, to show patience in the face of injustice is true evidence of Christian character. This enduring of unjust suffering is tolerable because the one enduring this pain is conscious of God. Notice the structure of Peter's argument.

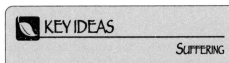

KEY IDEAS

SUFFERING

"For it is commendable if a man bears up under the pain of unjust suffering because he is conscious of God" (2:19).

"But how is it to your credit if you receive a beating for doing wrong and endure it?" (2:20).

"But if you suffer for doing good and you endure it, this is commendable before God" (2:20).

Suffering can be listed to your **credit** (2:20). The word *credit* implies honor, enhanced reputation, or prestige. But it all depends on whether servants are **doing wrong** or if they are **doing good** and still receive a beating simply because the master is cruel.

A CALL TO SUFFERING

Why is suffering for doing good commendable? The answer lies in what Peter refers to as the call on each Christian's life. Peter phrases it as **you were called** (2:21), which carries the idea of an invitation or summon. This call is in the passive voice, indicating it is God who calls. Notice how Peter refers to the concept of the call in several passages in his letter with important key ideas.

The above texts develop a very important teaching point for Peter. As Christ did not receive the crown of glory without the crown of thorns, this call for the believer also means that the expectation of privilege and light, blessing, and eternal glory will not come without the current experience of suffering patiently endured.[19]

CHRIST, THE MODEL SUFFERER

Thankfully, Christ has given us a model for Christian suffering. Peter begins to develop this model with the phrase **because Christ suffered for you** (2:21). The word *because* or *since,* as in the NASB, serves to introduce significant teaching that deals with the relationship between Christ and believers. Peter uses this technique elsewhere, as in 2:5; 3:18; and 4:1. Each text expresses a particular contrast between Christ and the believers. Here, "the commonality between Christ who suffered innocently and the innocent suffering of servants" is the point that Peter is making.[20] The fact that Christ suffered innocently is underscored by the fact "he suffered for you" where the preposition *for* has great theological importance.

The New Testament affirms Christ's total sinlessness in many passages.[21] If Christ, the sinless one, suffered, it must have been for someone else. This is where terms like "vicarious atonement" and "substitutionary atonement" become so important in any discussion of the doctrine of the atonement. An example of how the early Church understood this concept of Christ's vicarious atonement is found in Galatians 1:4 where Paul writes that the Lord Jesus Christ "gave himself *for* our sins."

The model of Christ's suffering leaves an example, which is Peter's way of informing his readers that Christ left them something that they are to follow. The suffering of Christ impacts our understanding of suffering in two ways. First, when Peter states that Christ suffered, he is using a word that becomes almost his personal word for passion. Out of the forty-two times it is used in the New Testament, Peter uses it twelve times. A reason for Peter's interest in this term is perhaps due to the fact the Jesus himself described His death as a suffering (Mark 8:13; 9:12).

The second interesting aspect of this example is that Peter intends that his readers will "follow this example" by following in Christ's footsteps. The theme of following Christ is a frequent one in the New Testament.[22] In fact, the phrase *follow in His steps* became a Christian technical term for being a follower of Jesus. Notice, for instance, this verb is of the same family as a verb used in the Jesus narratives of those who respond to the call of Jesus and follow Him, either in the physical sense of accompanying Him as disciples (Mark 1:16–20; Luke 9:57–62) or figuratively, as going the way of the suffering Jesus or living in His Spirit (Mark 8:34–9:1; 10:38–39; Luke 14:27).[23]

The believer is admonished to follow **his steps** (2:21). In the plural, this means the line of footprints. To follow an individual's footprints is to move in the direction he is going. Peter's admonition to follow in Christ's steps, and thus embrace the suffering which He embraced, is supported by a quotation from the suffering servant text, Isaiah 53:9. As He patiently endured wrong treatment, the believer is called to follow that same path.

In reference to Christ's sufferings, Peter notes that **when they hurled their insults at him** (2:23), He did not retaliate. The word *insult* carries the idea of cursing or speaking evil of. The tense of the verb indicates that this was done over and over again. What was Christ's response? He did not retaliate; He did not return or give back with abusive language. And again, just as the insults were repeated over and over again, so Christ's refusal to retaliate occurred over and over again.[24]

When [Christ] **suffered, he made no threats.** Literally, the word threat implies that He did not begin to threaten, or that he repeatedly made no threats. Either way of understanding this phrase, rather than get even, Christ **entrusted himself to him who judges justly**. The idea coming from *entrust* is to hand over, to give over, or to commit. One might miss the broad span of this act of entrusting everything to God. "Jesus entrusted not only himself but also the wrongdoers, and his followers, and indeed the entire situation 'to him who judges justly.'"[25]

Peter continues to speak of Christ's atonement by reminding his readers that **he himself bore our sins** (2:24). The verb *to bear* signifies to take up, bear the burden of, or take away. Peter stresses that Jesus did this act in His own physical body, therefore in history, in His crucifixion. The use of *tree* for a gallows, and in the New Testament for a cross, is a typical euphemism (Deut. 21:22; Acts 5:30; 10:39; 13:29; Gal. 3:13).

He bore sin in His body on the tree for the supreme purpose that we might **die to sins**. The phrase *to die* means to have no part in, to get away from, or to depart. Peter would have his readers to understand that he means to die in reference to sin. However, death to sins is only part of Peter's thought. Death leads to new life. Peter wants his readers to **live**

for righteousness (2:24) due to the fact that they have returned to spiritual health. Wayne Grudem points to the implications of this dying/living theme when he states that "the purpose of Christ's bearing our sin is that we might die to sin and live to righteousness. The verb 'die' is in the form of a participle indicating action prior to the main verb 'live to righteousness.' This gives the idea of 'we having died to sin, might live to righteousness.'"[26] Peter undergirds this important truth with a reference to Isaiah 53. Within the New Testament, 1 Peter manifests the most extensive use of Isaiah 52:13–53:12 in elaborating the details, significance, and soteriological effect of Jesus' suffering and death and in presenting Him as a model to be emulated. The correspondences in terminology and theme are abundant.[27]

Peter, to whom Christ gave the command to "feed my sheep" (John 21:15–17), uses the familiar simile of **sheep going astray** (Ps. 119:176, Isa. 53:6) to describe his readers' former lives. However, **now you have returned to the Shepherd** (2:25). Peter would have been familiar with this image of Christ from the teachings of Christ himself (Matt. 25:32; Mark 14:27; John 10:1–16).

Peter also calls Jesus the **Overseer of your souls**. The word is actually *bishop* in the Greek and carries the idea of one charged with the duty of seeing that things to be done by others are done rightly; it refers to any curator, guardian, or superintendent.

3. SUBMISSION TO SPOUSE 3:1-7

Just as Christians were to be subject to civil authorities (2:13–17) and servants were to be subject to their masters (2:18–25), Peter now exhorts wives to be submissive to their husbands (NIV, TNIV). Other versions translate the concept as "accept the authority" (NLT) and "be in subjection" (NASB). But in that Hellenistic culture, women, as well as slaves, were considered property. The general opinion of that day in regard to a woman was that she "lacked the capacity for reason that the male had, she was ruled rather by her emotions, and was as a result given to poor judgment, immorality, intemperance, wickedness, avarice; she was untrustworthy, contentious, and as a result, it was her place to obey."[28]

What a different view Christian teaching held of women! Jesus not only taught women, but included them as His disciples (Luke 8). Paul wrote that husbands and wives should submit to *each other* (Eph. 5:21) and appointed women as leaders in the church. And within this section, Peter admonishes husbands to treat their wives in a godly manner. So, Christian teaching elevated women from "chattel" to equals in the eyes of God. But just as Peter is not condoning slavery by admonishing slaves to obey their masters, he is making certain concessions so that believers can live peaceably in a pagan culture—and, perhaps, with unbelieving husbands.

THE PURPOSE OF A WIFE'S SUBMISSION

Peter begins his admonition with the phrase **in the same way** (3:1). This phrase could be understood as similar to Christ's example in 1 Peter 2:21–25, or similar to the way servants are to be submissive in 2:18, or simply "also," introducing a new subject.[29] Peter's intent in beginning this passage with "in the same way" argues that submission is not in any way a sign of inferiority, since Christ himself was submissive to His Father's will. ("In the same way" also refers to husband's submission in 3:7.)[30]

The wife is to be submissive to her husband for a purpose. The purpose clause is introduced with **so that** and spells out the purpose of submission, **if any do not believe . . . they may be won.** The particle word *if any* states a fact in this context, not a hypothetical possibility, that some women were married to unbelievers.[31] The husbands in question "do not believe the word." They were likely discouraging their wives' dedication to Christ and attendance at Christian activities.[32]

As submissive wives, they may win their non-believing husbands to Christ. The word *win* is used here in the sense of winning over or convincing persons, in this case the husbands, to becoming believers.[33] This winning is not a process of compulsion, but of attraction. In fact, Peter envisions the possibility of a wife winning her husband to Christ without saying a word. This will be done **by the behavior** of the wife. As Peter describes the possibilities, words are less important than the persuasive power of the wife's conduct.[34] In this regard, note the following contrast between the admonition given in 1 Peter 2:12 and that in 1 Peter 3:1c–2.

These verses suggest three things: the conduct of Christian wives is a particular instance of the honorable conduct required of all of the readers; non-believing husbands are a particular instance of non-believing Gentiles in general; and the goal of honorable conduct is the same in both passages, namely, the conversion of outsiders.[35]

THE POWER OF A WINSOME LIFESTYLE

How does Peter characterize the winsome lifestyle of a Christian wife that causes her non-believing husband to take note? Peter states the husband will **see the purity and reverence of** her life (3:2). The word purity implies clean, chaste behavior. This word does not simply mean sexual purity as in 2 Corinthians 11:2, but has a wider meaning of "Christian virtue" as in Philippians 4:8; 1 Timothy 5:22; James 3:17; and 1 John 3:3.[36] By this phrase, Peter reminds us that submission must never go so far as to include obedience to do something that is morally wrong. The classic example of such virtue in a woman is Augustine's tribute to his mother, Monica, who through a lifetime of virtue finally won her husband, Patricius, for the Lord.[37]

The persuasive power of chaste behavior leads Peter to a discussion of inner and outer beauty. The contrast is first developed from a negative point of view. Peter admonished Christian wives that their **beauty should not** come from external conditions. The NASB is even stronger, as it reads "must not be" based on externals. Beauty should not be based on **outward adornment** (3:3). The word basically refers to the focus of attention for her attractiveness, the thing she uses to make herself beautiful to others. Three examples of outward adornment follow: braided hair, the wearing of gold jewelry, and fine clothes. Peter's point is not that any of these are forbidden, but that they should not be a woman's "adorning," the source of beauty.[38]

The positive aspect of a woman's adornment is described as **instead**; beauty should be of the **inner self** (3:4). The word *instead* is the sharp contrast that is usually rendered "but." The "inner self" of a wife is described in various ways. It is usually understood as the wife's inward nature, her true personality. The concept of the "hidden inner self" is where Christian character is revealed and it expresses itself through the body. This phrase comes close to the atmosphere of some sayings of Jesus (Matt. 15:8, 18) as well as Paul's inner man/outer man distinction (Rom. 7:20–22; 2 Cor. 3:16).[39] What will the unbelieving husband see from a Christian wife's inner beauty? He will see the **unfading beauty of a gentle and quiet spirit.** These are qualities that are winsome and that will connect with the inner workings of God on behalf of the non-believer. These qualities are of **great worth** in God's sight. Thus, Peter reminds his audience that it is not only the non-believer that will see such inward qualities, but God sees them as well.

THE GODLY HERITAGE OF HOLY WOMEN

If the Christian wives in Peter's audience will live such godly lives, they will join a rich host of godly women across biblical history who have conducted themselves in similar fashion. The **holy women of the past** (3:5) serve as the example that Christian wives should follow. Although Sarah is soon to be introduced as the prime example (3:6), the plural *women* refers generally to godly women in the Old Testament. These holy women of the past used to make themselves beautiful in this manner. The tense of the verb *used to* indicates customary action; this was their habitual practice. And by this behavior, they were submissive to their own husbands.

The prime example of this kind of conduct is Sarah, the wife of Abraham. Of her it is said that she **obeyed** Abraham. The wives of Peter's audience, when they follow her example, become **her daughters,** or as the NASB renders it, "have become her children." Relationship to Sarah is evidenced when wives **do what is right and do not give way to fear** (3:6). When Peter uses Sarah as his example, he does not point to any specific action on her part. The ideas of doing right and not giving way to fear indicate a continuing pattern of conduct during her life.

THE HUSBAND IN SUBMISSION

Peter speaks briefly, but just as forcefully, to husbands. The last verse in this paragraph begins with **in the same way.** It carries the sense of also or continuing in the same area of discussion. Peter's admonition to husbands is to **be considerate as you live with your wives** (3:7). The word *considerate* means knowledge with understanding or consideration. In the present context, it means Christian insight and tact, a conscious sensitivity to God's will. This sensitivity is demonstrated in two distinct ways. First, **treat them with respect,** used in the sense of showing honor to someone. The phrase **as to the weaker partner** may mean being weaker physically, but may also refer to the wife's standing in the culture of the time mentioned earlier.

LIFE CHANGE

LIVING WITH AN UNSAVED HUSBAND

First of all—don't . . .

- constantly talk religion;
- assume external adornment will attract him to Christ.

On the other hand—do . . .

- be submissive to your husband;
- make certain your behavior is winsome;
- allow your "inner self" to dominate;
- remember you're in a long line of godly women.

Such action will allow God's "internal" persuasion to work.

The second way to demonstrate consideration for one's wife is to remember that the wives are **heirs . . . of the gracious gift of life** (3:7). This phrase serves as a reminder to Peter's male readers that their wives are still equal to them in spiritual privilege and eternal importance. (Paul teaches this in Galatians 3:28.) They are joint heirs. This twofold admonition to husbands serves not only to maintain harmony within the Christian home but also has a specific spiritual purpose in mind. Husbands who are considerate of their wives, who treat them with respect and acknowledge them as joint heirs of eternal promises, will not have their prayers hindered. The word *hinder* has the idea of preventing, cutting in on (Rom. 15:22; Gal. 5:7; 1 Thess. 2:18). Peter Davids outlines two specific reasons for this command to Christian husbands: (1) such action recognizes what society did not, that before God husband and wife are equal, joint heirs of God's gracious gift. (2) A failure to keep this relationship loving, giving in to the societal tendency to dominate and exploit one's wife, would injure one's relationship with God, hindering his prayers.[40]

ENDNOTES

1. See Paul Achtemeier, *1 Peter* (Minneapolis: Fortress Press, 1996), pp. 180–182, for extensive discussion on the contrast between 1 Peter 2:13–17 and Romans 13.

2. John H. Elliott, *1 Peter* (New York: Doubleday, 2000), p. 485. The call to do right rather than do wrong is found in the following texts: 2:14, 15, 20; 3:6, 10–11, 13, 14, 17, 18b; 4:1–4, 15, 18, 19.

3. Wayne Grudem, *1 Peter* (Grand Rapids: William B. Eerdmans, 2002 reprint) p. 118.

4. Achtemeier, *1 Peter*, p. 182.

5. As quoted by Gerald Bray, ed., *James, 1–2 Peter, 1–3 John, Jude* (Downers Grove: InterVarsity Press, 2000), p. 92.

6. See Grudem, *1 Peter*, p. 119, for a further discussion of the theological ramifications of this call to submission.

7. As Elliott reminds his readers, "the whether . . . or . . . construction introduces two specific civil authorities to whom subordination is due. (1) To the emperor, who in the Roman world of the first century, was the highest instance of human authority. (2) To governors, which can refer either to legates of the emperor in charge of imperial provinces or to pro-consuls who administered senatorial or 'public' provinces such as those in which the addressees resided, with the exception of Galatia," p. 490.

8. The interested reader can turn to Achtemeier, *1 Peter*, p. 184, for a complete review of the use of *do good* in 1 Peter.

9. Peter H. Davids, *The First Epistle of Peter* (Grand Rapids: William B. Eerdmans, 1990), p. 101.

10. Wayne Grudem concludes the following: "Because Peter's readers might think such extensive submission to authority would be oppressively restrictive, Peter explains that true freedom is consistent with obedience to God's will. He assures them that they are able to 'live as freemen.' The kind of freedom is not specified, but certainly the great freedoms of the Christian life are freedom from the impossible obligations to earn merit before God by perfect obedience, freedom from guilt, and freedom from the ruling power of sin," p. 121.

11. Achtemeier, *1 Peter*, p. 188.

12. Elliott, *1 Peter*, p. 497.

13. Achtemeier, *1 Peter*, p. 184.

14. See for instance William Klein, Craig Blomberg, Robert Hubbard, Jr., *Introduction to Biblical Interpretation* (Nashville: Thomas Nelson Publishers, 1993), p. 436. The authors remind the reader that numerous ancient Jewish and Greco-Roman sources contain sections of instruction for individuals in a relationship of

authority or submission. Often these instructions focused on relationships within the extended household: husbands and wives, parents and children, masters and slaves. Scholars refer to these materials as domestic or household codes. Three clear examples of this form are evident in the New Testament: Ephesians 5:22–6:9; Colossian 3:18–4:1; and 1 Peter 2:13–3:7. Probably the most significant discovery that emerges from a comparison of canonical and extra-canonical domestic codes concerns the radical nature of the value the Christians placed on each member of the relationship.

15. Achtemeier, *1 Peter*, p. 190.

16. Read Davids, *The First Epistle of Peter*, p. 105, for more details on this topic.

17. Achtemeier, *1 Peter*, p. 195.

18. See Achtemeier, *1 Peter*, p. 196 for further discussion of this important point.

19. See Davids, *The First Epistle of Peter*, p. 109, for a discussion of this point.

20. Elliott, *1 Peter*, pp. 513–524.

21. Consider for example: Matthew 27:4; John 8:29, 46; 18:38; 2 Corinthians 5:21; Hebrews 4:15; 1 John 3:5.

22. See for instance 1 Corinthians 4:16; 11:1; Ephesians 5:1; 1 Thessalonians 1:6; 2:14.

23. Review Elliott, *1 Peter*, p. 525, for his interesting treatment of this concept.

24. As Grudem, *1 Peter*, p. 130, states: "The reviling of Christ was intense during his trial and crucifixion (Matt. 26:67–68; 27:12–14, 28–31, 39–44; Luke 22:63–65; 23:9–11). The instinctive response of human beings when so abused is to try to get even, to hurt in return for being hurt."

25. Ibid., p. 130.

26. Ibid., p. 132.

27. See Elliott, *1 Peter*, p. 547.

28. Achtemeier, *1 Peter*, p. 206.

29. See Grudem, *1 Peter*, p. 135, for a full discussion of these possibilities. Grudem sees option two as the best choice in this context.

30. See Achtemeier, *1 Peter*, p. 209, for a full discussion of the intention of this passage.

31. But note Grudem's comments (p. 137) to the point that the phrase suggests that this would be an unexpected or uncommon occurrence. It implies that Peter expected that most Christian wives among his readers had Christian husbands.

32. For a discussion of the implications of living with a non-believer, see Davids, *The First Epistle of Peter*, p. 116.

33. This instruction in 1 Peter echoes Paul's admonition in 1 Corinthians 9:19–22. In the context of 1 Corinthians, Paul will do almost anything in order "to win as many as possible."

34. Turn to Elliott, *1 Peter*, p. 559, to see his development of the idea of "action, not simply words" as a tool of evangelism. He calls attention to the following texts: Matthew 7:21–27; 25:31–46 and James 2:14–26.

35. The interested readers can pursue this idea by reading John Elliott, *1 Peter*, pp. 560–561. On these pages he develops this contrast and discusses the implications of such a contrast.

36. Note Davids, *The First Epistle of Peter*, p. 116, for a fuller discussion of this expanded meaning of "Christian virtue."

37. As noted by Davids in a footnote on p. 117.

38. The interested reader can see Grudem's comments at this point for helpful insight. See p. 140.

39. See Davids, *The First Epistle of Peter*, p. 118, for interesting comments on this point.

40. Davids, *The First Epistle of Peter*, p. 123.

6

HOW TO LIVE AS CHRISTIANS

1 Peter 3:8–4:11

1. LIVING IN HARMONY 3:8–22

P eter is now ready to sum up his ethical exhortation on how to live properly in the world, and he does it by citing some general ethical imperatives for Christians in any situation. As one begins to work through this passage, keep in mind that while no other social code in the New Testament ends with such general exhortations, the content is familiar to Christian tradition (Matt. 5:44; Luke 6:27–28; Eph. 4:1–3, 31–32; Col. 3:12–14; 1 Thess. 5:13b–15).[1]

TWO SIDES TO ETHICAL CONDUCT

This passage begins with **finally**, an adverb used to introduce a fresh point and not simply to summarize what has gone before. Its use here facilitates the transition from specific ethical duty to a general statement of Christian conduct. The general qualities are charted:

KEY IDEAS

CHRISTIAN CONDUCT

General Term	Meaning of Term
Live in harmony.	Be one-minded, or like-minded.
Be sympathetic.	Share the same feeling, or be full of compassion.
Love as brothers.	Love fellow Christians.
Be compassionate.	Be tenderhearted or kind.
Be humble.	Be unpretentious.

The above qualities contain ethical commands in the positive. This is now contrasted with the negative side of the issue. Peter announces that the Christian cannot get caught up in a "payback" mentality. **Do not repay** (3:9) is Peter's warning. The phrase means to give back or to give in return. Just because evil is done to Christians, they cannot return **evil with evil**,[2] or for greater emphasis, **insult with insult**. The "evil" phrase represents the actual deed; the "insult" phrase implies a cursing, speaking evil of someone, or abuse as in 2:23.

Rather than get even, the Christian is to respond **with blessing**. The word *blessing* is frequently used in the sense of bestowing a blessing upon or acting graciously toward someone. The word is found with God or Christ as the subject, or with the idea of "praise," with God or Christ as the object. In this context, Peter uses the word in reference to one's Christian ethical duty. Peter admonishes his readers that this is part of what it means to be a follower Christ.

Believers should not be surprised at such radical conduct. For **to this you were called** (3:9). Why are you called? **So that**, which introduces the purpose clause, **you may inherit a blessing**. Inherit implies gaining possession of or being given something. At the heart of this phrase is the idea of inheritance as a free gift that comes without having to merit it.

The purpose clause is followed by the reason for such behavior. The reason is indicated by **for**, which introduces a quotation from Psalm 34:12–16, **Whoever would love life and see good days . . .** (3:10). The NASB reads: "The one who desires life, to love and see good days . . ." The words *love* and *see* are both infinitives connected by the conjunction *and*. The NASB seeks to retain that grammatical construction. Either reading, the idea is this: To attain the desired positive result demands resolute action. That individual must **keep his tongue from evil**, where "keep" carries the idea of stopping or abstaining from. Also, that individual must **keep his lips from deceitful speech,** which contains the idea of trickery or treachery.

Peter is not finished with this general admonition. The one who would love life and see good days must **turn from evil**, which carries the idea of reversing direction, turning aside, or turning away from and doing good. Also, Peter's readers must **seek peace and pursue it** (3:11). Peace is not easily found. It must be pursued; one must chase after or even to hunt it down. To pursue peace is an active and persistent effort on behalf of peace. The teaching of the Beatitudes (Matt. 5:3–11), underscores this very point. The purpose clause of verse 10, introduced with *for*, is now continued with another purpose clause at verse 12, which is also introduced with *for*. This second purpose clause is simply that the Lord takes notice of such activity. **The eyes of the Lord are on the righteous and his ears are attentive to their prayer**. Nothing escapes the notice of the Lord. But, on the other hand, **those who do evil** are noticed as well. The phrase *do evil* is in the present tense and emphasizes continual action of some activity. The **eyes of the Lord**, **his ears**, and **the face of the Lord** represent poetic figures of speech. References to eyes and ears attach human traits to God. To talk about "the face of God" is to refer to one part of the totality of God.

KEY IDEAS

BLESSINGS OF RIGHT CONDUCT

Verse	Right Conduct	Resulting Blessings in This Life
1:8	loving Christ	unutterable joy
1:9	continuing faith	more benefits of salvation
1:17	holy life with fear	avoiding God's fatherly discipline
2:2	partaking of spiritual milk	growing up toward salvation
2:19–20	trusting God and doing right while suffering	God's approval
3:1–2	submitting to husbands	husbands won for Christ
3:7	living considerately with wives	prayers not hindered
4:14	enduring reproach for Christ	spirit of glory and of God rests upon you
5:7	casting cares on God	He will care for your needs (implied)
5:9–10	resist the devil	God will restore, establish, and strengthen you

The general exhortations of 1 Peter are usually considered in reference to future blessings. This is particularly true in texts like 1:4–7, 13; 4:13; and 5:4. However, it would not be foreign to Peter's thought to emphasize present blessings resulting from right actions. In fact, 1 Peter contains several examples of blessings in this life, which are promised as a result of righteous conduct.[3] Note the examples in the chart on page 97.

The lesson to be learned from 1 Peter 3:8–12 is to understand that one motive for righteous living is the knowledge that such conduct will bring blessings from God in this life.

The remainder of chapter 3 contains two paragraphs: 3:13–17 and 3:18–22. The logic of these two passages flows from the statement of the basic premise (v. 13) that nothing can bring harm to the person who does what God wants. "The theme of this passage is 'Christian life in the midst of hostility.' And with this theme, one is dealing with the core of Peter's message to his readers who are facing social oppression and persecution."[4] With this passage, Peter begins a new section dealing specifically with the problem of persecution by unbelievers. This is the first time Peter confronts persecution as his primary subject and deals with it at length.[5]

HARMED FOR DOING GOOD?

Peter raises the question, **Who is going to harm you if you are eager to do good?** To understand the implications of this question, it is best to break it down into its components. First, **to harm** carries the idea of treating badly, being cruel, or forcing someone to do something, as in Acts 7:19. There is a future tense implied with this question, which is clear from **if you are eager to do good** (3:13). This implies a probable activity in the future. The word *eager* is the word from which we get our word *zealot*. Zealots were members of a Jewish nationalistic sect. These individuals were those who were zealous and eager for their particular political cause.

At first glance, it seems inconceivable to believe that someone would be harmed for being eager to do good. **But**, where strong contrast is again used, that is exactly the case. **Even if you should suffer** (3:14) carries the idea of future possibility.

But this potential for suffering brings with it a blessing. The idea of blessing in Scripture has two understandings. The Old Testament blessing reflects the belief that God rewards proper conduct with blessings in this life. Psalm 1 is the prime example of this understanding of blessing. The second meaning of blessing is reflected in the New Testament with the blessings in the Beatitudes in Matthew 5. In the Beatitudes, the idea is connected with a future action, as in "Blessed are the meek, for they *will* inherit the earth" (Matt. 5:5). This is to be understood as a particular blessing inaugurated now with the complete blessing fulfilled sometime in the future. The future is usually associated with the Second Advent. Peter uses Matthew's word for *blessed* which means happy or fortunate.

Facing the real possibility of persecution for doing good, what is a Christian to do? Peter's response is **in your hearts set apart Christ as Lord** (3:15). The phrase *set apart* implies to sanctify, to venerate, and to adore Christ. The result of such action will be the dispelling of all fear of humans. Peter tells the believers to **always be prepared to give an answer.** The implication is that the believers should constantly be ready to defend their faith. The concept behind the word *answer* is the word from which we get the term *apologetic*. The believer is to constantly be prepared to give a verbal defense or a reason for faith. The word *apologetic* is often used for the defense in a court of law. Paul uses this word to mean an informal explanation or defense of one's position of faith, as in 1 Corinthians 9:3 or 2 Corinthians 7:11. This answer is to be given to all who ask believers to give **the reason** for the hope in Christ that they have. This defense must be made properly, and so Peter admonished his readers to make this defense **with gentleness and respect**.

This proper defense will allow one to [keep] **a clear conscience** (3:16). The verb *to keep* carries the idea of possessing or maintaining a good conscience. A clear conscience will lead to a positive result. The introductory phrase **so that** introduces the result of maintaining a clear conscience: that those who **speak maliciously may be ashamed.** Anyone who dares to speak against good behavior should be shamed or disgraced. Their disgrace is their own **slander**, mistreatment, or their dealing despitefully with someone.

It is better (3:17), the comparative of good, **if it is God's will** to suffer now rather than later. A literal reading of this phrase would be "if the will of God should will." It is a real possibility that one should suffer for doing good. If this is so, it is much better to suffer for doing good than for doing evil. Those who do evil now will suffer God's wrath and judgment someday.

THE EXAMPLE OF CHRIST

Peter has set a high standard. It is better to suffer for doing good than for doing evil. And, as a further point of emphasis, this suffering appears to be the will of God. Has anyone ever endured such an experience? As a matter of fact, yes. **For Christ**, or because Christ has done something, Christians must also do something. This is a new application of the imitation of Christ motif. Because He suffered for doing good, we must imitate this kind of willful suffering if we must. What exactly did Christ do? Christ died **to bring you to God** (3:18). The purpose of Christ's death was to lead, to provide access for, or to bring about a right relationship. The word used for the phrase *to bring you to God* had various usages and could denote bringing people before a tribunal, presenting them at a royal court, or the ritual act of bringing sacrifice to God.

The mention of Christ's death is qualified by two phrases. First, it was **once for all**. By this phrase, Christ's death is placed within a particular place and time in human history. In direct contrast to the Old Testament, where sacrifices were ongoing on a daily basis, Christ died once. Thus, the superiority of His atoning death is paramount in Peter's mind.

It should also be noted that this death was for all. The universal application of Christ's death is here stressed. Neither Peter, the early Church, nor do we today believe in universalism. That would be the idea that ultimately, everyone will be saved. Sadly to say, some individuals will never accept the gospel offer, thus will go out into eternity and ultimately to hell. When the Church, speaking from a Wesleyan perspective, speaks about Christ dying for all, they mean objectively, Christ died for all humankind. The merits of Christ's atoning death are applied to each individual subjectively based on faith in Christ. The second qualifying phrase is **the righteous for the unrighteous**. By this phrase, the Church has always maintained the belief in the substitutionary aspect of the cross. The righteous died for the unrighteous. When one speaks of Christ as the substitute dying for all humankind, the implication to be drawn is that this death was vicarious. Christ died for others.

Peter adds one more contrast. Christ was put to death **in the body** or literally in the flesh, which refers to the reality of Christ's physical death. But, Christ **was made alive by the Spirit**. The expression "by the Spirit" could refer to either the Holy Spirit or to the spirit of Christ. The NASB reads "in the spirit" with a marginal reading "or Spirit."

First Peter 3:19 begins the most difficult passage in Peter's letter. It could very well be the most difficult in the entire New Testament: Jesus **preached to the spirits in prison**.

The verse begins with a relative pronoun **through whom**. Based on the context, the pronoun could refer to the word *spirit* and thus "through whom" could give the meaning of Christ, through the Holy Spirit. The pronoun could also be understood as in the NASB as "in which," where it could refer to the state or circumstances of something. The meaning here would be that Christ, in the state of His own spirit, did something. The point that Peter seems to make is that Christ, either through the Holy Spirit or in His own spirit, preached to the spirits in prison. In the words of a creedal statement, "He descended into hell." But what does that mean?

Thomas Oden has summarized the teaching on "the descent" concept by identifying five major types of emphasis:[6] (1) Jesus died and descended into the grave (the burial motif). (2) The descent points to Christ's emphatic suffering and participation in the depth of human alienation (the humiliation motif). (3) The descent points to Christ's victory over the demonic powers (the exaltation motif). (4) Christ's descent was for the purpose of preaching in the abode of the dead (the preaching motif). (5) The descent constituted the final phase of the humiliation and the beginning of the exaltation of Christ (the reversal motif).

The problematic phrase is **he went and preached to the spirits in prison**. The concept of *the descent* refers to the phrase *he went*. The phrase **preached to the spirits** is almost as confusing. Wayne Grudem addresses the complexity of this issue by summarizing three possible interpretations. Grudem's way of working through this problem is in the form of providing answers to three different key questions.[7]

KEY IDEAS

THE SPIRITS IN PRISON

Who are the spirits in prison?	What did Christ preach?	When did He preach?
unbelievers who had died	second chance for repentance	in the days of Noah
Old Testament believers who had died	completion of redemptive work	between death and resurrection
fallen angels	final condemnation	after His resurrection

The understanding of Grudem's three questions revolves around how one interprets the relative pronoun ("through whom") at the beginning of verse 19.

Option one would be the spirit of Christ speaking though Noah as he preached to his generation. The first option goes back to the life of Noah as found in the book of Genesis. Noah's life is reported in Genesis 5:1–9:28. In his day, the entire population was corrupt (6:12) and God's judgment was about to come on all inhabitants of the earth. Only Noah and his family found favor in the eyes of the Lord (6:8). The form of the impending judgment was the devastating flood that would cover the earth and kill all living creatures. Noah was instructed to do two things: (1) build an ark, which he would take a number of years to complete, and (2) as he built the ark, preach to his generation, warning them of the coming judgment of God.

Option two would be Christ himself preaching, in the place of the dead, to Old Testament believers. Thomas Oden reminds his readers of one teaching in the early Church by quoting Clement of Alexandria who wrote, "Christ preached the gospel in the place of the dead to bring salvation to awaiting believers."[8] This tradition continued into the teaching of various groups as is evident by Oden's reference to The Russian Catechism which reads: "Two reasons are assigned for the descent into the abode of the dead: (1) to preach his victory over death, and (2) to deliver the souls which with faith awaited his coming."[9]

It is interesting to connect 1 Peter 3:19 with that equally difficult passage in Matthew 27:51–53:

> At that moment the curtain of the temple was torn in two from top to bottom. The earth shook and the rocks split. The tombs broke open and the bodies of many holy people who had died were raised to life. They came out of the tombs, and after Jesus' resurrection they went into the holy city and appeared to many people.

One possible interpretation would be that between death and resurrection, Christ descended into the abode of the death and rescued Old Testament believers from the grip of death. They were delivered from that bondage and became the first to realize the privilege of believers, that at death they are "away from the body and at home with the Lord" (2 Cor. 5:8). Since Jesus' descent into "the abode of the dead," all believers who die are at once with the Lord.

As mentioned previously, there are a variety of interpretations of this difficult passage. After discussing many of these interpretations, Thomas Oden remarks, "Noting all the difficulties of these passages, it may be concluded that there is scriptural grounding for the belief that Christ descended into the abode of the dead, but hardly for speculation in detail upon precisely how or why this descent occurred."[10]

But this does not mean that there is nothing to be gleaned from this text. The theological importance is clear. This passage is intended to show why Christians will, in the end, triumph over the powers currently arrayed against them. Christ, the righteous one, can lead them, the unrighteous, to God because by His suffering and resurrection, He has overcome all powers that can hinder such access.[11]

2. LIVING FOR GOD 4:1–11

With this paragraph, Peter concludes his ethical section. This section was introduced in 2:11 with the phrase **dear friends**. The conclusion will be the doxology at 4:11 "To him be the glory and the power for ever and ever. Amen." The manner in which this section begins and concludes marks it off as a complete section within itself. This final paragraph may be divided into two sub points: (1) the way Christians are to live within their contemporary culture, verses 1–6; and (2) the way Christians are to live with one another, verses 7–11.

Thus far, the ethical instruction, begun back at 2:13, has emphasized submission. The Christian is to live a life of submission to others, following in the steps of Christ himself. The emphasis now will be on the theme "living for God." The paragraph is introduced by **therefore** (4:1), which serves to introduce the concluding point and may in fact be the main point of the entire section (2:13–4:11). The point is the word *therefore* leads to the implications of something previously stated. Does *therefore* refer to the previous paragraph (3:8–22)? That would mean the admonition of that paragraph, "live in harmony," leads to the thought in 4:1–11: "living for God." If the "therefore" of 4:1 serves as the conclusion of the entire section 2:13–3:22, then this last paragraph will bring the theme "accepting submission and living for God" to a conclusion.[12]

THE PROPER ATTITUDE

Peter begins his instruction on living a Christian life in the contemporary culture with the admonition to **arm** themselves. The word Peter uses for arm yourself carries with it the basic idea of putting on your armor. Here, Peter echoes the teaching of Paul of putting on spiritual armor or using spiritual weapons.[13] But arm yourself with what? Peter's armor consists of **the same attitude** that Christ had. The word *attitude* contains the basic idea of thought, intention, or purpose. But Peter is talking about something more than just maintaining a positive attitude. This is "not so much attitudes of mind but the 'insight' which one has gained into the nature of God's dealings with people."[14] Probably the best commentary of this topic is Paul's description in Philippians 2:5–8 of Christ "[humbling] himself and [becoming] obedient to death—even death on a cross!" The dying life voluntarily accepted and put on as armor finds expression in the meek and courageous pursuit of the spiritual life.

He who has suffered in his body **is done with sin** (4:1). At first, this may appear to be a proverbial expression related to Romans 6:7, and the suffering is meant to convey dying in the sense of dying to sin. But notice the contrast. Paul, in texts like Romans 5:12–13, 20–21; 6:1, 10, 12–14; and 13:14, views sin as a condition or external power. On the other hand, Peter, in texts like 2:22, 24; 3:18; and 4:8 views sin as active wrongdoing contrary to the will of God.[15] Peter's point is that those who have suffered in his body **for doing good** (2:20) have ceased from committing sins.

A CHOICE TO MAKE

What will result from being done with sin? **As a result**, we have a choice to make. This phrase introduces a purpose clause in which we have a choice as to how to live our life. We can choose to live for **evil human desires** or for **the will of God** (4:2). The contrast could not be more sharply drawn. The will of God is His intent for every individual. God has a personal interest in each of us and desires the very best for us. To live for evil human desires implies that someone else has an interest in us, but for a negative purpose. Living for the will of God implies that He has a specific will and plan for each of us, but for a positive purpose. Living for evil human desires takes a toll on us.

Peter reminds his readers that previously, they had **spent enough time** (4:3) living in a sinful way. The phrase *spent time* implies more-than-sufficient time or far too much time. The former lifestyle of Peter's audience is **in the past**. This part of their past is a closed chapter. That part of the story is over and done with. Peter describes this past life as **doing what pagans choose to do**[16]—**living in debauchery**. The word *living* is used in the Jewish sense of walking or conducting one's life. The life of debauchery is one of sensuality, indecency, vice, with unbridled and unrestrained living. What follows is another example of the vice list. It follows Paul's example in Romans 13:13; 1 Corinthians 5:10–11; 6:9–10; Galatians 5:19–20; and Colossians 3:5.[17]

◼ KEY IDEAS

SINFUL ACTIONS

Particular Vice	Definition of the Term
debauchery	living without any regard for moral restraint; giving oneself over to acts of sexual immorality
lust	sinful human desires that can be allowed to exert strong influence on one's behavior
drunkenness	characteristic of a life bent on following physical desires
orgies	banquets and feasts given to wild immorality
carousing	drinking parties or drinking bouts
detestable idolatry	lawless acts of idol worship; evil kinds of idol worship, which involved or incited people to kinds of immorality even forbidden by the laws of human governments

The prominent point of this vice list[18] is its emphases on sexual and alcoholic excess with the stress on idolatry. The reason for living not "by human passions" but "by the will of God" is that Peter's readers have done enough living like that described in the vice list in "the time that is past." The list accurately describes Greco-Roman life as morally out of control. Christians are encouraged to abandon that kind of activity in which they once shared, common in secular culture but contrary to God's will.

The following verses build on this concept. The NASB makes the transition by stating "in all this" **they think it strange you do not plunge with them into the same flood of dissipation** (4:4). The concept behind "thinking it strange" is the idea of being surprised or entertained by the novelty of a thing. It also carries the idea of being upset at a new turn of events. The vice list indicated behavior that was the normal life of these Christians before their conversion. Their neighbors are now surprised that they do not join them in this lifestyle.[19] More in line with Peter's context, the word for "think strange" includes the thought of taking offense, as ignorant people often feel an unreasonable resentment of anything that does not fit into the pattern of life familiar to them.

Peter's readers amaze their non-Christian neighbors by not plunging into the pagan lifestyle. The word *plunge* means to run together or to join with others. The word suggests joining in a mad race. The believer does not join in the same flood of dissipation or reckless living. By the use of this word, Peter has described the contemporary culture of the day, which reflects the frantic pace of people rushing in every direction in a mad search for pleasure. His readers used to join that crowd, but their faith in Christ has turned them in a new direction. Peter pictures the life of paganism as a feverish pursuit of evil, wherein people vie with one another in pouring forth a life abandoned to vice and are recklessly licentious.

JUDGMENT IS COMING

The question now comes, "How do people respond when you refuse to join them in this pagan lifestyle?" The answer is simply stated, **they heap abuse on you (4:4)**—to speak against God, blaspheme, slander, or speak evil against. In this context, it indicates to defame someone, or to injure the reputation of someone.[20]

But the experience of receiving abuse now is not the end of the matter. Peter reminds his readers that there is a Day of Judgment coming. Individuals committed to a pagan lifestyle **will have to give account to him who is ready to judge (4:5)**. The reference is, of course, to God himself. To *give account* is to pay back. This word is used in a variety of contexts: of human accountability to an employer (Luke 16:2), or to government authorities (Acts 19:40), and also of men and women's accountability to God at the final judgment (Matt. 12:36; Heb. 4:13). God stands ready and prepared to judge all people who are committed to such a life of paganism. The fact that God is the judge of all people leads Peter to **the reason the gospel was preached even to those who are now dead (4:6)**. The reference to the dead may be to those who are spiritually dead, but it seems better to understand the term as referring to those whom the gospel was preached during their lifetime and they have since died physically. The fact of the common experience of physical death should not trouble the minds of those left alive, for short of the second coming of Christ, the gospel was never intended to save people from physical death.[21] The gospel was preached to people **so that** they might be judged. It is interesting to note that the NASB has a marginal reading of "preached in their lifetime." The gospel was preached to people in this life, and they will stand someday and give an account of what they did with this gospel.

The certainty of judgment leads Peter to the fact of the Second Advent. He introduces this concept by stating that **the end of all things is near** (4:7). Peter shows a wide understanding of the implications of eschatology for believers as they live out their Christian faith.[22]

KEY IDEAS

THE END TIME

Text	Implications of Eschatology for Everyday Living
4:7	Reference to the impending end as the basis for ethical conduct. Knowledge that there is an end of time and a judgment gives to the present its seriousness and its meaning.
4:17–19; 1:17; 4:5	References of imminent judgment.
1:4–5; 1:13; 4:13; 5:10	Events accompanying the end time.

Peter's teaching on last things is in keeping with the truth of the entire New Testament. Jesus is introduced to Mark's audience with the message "The time has come, the kingdom of God is near" (Mark 1:15). The concept of the Kingdom is tied with the Kingdom concept. The Kingdom was fulfilled at the First Advent of Christ; it will be consummated at the time of the Second Advent.

While the NIV and KJV use "is near," Peter used a Greek word that literally means the end of all things *has drawn near*. The verb tense indicates a past action with implications that carry into the present. Thus, the end of all things is not an arbitrary point in time, but rather the result of a plan formulated prior to the creation of the world. This plan has the ultimate purpose of bringing about God's desire to save a lost world. The implication of Peter's use of the phrase **has come near** would be the fact that all the major events in God's plan of redemption have occurred, and now all things are ready for Christ to return and rule. The last act, the Church age, had been continuing for about thirty years by the time Peter wrote this letter. Thus the curtain could fall at any time, ushering in the return of Christ and the end of the age. "Rather than thinking of world history in terms of earthly kings and kingdoms, Peter thinks in terms of 'redemptive history.' From that perspective all the previous acts in the drama of redemption have been completed."[23]

Since this is true, Peter is intent on describing the required Christian lifestyle for believers living in the expectancy of the end of all things. Not only is there a prescribed manner of living in a pagan culture, but there is also a Christian lifestyle for living among those of like faith. The concluding subsection (4:7–11) describes this way of life. The first trait that will enhance living among fellow believers is [being] **clear minded**. The phrase means to be in one's right mind or to be sensible or serious. The word points to a cool head and a balanced mind that exercises self-control and moderation. To that characteristic is added being **self-controlled**, which implies being sober, or keeping a clear head. Above all, believers should **love each other deeply** (4:8), which carries the idea of a constant, unfailing love for each other. The reason for this call to intense love is **because love covers over a multitude of sins.** The mention of "covering over sins" does raise the interesting question, "Whose sins are covered?" Paul Achtemeier suggests four possible ways this phrase could be understood: (1) The sins of the one who loves the other are covered by that love. (2) The sins of the one loved are covered by the one who loves. (3) The sins of both the one loving and the one loved are covered. (4) The sins of the one loved, which causes that person to repent, are truly covered.[24] Achtemeier, after evaluating each possibility, favors option number two and concludes that the one who loves another overlooks the other person's offenses, whether against the one loving or against others in the community.

Peter now produces two ways to demonstrate deep love for one another. First, he commands his audience to **offer hospitality** (4:9) to others. The word implies the entertaining of strangers. Those committed to a pagan lifestyle treat others as strangers. On the other hand, Christians are to offer hospitality to strangers and do it **without grumbling**, murmuring, or complaining. The lack of a network of decent hotels for ordinary people necessitated a readiness to provide board and lodging for friends and other suitably sponsored travelers. Thus, hospitality was even more esteemed than it is today. And this hospitality is to be done without grumbling, which brings a touch of realism to this command. Hospitality can be abused. Peter reminds us that hospitality must be shouldered cheerfully if it is to be worthwhile.

The second way Peter writes that believers can demonstrate deep love is by using spiritual gifts. The word for **gift** (4:10) is *charismata*, which means gift or gracious gift. It comes from the root word for grace. Paul is known for providing us with lists of spiritual gifts: Romans 12:6–8, where seven gifts are mentioned, and 1 Corinthians 12:7–11, where he identifies nine. Peter, in contrast, provides two basic categories under which all gifts fall: gifts of speaking and gifts of action. As far as action is concerned, Peter reminds his readers that spiritual gifts are to be used to **serve others**. The word *serve* is the word from which we get our concept of a deacon. The act of serving others carries the idea of spiritual ministry as Acts 6:3–4 indicates. Service must be done with **the strength God provides** (4:11). This is why serving others is a spiritual gift. The second example of *charismata* is the

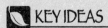 **KEY IDEAS**

EARTHLY LIFE AND LIFE IN THE SPIRIT

Peter divides "time" into two categories: earthly life and resurrection life. Earthly life is life in the flesh. This "time" of earthly life can be subdivided into two parts—life prior to Christian conversion and the rest of one's earthly life. These concepts are based on texts like 1 Peter 1:14, 18; 2:1, 9–10.

Peter's concept of resurrection life is described as life "in the spirit." It is the glorified existence in heaven of the believer. The "time" of this existence is at hand. The support for this concept is a text like 1 Peter 3:18.

believer's speech, which should be used as though speaking the very words of God. The phrase **words of God** has a technical use, meaning Scripture or divine utterance. In this context, Peter admonishes his readers to so guard their speech that their everyday conversation may be likened to the words of God.

ENDNOTES

1. The interested reader can turn to Paul Achtemeier, *1 Peter* (Minneapolis: Fortress Press, 1996), p. 221, for a detailed discussion of the relationship between this passage and other social codes.

2. Wayne Grudem, *1 Peter* (Grand Rapids: William B. Eerdmans, 2002 reprint), p.147, reminds us that the reason given in the gospels is that followers of Jesus ought to imitate the goodness of God even to undeserving sinners (Matt. 5:45, 48; Luke 6:35–36), goodness which is meant to lead them to repentance (Rom. 2:4).

3. Ibid., p. 149.

4. Achtemeier, *1 Peter*, p. 228.

5. Read Grudem, *1 Peter*, p. 151, for a discussion of this new emphasis in 1 Peter.

6. Thomas Oden, *The Word of Life: Systematic Theology*, vol. 2 (San Francisco: Harper-Collins, 1992), p. 440.

7. Grudem, *1 Peter*, p. 158. Grudem prefers the first option, that Christ was preaching through Noah when the ark was being built.

8. Oden, *The Word of Life*, p. 439.

9. Ibid., pp. 444–445.

10. Ibid., p. 450.

11. See Achtemeier, *1 Peter*, pp. 246–247, for a thorough discussion of the theological importance of this text.

12. Note for instance that Peter Davids, *The First Epistle of Peter* (Grand Rapids: William B. Eerdmans, 1990), p. 147, suggests that this paragraph jumps back to 3:18 to pick up the point Peter wishes to apply to his readers' lives: Christ suffered in the flesh. This same concept will reappear at the close of the first sub-point (4:6).

13. See Davids, *The First Epistle of Peter*, p. 148, for a discussion of this point and his references to passages like Romans 6:13; 13:12; 2 Corinthians 6:7; 10:4; and Ephesians 5:17–23.

14. Grudem, *1 Peter*, p. 166.

15. Turn to John Elliott, *1 Peter* (New York: Doubleday, 2000), p. 715, for an introducing discussion of this contrast.

16. Recall similar terminology by Paul when, in Galatians 1:13–17, he describes his own "previous way of life."

17. Note Achtemeier, *1 Peter*, pp. 281–282, where he discusses the point that such lists in the New Testament reflect a Christian perspective. However, some of the individual vices were also condemned by secular writers as well.

18. The interested reader can refer to Grudem, *1 Peter*, pp. 168–169, for an interesting discussion of the vice list.

19. See Grudem, *1 Peter*, p. 169.

20. But note Achtemeier's comment as he clarifies the question of abuse: "The abuse Christians suffer at the hands of their non-believing contemporaries does not have to do with Roman concerns over foreign religions and hence with any official governmental attempt to suppress the Christian religion. It has rather to do with the fact that people who have become Christians, who once took part in the cultural activities and the lifestyle of their times, no longer do so, and it is that refusal of further participation that brings abuse upon them," p. 276.

21. Read Grudem, *1 Peter*, p. 171, for his interesting discussion of this point.

22. See Achtemeier, *1 Peter*, p. 294, for further discussion of Peter's understanding of his statement "The end of all things is near."

23. Grudem, *1 Peter*, p. 172.

24. Achtemeier, *1 Peter*, pp. 295–296.

Part Three

Three Things That Bind Us Together

1 PETER 4:12–5:14

7

SUFFERING AS
A CHRISTIAN

1 Peter 4:12-19

This passage concludes the body section of Peter's letter. It is the shortest of the three sections. The language of this third section imparts something of the flavor of a final and summarizing admonition to the reader.[1]

The question may be raised as to why this short section should be designated as part three rather than a continuation of part two of 1 Peter. The decision to make this a separate section is made on structural grounds. Just as the second section began with "dear friends" (2:11), and concluded with a doxology (4:11), so this section begins with "dear friends" (4:12) and concludes with a doxology (5:11). On structural grounds it appears that this is a distinct, separate section in Peter's overall writing.

If this is, in fact, a separate section in 1 Peter, what is the point of this new material? As will become clear, it is not new material. Two themes already treated at some length in 2:11–4:11, the conduct of Christians within their community (2:18–3:7) and the suffering they must endure within a hostile society (3:8–4:11), are to be found in this third section (suffering: 4:12–19; 5:6–11; conduct within the community: 5:1–5) with more emphasis here on Christian suffering. This makes for an interesting structure that must be understood to fully appreciate Peter's purpose. We find the following: biblical texts directed outward to the suffering experienced *outside* the community (4:12–19); material directed *inward* to appropriate behavior within the Christian community (5:1–5a); and biblical material again directed outward, to the suffering experienced *outside* the community (5:5b–11).

There are common themes that keep appearing within these three paragraphs. Three themes predominate the third section: suffering, the relation of believers to God, and references to future glory, salvation, or the blessing awaiting the faithful.[2] But while the themes have been discussed previously, two new considerations are introduced in this third section of the body. Suffering is now seen in a new context. First is the announcement that Christian suffering, universal in its scope (5:9), represents the beginning of the final judgment, which will then be extended to include those outside the community (4:17–19). The second new consideration is the identification of the devil as the true adversary of the Christians (5:8–9).

Peter's insight into the proper Christian response to suffering comes from a particular theological perspective that becomes clear as readers work their way through this third section of the body of his letter. The theological point of the two new considerations mentioned above is that Christians should know that the extent of suffering is bigger than just the Christian community. They have not been singled out for such treatment. The suffering that has begun with the believers will soon be extended to non-Christians as well. Theologically speaking, the suffering of the believers is just the beginning of what will ultimately be the end of society in general that will be eliminated in God's final judgment.

The overall theme that controls this last section of the body of this epistle into a coherent whole is the mention of things that bind together the Christian community. The first thing Peter mentions is the experience of suffering as a Christian. The theme of suffering has previously been mentioned in this letter, but that does not mean that the material contained in this paragraph is merely a repeat of previous ideas. There are two new features in Peter's comments on suffering. First, Peter reminds his audience that the name "Christian" makes the bearer liable to persecution and suffering. Second, Christian suffering represents the beginning of God's final judgment.[3] These twin concepts are developed in this paragraph.

116

1. SUFFERING FOR BEING A CHRISTIAN 4:12–14

The paragraph begins, **Dear friends, do not be surprised** (4:12). This term of endearment, previously used in 2:11, is appropriate for the subject matter that is to be developed. Who might be surprised by the experience of suffering? Certainly not Jewish converts to the Christian faith. They had a long history of being a persecuted people. But individuals who have come from a pagan background and have accepted the Christian faith might not have expected suffering to be one of the side effects of becoming a Christian. This is perhaps another clue as to the composition of Peter's audience.

The suffering Peter has in mind is described as **the painful trial you are suffering** (4:12). This term, rendered as "fiery ordeal" by the NASB, indicates a refining fire. It is Peter's contention that the suffering he is about to explain purifies and strengthens the Christian. As has been noted already, the theme of suffering is a key concept for Peter. How he uses this concept in his letter is interesting. Sometimes suffering is just a possibility (1:6–7; 2:12, 21; 3:14; 4:1–2, 14, 16). Sometimes, some kind of unjust treatment is actually happening (2:15, 18–20; 3:9, 14, 16; 4:4, 17, 19; 5:9–10).

There are also two clear statements about present persecution as the characteristic of the Church generally.[4] Christians should not be surprised when they experience suffering or think that this is a strange occurrence. Rather, the inevitability of such suffering is a general Christian insight. The early Church was instructed to expect suffering (Acts 16:22; 20:19; 1 Thess. 3:3; 2 Tim. 3:12; 1 John 3:13). This insight was based on the words of Jesus (Matt. 10:24–25; John 15:18–21; 16:1–4, 33).[5] Rather than act surprised, **rejoice that you participate in the sufferings of Christ** (4:13). It is amazing to think that increased sufferings seem truly to increase the believer's joy in the Lord, but this is so! To substantiate this point, see for example Acts 5:41, 16:25; Romans 5:3; Colossians 1:24; and Hebrews 10:34.[6] The phrase *to participate in* implies to share in or to have fellowship with another. Suffering as a Christian confirms to us the fact that we are indeed Christ's. The present tense of *rejoice* calls for a continual act of rejoicing: keep on rejoicing. This continual rejoicing has a purpose.

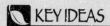

KEY IDEAS

A CHRISTIAN VIEW OF SUFFERING

- A means of testing the Christian (4:12)

- A cause for joy (4:13b)

- A way of sharing Christ's suffering (4:13a)

- A way of glorifying God (4:14, 16)

- Useless if deserved for non-Christian reasons (4:15)

- The beginning of final judgment (4:17)

- Judgment will be harder on their tormentors than on the Christians (4:17b–18)

The purpose of suffering is introduced by a purpose clause, **so that you may be overjoyed when his glory is revealed** (4:13). Peter connects present history with future expectation. The term for this is eschatology. Peter's thought is that the ability to rejoice in suffering *now* will certainly lead to great rejoicing in Christ's presence when He returns in the Second Advent.[7] To be overjoyed when His glory is revealed carries with it the idea of rejoicing with exultation, being exuberantly happy, or having extreme joy and gladness.

Paul Achtemeier has clearly outlined the concept of suffering as presented in 4:12–19. He identifies present suffering (4:12–16), suffering in an eschatological perspective (4:17–18), and a final admonition regarding suffering (4:19).[8] What follows is not a hypothetical situation, but the sentence structure emphasizes the reality of the assumption that Christians will be reproached, and hence has the force not so much of *if* as of *when*. **If you are insulted . . . you are blessed** (4:14). The word *insult* means to reproach or to denounce. The history of the word *insult* includes reproaches heaped on God and His saints by the wicked, and in the New Testament becomes associated with the indignities and maltreatment that Christ had to endure. But why are Christians blessed when this occurs? Because the Spirit of glory and of God **rests** on that Christian. "Christians are to rejoice in trials (v. 13) because the presence of such sufferings means they are blessed by the presence of God's Spirit, and have already a share in the eschatological glory yet to be revealed."[9]

2. SUFFERING FOR THE RIGHT REASON 4:15–16

Any discussion concerning suffering reminds the reader that one may suffer for doing right or for doing wrong. Peter reminds his audience, **if you suffer** (note the NASB which reads "make sure that none of you suffers"), it should not be because one deserves to suffer. What does Peter have in mind? He lists three categories of activity that bring deserved punishment: **a murderer or thief or any other kind of criminal activity, or even as a meddler** (4:15). While there may be a wide spectrum between being a murder as opposed to being a meddler, these kind of activities all have one thing in common: they open the individual to insult, reproach, and suffering.

On the other hand, if you suffer as a Christian, that experience may produce a positive blessing. Note first, that like the previous sentence that began with if, this is not a hypothetical situation. This is the second use of a sentence that assumes the reality of what is spoken about. Peter's admonition is, **if you suffer as a Christian . . . you bear that name** (4:16). The identification of the reader as "Christian" follows a common practice of forming a description of followers that included the name of the leader. This term *Christian* is only used three times in the New Testament: Acts 11:26; 26:28; and 1 Peter 4:16. By reviewing the context in the book of Acts, the name "Christian" was apparently coined by outsiders. Believers referred to themselves with terms like "disciples" (Acts 6:1; 19:9), "saints" (Rom. 1:7; 2 Cor. 1:1), or "brothers" (Rom. 1:13; 1 Cor. 1:26).[10]

Peter gives two commands for Christians who experience suffering for doing what is right. First, in the negative, **do not be ashamed** (4:16). The second command is in the positive, **praise God**, that is, to *continually* praise God. The two commands are in the context of bearing the name "Christian." Because they are Christians, they should not be ashamed and should continually give praise to God. There is another possible way of understanding Peter's commands. The NASB renders the last phrase of 4:16 as "glorify God in this name." This suggests that triumphal living, characterized by not being ashamed and by continually praising God, is done in the name of God himself.

3. CHRISTIAN SUFFERING POINTS TO FINAL JUDGMENT 4:17–19

This positive approach to the potential of suffering as a Christian must be seen in the total context of God's redemptive plan. Any present suffering must not be compared with eternal reality. This is what is meant by the eschatological understanding of suffering: something once begun that will ultimately find its conclusion. It is the contrast between the present evil age, with its suffering, and the better future, with its salvation. The Christian is called to suffer now **for it is time for judgment to begin** (4:17). The word *judgment* is a neutral word. It is a judgment that can result in either a good or bad evaluation. It can result in approval or discipline, as well as condemnation.[11] Judgment is to begin with the family of God. This process is being accomplished in part by the suffering for doing good that is the common experience of the believers in Peter's audience. God has begun judging within the Church and will later move outward to judge those outside the Church. This is a further reason why glorifying God in suffering is both possible and necessary: such suffering "represents the beginning of God's final judgment on all people."[12] It is common in today's Church to hear individuals talking about wanting God to bring judgment on the unbeliever. What is not so common is to hear those same individuals pleading for Christian

 KEY IDEAS

PETER ON CHRISTIAN SUFFERING

- Don't be surprised; suffering is not foreign to communion with the suffering Christ.

- Suffering just because one is a Christian is proof of faith and trust in God.

- Suffering should lead to rejoicing with exultation.

- Suffering is blessed by the presence of the divine Spirit of glory and a sign of being honored by God.

- If one suffers as a Christian, this is not a cause for feeling shamed, but an occasion for glorifying God.

- Suffering is a sign of the divine judgment that has begun with God's own people. It is thus a further indication of the presence of the end.

- All who suffer innocently can confidently entrust their lives to their faithful Creator and thereby persevere in doing what is right.

suffering. Do you want God's final judgment to come on ungodly individuals? Then plead for suffering. This is the beginning of God's final action in bringing this world to its ultimate conclusion.

Peter reinforces the teaching of 4:12–19 with a quotation from Proverbs 11:31, though the concepts in 1 Peter are closer to the picture presented in Malachi 3. The quote from Proverbs begins with the phrase **if it is hard for the righteous to be saved.** *Hard* is an adverb meaning with difficulty or scarcely. This same adverb is used five other times in the New Testament: Acts 14:18; 27:7, 8, 16; and Romans 5:7. In those contexts, the word means barely or with difficulty, rather than scarcely. The point is not so much the scarcity of salvation, or doubt about it, as it is the difficulty presented to God to save even a righteous person. Given that fact, how sure it is that those who reject God's good news will not find salvation.[13]

The summary admonition (v. 19) is introduced by **so then.** This phrase normally indicates result, effect, or consequences. Building on this idea, John Elliott summarizes this passage by listing the following key points, which he claims to be the most sustained comments on Christian suffering to be found in the New Testament.[14]

- Don't be surprised; suffering is not foreign to communion with the suffering Christ.

- Suffering just because one is a Christian is proof of faith and trust in God.

- Suffering should lead to rejoicing with exultation.

- Suffering is blessed by the presence of the divine Spirit of glory and a sign of being honored by God.

- If one suffers as a Christian, this is not a cause for feeling shamed but an occasion for glorifying God.

- Suffering is a sign of the divine judgment that has begun with God's own people. It is thus a further indication of the presence of the end.

- All who suffer innocently can confidently entrust their lives to their faithful Creator and thereby persevere in doing what is right.

One final word may be in order at this point. Seeking out martyrdom is not an issue in this text. Peter is talking of joy *in* suffering, not a joy *for* suffering.

ENDNOTES

1. Turn to Paul Achtemeier, *1 Peter* (Minneapolis: Fortress Press 1996), pp. 301–302, for detailed information concerning the relationship between this third section of the body of 1 Peter and the previous two sections.

2. John Elliott, *1 Peter* (New York: Doubleday, 2000), p. 768.

3. Achtemeier, *1 Peter*, p. 304.

4. Explore the concept of suffering in 1 Peter by turning to Wayne Grudem, *1 Peter* (Grand Rapids: William B. Eerdmans, 2002 reprint), pp. 177–178.

5. See Achtemeier, *1 Peter*, p. 305, for further treatment of this point.

6. See Grudem, *1 Peter*, p. 179.

7. Turn to Grudem, *1 Peter*, p. 179, for further development of the eschatological significance of present suffering.

8. Achtemeier, *1 Peter*, p. 304.

9. Ibid., p. 309.

10. Read Achtemeier, *1 Peter*, p. 313, for further discussion of this point.

11. See Grudem, *1 Peter*, p. 181, for further development of the word *judgment*.

12. See Achtemeier, *1 Peter*, p. 315.

13. Turn to Achtemeier, *1 Peter*, p. 317, for further discussion of this adverb and its implications.

14. Elliott, *1 Peter*, pp. 807–808.

8

UNITY AND TRUST

1 Peter 5:1-14

1. UNITY AMONG ELDERS AND YOUNG MEN 5:1-5A

Previously, it was suggested that the common experience of suffering for doing good served to bind the believers together (4:12-19). This paragraph will illustrate the second thing that also binds believers: unity among church leaders. But why does Peter place this material at this point in his letter? The discussion of the necessary characteristics of leaders within the Christian community is placed here, not to provide advice on how the community is to be organized, but because of the testing situation discussed in 4:12-19. Effective pastoral leadership is indispensable if the community is to survive.[1] In addition to the general theme of 4:12-5:11, demanding some type of discussion of pastoral leadership, it was somewhat common in New Testament epistles to place instructions to church leaders at the end of a letter before the epistolary conclusion.[2] If the readers of Peter's letter heed his appeal, they will be bound together due to the action of responsible elders and subordinate younger persons.

The call to unity comes from Peter to the **elders** (5:1) and **young men** (5:5). The elders represent individuals who acted as pastoral leaders of the congregations. Advice to church leaders is a common theme in what is known as the pastoral epistles: to bishops (1 Tim. 3:1-7; Titus 1:7-9), to deacons (1 Tim. 3:8-13), and to elders (1 Tim. 5:17-19; Titus 1:5-6). To this group of church leaders, Peter makes his **appeal** (5:1). This word *appeal* implies to beseech or to encourage. It is the identical word Paul used in Romans 12:1. This appeal represents the purpose of the verse, if not the entire letter. That purpose is to encourage those addressed to see in their leadership an extension of the apostolic ministry and authority of Peter himself.[3] The appeal is the command found in the next verse: **be shepherds** (5:2). This appeal implies that Peter was in some position of authority that enabled him to make this appeal. But Peter refers to himself as a **fellow elder**, which would suggest that he considered himself to be on their level of authority and not someone over them who could make an appeal to them.

CHURCH ORGANIZATION

The terms **elder** and **fellow elder** bring into question the level of organization exhibited in the Church during Peter's ministry. The discussion of leadership roles in the community (4:10–11) assumes that all are involved because of their spiritual gifts since there is no mention of elders. This appears to point to the lack of specific organization in the churches addressed.[4]

Why does Peter refer to himself as a **fellow elder**? There is no historical evidence that Peter ever served as a pastor of a local congregation in the early Church. On the other hand, Peter could be considered as the pastor of the early leaders in Acts, and he certainty was the apostle to the Jewish people as Galatians 2:7–10 demonstrates. Also, after the episode at the house of Cornelius (Acts 10), Peter's ministry encompassed both Jewish people and the Gentiles. In a very real way, the world was Peter's parish. The term he used to designate himself is unique to the New Testament. This is the only place **fellow elder** is found. It does have similarities to a number of compound terms Paul used for the men and women who worked with him in his mission: fellow worker (Rom. 16:3, 9, 21; Phil. 2:25; 4:3; Col. 4:11; 1 Thess. 3:2; Philem. 1, 24), fellow soldier (Phil. 2:25; Philem. 2), fellow servant (Col. 1:7; 4:7), and with a somewhat different meaning, fellow prisoner (Rom. 16:7; Col. 4:10; Philem. 23).[5]

Peter employs three descriptive phrases to identify a fellow elder.

◗ KEY IDEAS

Descriptive Phrase	Implication for Fellow Elder
fellow elder	one with apostolic authority and who is involved in the functioning of an elder
witness of Christ's sufferings	an eyewitness to Christ's crucifixion, or a witness to the events of Jesus' passion
participant in future glory	eschatological glory in which all who remain faithful to Christ will one day share

These descriptive phrases raise a number of interesting questions. The aspect of Peter serving as an elder has already been addressed. But why would Peter mention being a **witness of Christ's sufferings**? Peter could mention being a witness to the Transfiguration or Resurrection, but how could this denier of Christ—who deserted Him during His trial and crucifixion—be a witness to His sufferings? The word *witness* is the word from which we get *martyr*. Perhaps Peter is using the same concept that Paul employed when he spoke of sharing in Christ's suffering through the beatings and stonings he received for his faith. Also, those who are witnesses of the grace and goodness of Christ may very well end up as a martyr for their faith as Peter did. (According to tradition, Peter was also crucified.) The apostle states that he will **share in the glory to be revealed**. The glory refers to Christ's Second Advent. From Peter's perspective, this great event was about to be revealed. When this does occur, Peter and his audience will share as partners in this glorious event.

SHEPHERDS OF GOD'S FLOCK

Based on this three-fold description, Peter commands the elders to **be shepherds of God's flock** (5:2). Peter uses an image that has a rich biblical background. The motif of shepherd is used through the Old Testament (Ps. 23; Isa. 40:11; Jer. 23:1–4; Ezek. 34:1–31) and the New Testament (Matt. 18:10–14; 26:31; Luke 12:32; John 10:1–18; 21:15–17; Heb. 13:20). The word translated shepherd is the word *presbyters*, which carries the idea of tending the flock of God entrusted to an individual.

The verb tense for this command may be understood as stressing the beginning of an action, which gives the sense of "take up the task of shepherding." The local congregation being called "the flock" continues the imagery of a shepherd leading his sheep. The individuals you lead are **under your care**, with the connotation of the elder serving as an overseer or guardian.

The attitude towards "being a shepherd of the flock" is as important as assuming the responsibility itself. Thus, Peter describes the proper attitude required of the shepherd by means of three pairs of contrasting phrases. The right attitude is important for unity.

LIFE CHANGE

HOW TO SHEPHERD GOD'S FLOCK

Negative	Positive	The Right Way to Shepherd
not because you must	but because you are willing	not under pressure, but willingly
not greedy for money	but eager to serve	not because of any stipend but eagerly
not lording it over	but being examples to the flock	not by harsh command but by example

Two observations are in order. First, as Peter Davids reminds his readers, "The three sets of contrasts are not to suggest that there is no reward for ministry done properly. There is a reward, but it comes at the Second Advent."[6] The second observation is from John Elliott who states, "The qualities enumerated are not qualifications for persons applying for the role of elder/overseer but attitudes according to which the elders are to lead and shepherd the flock."[7]

There is reward for ministry done with proper motives and attitudes. The time of reward will be when the **Chief Shepherd appears** (5:4). This is the only occurrence of the word *Chief Shepherd* in the New Testament, and it will reappear in later writings of the Church Fathers. That Christ is the Chief Shepherd implies that the elders who shepherd God's flock are continuing, in part at least, Christ's ministry. It also implies, perhaps, that they will stand before Christ to be judged on how they have functioned as such shepherds of His flock.[8] When the Chief Shepherd appears, proper service will be rewarded. The word **appears** refers in the New Testament both to Christ's incarnation (1 Tim. 3:16; Heb. 9:26) and to His second coming (Col. 3:4; 1 John 2:28; 3:2). It is the second coming that is meant here. When Christ comes again **you will receive the crown of glory**. The promise of receiving is the promise of eschatological recompense, whether positive (Eph. 6:8; Heb. 10:36) or negative (Col. 3:25).[9]

The reference to the crown of glory reflects the first-century practice of rewarding an athlete who won a race with a wreath. This prize was the cause of boasting, as in Philippians 4:1 and 1 Thessalonians 2:19. But Peter has a rich biblical context in which to develop this concept. Jewish wisdom literature has several references to the crown (Prov. 4:9; 12:4; 14:24; 16:31; 17:6). In the New Testament, the crown takes on the aspect of "eschatological recognition" (1 Cor. 9:25; 2 Tim. 4:8; James 1:12; Rev. 2:10; 3:11).[10] This crown is qualified by two phrases: (1) a crown of glory—unique in the New Testament, symbolizing eschatological reward, and (2) unfading—by which the permanency of this reward is emphasized. "This crown is the divine, unfading crown, emblematic of God's approval and reward that awaits those elders/shepherds who bear their responsibility appropriately and effectively."[11]

YOUNG MEN ALSO HAVE RESPONSIBILITIES

In the same way, others also have responsibilities. Young men are to **be submissive to those who are older** (5:5). Does Peter have in mind simply the fact that younger men should be respectful of their elders, or does he have something else in mind? In the context of elders and "shepherds of the flock," it is probably true that Peter has in mind younger men who are in some way junior leaders. Such individuals would be ready to learn and assist those directing the church. But youth can sometimes be impatient with their leaders. The unity among elders and junior leaders can become strained just at this point. Elders are sometimes characterized by conservatism, and the pastoral wisdom of the elders may at times appear to the junior leaders as out of date and not responsive to the contemporary situation.[12]

LIFE CHANGE[13]

LEADERSHIP SKILLS 101

1. Mutual respect and humility is necessary within a community under outside pressure, if that community is to survive.

2. Leaders must function pastorally, not dictatorially, if those wounded by external social pressures are to remain within the community.

3. There must be mutual trust within the community, especially between those with leadership responsibilities and the other members, since lack of trust within the community in the presence of severe pressure against the Christian faith in the external world would doom the community.

4. Only with good leadership and mutual respect will the community and its individual members survive to share in the glory that is to come when the divine judgment has run its course.

—Paul Achtemeier

But three things bind the believers together. The first is the common experience of suffering for doing good. This present paragraph mentions the fact that good spiritual leadership will bind the believers together.

2. TRUST WITH HUMILITY 5:5B–11

This paragraph is the final teaching section in 1 Peter. It concludes the three-fold theme of things that bind believers together. Previously, Peter discussed the fact that suffering for doing good binds believers together (4:12–19). Then, he discussed the fact that unity between the elders and younger leaders is essential (5:1–5a). Now, Peter turns to the Christian virtue of trust in God that springs from a humble spirit.

But how does humility fit into Peter's argument? Simply that it is a humbling experience to accept one's experiences in life, particularly if it involves oppression and suffering. Peter's response is that a humble acceptance of whatever may come about is predicated on trust in God. The Christian life is an example of acts and consequences. The act of placing one's trust in God will produce certain consequences. There will be some good consequences of which Peter has spoken about in detail. But there are also bad consequences as a culture that is against God will extend their hatred of God to His followers as well. This will bind fellow believers together.

LIFE IS A HUMBLING EXPERIENCE

Peter begins this last teaching text with a reference to **all of you** (5:5). This reveals its universal application. The admonition is that you all should **clothe yourselves with humility**. The word **clothe** means to put on, to tie, or to firmly fasten something on one's self. Humility is to be worn as a suit of clothing. The word *humility* in this context means to have lowly thinking, as in Colossians 2:18, 23. The quotation from Proverbs 3:34 helps to make clear what Peter means by "lowly thinking." But **God opposes the proud**. This term, *proud,* refers to those who think themselves above others or those who are arrogant. It is used in reference to those who hold too high an opinion of themselves. It is these individuals that God opposes. This means that He lines up against or resists them. The attitude of wearing humility as a suit of clothes enables one to accept life as it comes because of a deep trust in the ultimate victory of God and His people.

Therefore, which serves to introduce the conclusion of the matter, Peter writes, **humble yourselves under God's mighty hand** (5:6). With this admonition, the focus has shifted from being humble within the community (5:5) to accepting the humble status forced upon Christians by the rejection and hostility of the surrounding culture (5:6), a situation faced by all Christians of whom the author is aware (5:9).[14]

The humble status is one of persecution. Remember what Peter has already said concerning the persecuted Christian. Peter Davids wrote, "The duty of the believer is not to resist, but to humble himself under the mighty hand of God."[15] The double image of humbling and God's hand could mean

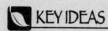

KEY IDEAS

CHRISTIAN PERSECUTION

- Persecution comes to faithful Christians according to God's will (3:17).

- Persecution is not foreign to their existence as followers of Christ (4:12–16).

- Persecution is in fact God's purifying fire (4:17–19).

judgment (Ps. 106:42 KJV) or obedience. The context determines the exact meaning. Peter is asking his readers to accept the present circumstances because of what they know concerning their future commencing with the Second Advent. This is the "reversal-of-fortunes" theme that is in the Old Testament (1 Sam. 2:7–8; Ezek. 17:24) and is developed by Jesus' teaching (Matt. 23:12; Luke 1:52; 14:11; 18:14). This theme emphasizes the point that humiliation in the present leads to exaltation in the future. The contrast is for believers to be "under" so that God may "lift them up." The contrast between lowliness and exaltation is a common New Testament teaching point.

KEY IDEAS

REVERSAL OF FORTUNES

Saying of Jesus	Matt. 23:12; Luke 14:11; 18:14
Jesus' life	Luke 1:51–53; 2 Cor. 8:9
Particularly death and resurrection	Phil. 2:8–9; 2 Cor. 13:4a
Normative for Christians	2 Cor. 11:7; Phil. 2:3–4; James 1:9–10

This reversal-of-fortunes theme is brought about by God's mighty hand.[16] This reversal will take place **in due time** (5:6), which has a rather general sound to it. This phrase refers to "the time God deems best, whether in this life or in the life to come."[17]

GOD CARES FOR YOU

Believers who live under God's mighty hand will need to **cast all anxiety on him** (5:7). That is their only recourse. The word **cast** implies the idea of throwing on. In Luke 19:35, the identical word is used in the context of throwing clothes on a donkey for Jesus to ride. In similar fashion, every care, concern, and worry is to be thrown on God. This action of casting all anxiety is to be connected with the command to "humble yourselves." The true Christian attitude is not self-abandonment or resignation, but it is a positive expression of bowing before God and trusting Him for everything in life.

The reason for such action is **because he cares** (5:7) for the individual believer. This verb *to care* means there is a constant care and concern for the individual on God's part.

The fact that two contrasting entities are interested in the believer introduces two commands: **Be self-controlled and alert** (5:8). Christians are always to be characterized by these two commands, but are to be especially so as the final events leading up to the Second Advent nears.[18] These two commands call on the believer to begin being alert and watchful, then continue doing that until the return of Christ.[19] The verb **be alert** comes from a military context and refers to a soldier on watch; it is in contrast to mental and spiritual lethargy. Trust in God must not lead to slackness. The spiritual warfare that Christians wage demands vigilance.

THE ENEMY IS ALSO INTERESTED IN YOU

But why must you be vigilant? Because **your enemy** (5:8) is after you. With this fact made evident, we have another indication that we are nearing the close of Peter's letter. Finally, the true nature of the Christians' opposition is made clear: it is the embodiment of supernatural evil, the devil.[20] The word for "enemy" originally meant a legal adversary, an opponent in a lawsuit. With later usage, the word came to cover an enemy in general. Here, the enemy is clearly identified as the devil.[21] A sober and watchful Christian should recognize the results of what may be demonic influence.

KEY IDEAS

	DEMONIC INFLUENCES
Mark 1:24; 5:2–5; 9:18; Acts 16:16–18; Rev. 2:10	bizarre or violently irrational, evil behavior, especially in opposition to the gospel or to Christians
John 8:44; 1 John 4:1–3	malicious slander and falsehood in speech
Mark 5:5; 9:20	increasing bondage to self-destructive behavior
1 John 4:1–6	stubborn advocacy of false doctrine
1 Cor. 12:10; Eph. 6:16	sudden and unexplained onslaughts of emotions (such as fear, hatred, depression, anxiety, violent anger)

The devil has a precise agenda. He **prowls around like a roaring lion** (5:8). This is the only place in the Bible that the devil is called a lion. There is, however, an Old Testament background for this image of the lion (Jer. 50:17; 51:34–38; Isa. 15:9; Ezek. 22:25). As these references indicate, the lion in the Old Testament is a description of the opponents of Israel. Both "prowl" and "roaring" indicate continual action. Our enemy is constantly on the move; he is constantly prowling and roaring. Why? Because he is **looking for someone to devour**. The word *devour* is literally to drink down. It is used in the sense to swallow down or to eat up. Since he is constantly on the move, seeking to fulfill his destructive agenda, there is no escape from such experiences. The believers cannot avoid the attack of the devil. Only by completely abandoning the gospel and the community shaped by it can they escape the persecutions they otherwise face.

What is the Christian to do? Peter's response to Satan sounds so simple: **resist him** (5:9). This word means to stand up against or to withstand. The tense of this command may be another of those situations where the idea is to begin to stand against. Resistance comes from a trusting relationship and **standing firm in the faith**. The concept of being firm in the faith has two meanings. It often means holding to certain doctrines firmly, as in 1 Timothy 1:19; 6:20; 2 Timothy 1:13. Here, Peter's emphasis is on one's trust in God.[22] The twin idea of resisting and standing firm has a similar reference with James 4:1–7. There are subtle differences however, even though both speak to firmness in faith.

KEY IDEAS

PRESSURES WITHIN AND WITHOUT

1 Peter 5:9	James 4:1–7
The believer is under external pressure.	The believer is under internal pressure.
The devil works through persecutors.	The devil works through the evil impulse within.

Christians are able to "stand firm" because they know some important things: the "general" of the army has not abandoned his "troops" and the battle itself is temporary. They also know that the **brothers . . . are undergoing** (5:9) the same kind of suffering. The abusive sufferings that Peter's readers are experiencing are also being experienced by Christians throughout the world. But Peter reminds his readers that the origin of suffering is not God but the devil.

CHRISTIAN SUFFERING HAS ITS REWARD

If, for a little while, the Christians can victoriously endure sufferings, God will do something great. **Grace** and the call of God (5:10) will be evident in their lives. The contrast will be evident between suffering **a little while**, where the temporary aspect of suffering is clear, and ultimate glory, which is **eternal**. The call of God will finally be accomplished as described by four powerful images of what God himself will do.

Peter intends to make a sharp distinction between these four words. "What Peter has done is pile up a number of closely related terms that together, by their reinforcing one another,

GREAT THEMES

THE GOOD GOD INTENDS

Term	Description and Definition
restore you	to put in order, to mend, or in the medical sense of setting a broken bone
make you strong	to strengthen or support
hold you firm	to make strong
keep you steadfast	to make a foundation, provide a solid foundation, or ground firmly

give a multiple underscoring of the good that God is intending for them and even now is producing in their suffering."[23] It is no wonder that Peter concludes this section with yet another doxology: **To him be the power for ever and ever. Amen.**

3. CONCLUSION 5:12–14

The letter is now finished. It only remains to draw the letter to a conclusion, and even here, there is a specific structure for the conclusion of a letter. The normal Greek letter ended with a short closing word, perhaps preceded by such items as an oath, a health wish, a purpose statement, and mention of who was carrying the letter.[24] The New Testament writers expanded this into a relatively lengthy conclusion. Four specific items usually appear in a New Testament epistle: a greeting, some comment about the messenger, a statement as to the purpose of the letter, and a blessing or prayer as the concluding line.[25]

Peter begins his conclusion with mention of the **help of Silas** (5:12). Peter says that this letter was sent with his help. But to what extent did Silas help? Under our discussion of authorship in the introduction, this question was addressed. The phrase "with the help of" is ambiguous. Seeking to clarify this phrase, the NASB renders this as "through Silas" this letter has been sent. Some has interpreted this phrase to mean Silas wrote the letter as Peter dictated the contents. Others have determined that Silas brought this letter to its intended readers. This latter view is the one taken in this commentary.

Who is Silas? Peter used the shorter form of the name. The long version is Silvanus. Most writers agree that shortening names was not uncommon in the first century. In the letters of Paul, we become acquainted with Silvanus (2 Cor. 1:19; 1 Thess. 1:1; and 2 Thess. 1:1). If Silvanus is identical to Silas in the book of Acts, we know a few more things about him. Silas was a leading man among the Christians (15:22), a prophet (15:32), and a companion of Paul in some of the latter's missionary journeys (15:40; 16:19, 25, 29; 17:4, 10, 14; and 18:5).

In addition to this, Peter regards Silas **as a faithful brother** (5:12). The word **regard** implies to reckon or to count as. This does not need to imply that others have doubted the ability of Silas, but it serves to emphasize Peter's confidence in Silas.[26] The phrase **I have written** illustrates a special verb tense used by writers when they put themselves in the position of their readers and look back on the time of writing as a past event. Almost every conclusion of a New Testament epistle will have this feature.

This letter was to have two overriding purposes. They have been discussed and elaborated on in the previous five chapters. In this conclusion, Peter returns to these twin themes: to encourage them, probably due to the suffering they were experiencing, and to testify concerning certain aspects of the faith. With these two purposes, the entire letter is summarized.

The content of this letter represents **the true grace of God** (5:12). He speaks of grace in the form of truth given, and grace as the needed encouragement in the time of trial. What did Peter expect his readers to do with this letter? He expected them to **stand fast in it**. The tense of the

> ### ◪ KEY IDEAS
>
> #### PURPOSES OF 1 PETER
>
> | To Testify Concerning Faith | To Encourage in Suffering |
> |---|---|
> | 1:3–12, 18:21; 23–25 | 1:13–17, 22 |
> | 2:6–10, 21–25 | 2:1–5, 11–20 |
> | 3:10–12, 18–22 | 3:1–9, 13–17 |
> | 4:4–6, 17–18 | 4:1–3, 7–16, 19 |
> | 5:10–11 | 5:1–9 |

verb implies, "Begin to take your stand." Peter has given his readers the witness of the faith and encouragement in their time of need. Now, they are to stand fast in the truth of what they have received. "Now is not the time to give up, but rather the time to stand fast in faith and hold on to what they already have, that is, God's grace. This is the major purpose toward which the whole letter is directed."[27]

Peter now sends greetings to the believers he has addressed. She who is in **Babylon** (5:13) cannot refer to the ancient Babylonian Empire, for it laid in ruin at this point in history. On the other hand, in the first century *Babylon* was a familiar code word that stood for the city of Rome (Rev. 14:8; 16:19; 17:5; 18:10). In the present context it probably means the church at Rome. This church is identified by two qualities: it is **chosen** by God, and they **send greetings** to Peter's audience. The fact of being chosen by God identifies them spiritually with all believers in general and specifically with Peter's audience (1:2). The fact that they send greetings includes them in the mutual bond of all true believers.

Mark (5:13) sends greetings as well. The "Mark" that is given ample attention in the New Testament is John Mark.[28] Peter refers to Mark as **my son**. This is to be understood not in the biological sense but as Peter's son in the faith. Peter exhorts the readers to **greet one another with a kiss of love** (5:14). Peter's phrase **kiss of love** is similar to Paul's phrase "greet one another with a holy kiss" (Rom. 16:16; 1 Cor. 16:20; 2 Cor. 13:12; 1 Thess. 5:26). Both Peter and Paul use this phrase in the concluding paragraphs of their writing. By this practice of kissing on the cheek, forehead, or hand, mutual Christian love was demonstrated. This entire letter has emphasized the point of mutual love (1:22; 2:17; 4:8); and love is also reflected in the term "dear friends/beloved" at 2:11 and 4:12.[29] The letter ends with this prayer: **Peace to all of you who are in Christ**.

ENDNOTES

1. See Paul Achtemeier, *1 Peter* (Minneapolis: Fortress Press, 1996), p. 322, for further discussion of the placement of this information at this point in 1 Peter.

2. Peter Davids, *The First Epistle of Peter* (Grand Rapids: William B. Eerdmans, 1990), p. 175, directs attention to such examples as 1 Corinthians 16:15–16; 1 Thessalonians 5:12–15; and Hebrews 13:7, 17.

3. Achtemeier, *1 Peter*, p. 324.

4. Turn to Achtemeier, *1 Peter*, pp. 322–324, for a detailed discussion of the implications of organization for Peter's audience.

5. For a full discussion of these terms and their implication, see Davids, *The First Epistle of Peter*, p. 176.

6. Davids, *The First Epistle of Peter*, p. 181.

7. John Elliott, *1 Peter* (New York: Doubleday, 2000), p. 815.

8. For more discussion of this point, turn to Achtemeier, *1 Peter*, p. 329.

9. See Achtemeier, *1 Peter*, p. 329, for further discussion of this dual aspect of "receiving."

10. Wayne Grudem, *1 Peter* (Grand Rapids: William B. Eerdmans, 2002 reprint), p. 191, suggests that in other New Testament references to "crown," these passages seem to be a metaphor for the heavenly life in general.

11. Achtemeier, *1 Peter*, p. 330.

12. See Davids, *The First Epistle of Peter*, p. 184, for more discussion of the dynamic between elders and young men.

13. Achtemeier, *1 Peter*, p. 322.

14. Read Achtemeier, *1 Peter*, p. 338, for the author's development of this shift in focus.

15. Davids, *The First Epistle of Peter*, p. 186.

16. This is the only occurrence of this term in the New Testament. The Old Testament has regular uses of the "hand of God" as a figure of God's power, particularly in relation to the Exodus of Israel from Egypt.

17. Grudem, *1 Peter*, p. 194.

18. See for example the theme of Jesus' teaching in Matt. 24:42–43; 25:13; 26:38–41; and the New Testament in general, 1 Thess. 5:6; 2 Tim. 4:5; Acts 20:31; 1 Cor. 16:13; Col. 4:5; Rev. 3:2–3; 16:15.

19. See Davids, *The First Epistle of Peter*, p. 189, for further implications of the tense of these two commands.

20. See Achtemeier, *1 Peter*, p. 337, for the implications of this disclosure in regards to the structure of 1 Peter.

21. The primary meaning is slanderer or accuser. In the New Testament, it represents the devil as the rebellious prince of evil (Matt. 4:1; John 13:2; Rev. 2:7–9). This one is the enemy of God's purposes (Matt. 13:39; Acts 10:38; Eph. 6:11; 1 Thess. 2:18; 2 Thess. 2:8–10; Rev. 12:9–10, 13–17) and the originator of lying and deceit (John 8:44; Acts 5:3; 2 Thess. 2:9–10; Rev. 12:9; 20:10).

22. Notice some other implications of a "firm faith." Acts 16:5 notes the new churches became firm in the commitment to Christ. The same idea is found in Colossians 1:23 but with a different word: "Continue in the faith, stable and steadfast, not shifting from the hope of the gospel that you heard" (ESV). Colossians 2:5 reads "rejoicing to see your good order and the firmness of your faith in Christ" (ESV). In Revelation 12:9–11 the effect of such firm commitment on the devil is that "they have conquered [the devil] by the blood of the lamb and by the word of their testimony, for they loved not their lives even unto death" (ESV).

23. Davids, *The First Epistle of Peter*, p. 196. Also see John Elliott, *1 Peter* (New York: Doubleday, 2000), p. 867, where he suggests that Peter has intentionally developed the idea of a building activity suggesting "all four actions pertain to the securing, fortifying, and up-building of the community as the household of God."

24. See Davids, *The First Epistle of Peter*, p. 197, for further discussion of the structure of a secular letter.

25. Ibid.

26. See Achtemeier, *1 Peter*, pp. 351–352, where he comments that it was a common ancient custom to commend the one who delivers a letter, a custom reflected in early Christians letters as well (Rom. 16:1; Eph. 6:21; Col. 4:7).

27. Davids, *The First Epistle of Peter*, p. 201.

28. Turn to Davids, *The First Epistle of Peter*, p. 203, for a summary statement concerning John Mark. As Davids reminds his readers, John Mark's house was apparently a main meeting place for Peter (Acts 12:12–17). He had traveled with Paul and then abandoned the mission (Acts 12:25; 13:13). Later, he apparently had a change of heart that convinced his relative Barnabas, but not Paul, although the latter eventually came to value him highly since he was with Paul during his Roman imprisonment (Col. 4:10; 2 Tim. 4:11; Philem. 24). It was natural, then, for him also to become a close associate of Peter when Peter came to Rome.

29. See Achtemeier, *1 Peter*, p. 355, for further discussion of this early Christian practice.

2 PETER

INTRODUCTION TO
2 PETER

B efore one can begin to interpret the text of 2 Peter, there are several items that must be addressed by way of special introduction. There is probably no other book in the New Testament canon that has undergone such intense study as 2 Peter. The scope of this commentary is not to be a critical analysis of such issues. But that does not mean that the interested reader should not be aware that such issues do in fact exist. The bibliography will provide ample opportunity to read further on such issues. The intent of this commentary is primarily to investigate the meaning of the text and suggest application for our contemporary situation. This can be attempted without a scholarly investigation of all issues involved.

Topics that will be discussed by way of introduction to 2 Peter include: (1) authorship, (2) the recipients of this letter, (3) a discussion of the kind of literature 2 Peter represents, (4) the occasion and date of writing, (5) an attempt at identifying the false teachers referred to in this letter, (6) a discussion of what the author was trying to "prove" in this letter, (7) a brief review of the literary relationship between 2 Peter and Jude, (8) and an outline of 2 Peter.

AUTHORSHIP

Any discussion concerning authorship of a New Testament book requires investigation into both external and internal evidence. For the purposes of 2 Peter, our brief examination of external evidence will be to see how this book was understood by early Church fathers.[1] Chrysostom (344–407), Origen (185–254), Cyril of Jerusalem (315–386), Hilary of Poitiers (315–367), Ambrose (333–397), and Novatian (235–258) all expressed their positions on the authorship of 2 Peter.

The Church fathers all recognize that there were great differences between the first and second letters attributed to Peter, but they explained

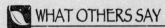

WHAT OTHERS SAY

PETER AS AUTHOR

There used to be many people who thought that this letter was not written by Peter. But it is enough to read this verse (1:17), and you will soon see that it was Peter who stood with Jesus on the Mount of Transfiguration. It is therefore the same Peter who heard the voice testifying to the Lord who wrote this letter.

—Gregory the Great (540–604)

these variations in different ways.[2] While some rejected the authenticity of the second letter and refused to accept it as part of the canon, the majority were unwilling to go that far. The quote from Gregory the Great expresses the majority viewpoint in regards to the question of authorship.[3]

Representative of the evangelical position is Donald Guthrie's evaluation of the impact of the Church fathers' positions. "It would seem as a fair conclusion to this survey of external evidence to submit that there is not evidence from any part of the early Church that this epistle was ever rejected as spurious, in spite of the hesitancy which existed over its reception."[4]

Why the hesitancy? It came about due to the strength of the internal evidence and the various ways of interpreting that evidence. The first place to begin is with the epistle's own claims regarding authorship. There are six texts that reveal that claim: 2 Peter 1:1, 14, 16, 18; 3:1, 15.

Those who favor Peter as the author of 2 Peter understand these texts as clearly referring to the apostle Peter as the author of 2 Peter.[5]

In addition to the epistle's own claim regarding authorship, there are four specific areas of evidence that scholars have identified and evaluated that must be reviewed before a final decision can be made. These four areas include the use of personal allusions,[6] certain historical problems, key literary issues, and proposed stylistic problems. How one resolves these issues will determine the issue of authorship for 2 Peter. The position of this commentary is in favor of the apostle Peter being the author of this epistle.[7] It is also good to remember that the question of whether or not 2 Peter is the inspired Word of God is not pending on the outcome of the determination of authorship of this epistle. The fact that 2 Peter is part of the New Testament canon indicates that its divine authority was recognized by the early Church.

THE RECIPIENTS OF 2 PETER

In 2 Peter 1:1 we read, **to those who the righteousness of our God and Savior Jesus Christ have received a faith as precious as ours**. Rather than providing an answer to the question of the letter's recipient, one is struck by the general tone of this "to" section. It is in contrast to the very specific recipients of the "to" section in 1 Peter where "strangers in the world, scattered" in five provinces of Asia Minor are mentioned (1 Pet. 1:1–2).

It was suggested in the introduction of 1 Peter that the author was writing to those individuals living in the five provinces of Asia Minor whom he did not personally know. It was, in fact, a general letter written to Christians to encourage them in their Christian walk. Are these the same individuals to whom 2 Peter was written? On the evidence of 2 Peter 3:1, the answer would appear to be yes. That text reads, "Dear friends, this is now my second letter to you."

However, there are texts in 2 Peter that appear to read as if Peter knew his audience. For instance, "We did not follow cleverly invented stories when we told you about the power and coming of our Lord Jesus Christ" (2 Pet. 1:16). "This clearly presupposes a period of previous mission work among the readers."[8] Also, the mention of the activities of the false teachers in 2:10–22 is described with present tense verbs. It sounds as if the false teaching is going on at the time of writing of this letter, and Peter is aware of it. If this is true, it is hard to reconcile that with 1 Peter, which was written to "strangers" in five provinces. The various commentaries in the bibliography will review this issue for the interested reader. Note Guthrie's conclusion of the matter. He states, "In absence of sufficient data there is no option but to leave the location of the readers as an open question."[9]

WHAT KIND OF LITERATURE IS 2 PETER?

As with 1 Peter, this second epistle has been identified by various literary categories. It is known as "The Second Epistle of Peter" and this designation implies that the contents contain the ingredients of a formal letter written in the first century. This is most evident at the beginning and conclusion of the letter. The beginning (1:1–2) contains the familiar "from . . . to . . . greetings" style. This is consistent with a salutation from the first century. The "from" part identifies the author and any descriptive phrases that will enable the intended audience to better understand and appreciate the author. The "to" aspect of the salutation identifies the readers of the epistle. The greetings part of the salutation is a Christianized version of the standard greeting of a secular letter. In a secular setting, this might mean no more than a wish for good health and well-being. In a New Testament epistle the secular greeting is changed to "grace and peace." This two-fold greeting affirms what the recipients of the letter already experience, namely the grace and peace of God. This Christian greeting also serves to express the desire that grace and peace may be experienced in greater measure in the lives of those reading the epistle.

The conclusion of 2 Peter also reveals characteristics of an epistle. Here one expects to find a summary of previous teaching, final words of admonition, and a prayer or doxology. The conclusion of 2 Peter (3:14–18) contains this type of material.

On the other hand, it is acknowledged that Peter's first audience heard this letter read aloud to them rather than each one having their own copy. Thus, 2 Peter must bear the traits of a formal speech. The structure of Peter's speech would resemble a speech from the first century, and his introduction is the first element that demonstrates this fact. Peter's introduction includes an announcement of the intention of the writer, the mention of key topics that will be developed in the remainder of the letter, and a call for a serious hearing on the part of the audience. This material is found in 2 Peter 1:3–15.

The major section of 2 Peter is the writer's response to five objections to the Christian message taught by false teachers within the body of believers. Peter's response to these objections is the rebuttal of each objection. The rebuttals are classified as proof material. In this type of material, the task turns on persuading the audience of the legitimacy of the author's case. This will necessitate refuting the arguments of the false teachers as well as demonstrating the truth of the author's own position. The proof section of 2 Peter is found at 1:16–3:13, with a brief digression at 2:10–22.

The third ingredient of this speech is the conclusion of 2 Peter, (3:14–18). This material includes a recapitulation of previous key points and an emotional appeal to the audience.[12] When one places the concept of 2 Peter structured as a letter alongside of it being structured as a speech, it becomes clear why many writers regard New Testament epistles as a "letter-speech."

Recent investigations in interpretation have provided yet another way to regard writings similar to 2 Peter. It has been suggested that 2 Peter is an example of what is known as a "farewell speech."[13] In this type of writing, authors refer to their old age or imminent death and exhort the hearers to live along a certain line in the future.[14]

THE OCCASION AND DATE OF WRITING

From reading 2 Peter one can ascertain some of the reasons the author had in mind when he wrote this letter: to remind his audience of certain fundamental Christian concepts (1:12), to refresh their memory (1:13), to stimulate them to wholesome thinking (3:1), to help them remember the words of the prophets and the commands of Jesus (3:2), to warn his audience (3:17), and to exhort them in godly living (3:18).

Some of the themes that are prominent in this short letter demonstrate urgency in writing. There are warnings against false teachers, a call to holiness and godly living, and a reaffirmation of the belief in the Second Advent.

The question of date of writing is directly tied to the bigger issue of authorship. For those who accept Peter as the author of this letter, a date of writing somewhere in the early to mid 60s of the first century would fit the available evidence for the time of his martyrdom. Those who reject Peter as the author of this letter would propose a date between A.D. 150 and 200 as possible for the writing of 2 Peter.

THE FALSE TEACHERS

The book of 2 Peter is only three chapters in length with the appearance of false teachers and the description of their activities dominating two-thirds of this letter. They are mentioned first in 2:1, and a discussion of their influence continues throughout the remainder of the book. The first mention of false teachers is contrasted with Peter's prior instruction on the priority of Scripture (1:12–22). Peter acknowledges the fact that his readers are "firmly established in the truth" (1:12). He reminds them that the teaching concerning the Second Advent is not based on "cleverly invented stories" (1:16). Peter regards prophetic utterances as "more than certain" (1:19) and reminds his audience that "prophecy never had its origin in the will of men. But men spoke from God" (1:21).

It is against this backdrop that Peter introduces the appearance of false teachers (2:1). They are never identified by name, so we only know them by what they teach and how they live. They are called false teachers as counterparts to "false prophets [who were] among the people" in the days of the Old Testament prophets. This raises the question, does Peter mean to make a distinction between false teachers and false prophets? Perhaps Peter is simply reminding his audience that these individuals are within the Church; they consider themselves to be believers and see their mission as instructing other Christians in their view of truth. Peter's objective is to demonstrate that their teaching is false and their lifestyle is pagan.

Their falsehood is often described in general terms. They introduce destructive heresies (2:1), and they exploit "with stories they have made up" (2:3). Specifically, they scoff at the mention of the Second Advent (3:1–10).

Their lifestyle is one characterized as that which follows the corrupt desire of the sinful nature (2:10), reveling in their pleasures (2:13), and their never-ending sinning (2:14). They make great spiritual claims but produce little (2:17), they carouse in broad daylight (2:13), and they speak the error of lawless men (3:17). "This is the kind of threat that one would expect [as] soon as Christianity challenged its pagan environment. Indeed it was found in the Corinthian church in Paul's day and in the Asiatic churches reflected in Revelation 2–3."[15]

WHAT WAS PETER TRYING TO PROVE IN THIS LETTER?

As was mentioned previously, the content of 2 Peter could be identified as a "letter-speech." When analyzing 2 Peter as a speech, the main section of its contents was identified as a proof section rebutting the teaching of false teachers. While considering themselves to be believers, they rejected key theological doctrines that the early Church maintained. They denied, for instance, the sovereign Lord (2:1), and the scoffed at the idea of the Second Advent (3:1–10). To support their false teaching, these individuals offered five propositions. Peter confronted these false ideas and offered his rebuttal of each. The false propositions and Peter's rebuttals are found in the following chart.

GREAT THEMES

FIVE FALSE PROPOSITIONS

False Propositions	Peter's Rebuttal
The apostles based their preaching of the second advent on human-made myths (1:16–18).	The Second Advent is not based on cleverly invented stories because Peter was an eyewitness of His majesty.
Old Testament prophecies were the products of human minds (1:19–21).	Prophecy never had its origin in human will because men spoke from God.
Divine judgment never happens (2:1–10).	Biblical history tells of divine judgment on angels who sinned, the ancient world, the cities of Sodom and Gomorrah.
Ever since our fathers died, everything goes on as it has since the beginning of creation (3:1–7).	Long ago, by God's word, the heavens existed and the earth was formed. But that world was destroyed. By the same word, the present heavens and earth are reserved for fire.
The expectation of the Second Advent is disproved by its delay (3:8–13).	The Lord is not slow in keeping His promise, as some understand slowness. He is patient, not wanting anyone to perish, but everyone to come to repentance.

THE RELATIONSHIP BETWEEN 2 PETER AND JUDE

One of the issues that kept 2 Peter from being immediately accepted as part of the New Testament canon was the striking similarities between some of the material in 2 Peter and that of the epistle of Jude. Nowhere is this more evident than when reading each respective writer's description of false teachers in the Church. Based on these striking similarities, four positions have been taken in regard to the relationship between the two books.

The first view is that both writings are independent writings, and any similarity in content between the two is due to the inspiration of the Holy Spirit. The three remaining views are built around some sort of belief of interdependence between 2 Peter and Jude. For instance, 2 Peter may be dependent on Jude, which implies that the writer of 2 Peter copied some material from the writer of Jude. The reverse could also be possible. The writer of Jude could be dependent on 2 Peter and copied some of his material that described false teachers. A final possibility could be that both of

KEY IDEAS

2 PETER 2 COMPARED TO JUDE

2 Peter 2:10–18	Jude 8–16
[T]hese men are not afraid **to slander celestial beings** (2:10).	[T]hese dreamers . . . **slander celestial beings** (8).
yet even **angels** . . . (2:11).	But even the arch**angel, Michael** . . . (9).
But these men **blaspheme in matters they do not understand.** They are like **brute beasts, creatures of instinct,** born only to be caught and **destroyed** . . . (2:12).	Yet these men speak **abusively against whatever they do not understand**; and what things they do understand **by instinct, like unreasoning animals**—these are the very things that **destroy** them (10).
They are **blots and blemishes, reveling . . . while they feast with you** . . . (2:13).	These men are **blemishes at your love feasts** . . . (12).
They . . . follow **the way of Balaam** . . . (2:15).	They have rushed for profit into **Balaam's error** . . . (11).
These men are **springs without water and mists driven by a storm** . . . (2:17).	They are **clouds without rain, blown along by the wind** . . . (12).
Blackest darkness is reserved for them (2:17).	. . . for whom **blackest darkness has been reserved forever** (13).
For they **mouth empty boastful words** . . . (2:18).	. . . they **boast about themselves** . . . (16).

the writers of 2 Peter and Jude were dependent on an unknown source from which they both copied material and placed in their respective letters.

This complex issue is beyond the scope of this commentary. The commentaries listed in the bibliography will discuss the issue and implications of literary independence or interdependency. One thing that should help in navigating a straight course through issues like this is the fact that the understanding of the text of 2 Peter does not depend on how some of these complex issues are finally resolved.

ENDNOTES

Sidebar: Gregory the Great, "Sermon in Ezekiel" 2.6.11, P. L. 79:1099.

1. Gerald Bray, ed., *James, 1–2 Peter, 1–3 John, and Jude: Ancient Christian Commentary on Scripture* (Downers Grove: InterVarsity Press, 2000), pp. 129–163.

2. Ibid., p. 129.

3. Ibid., p. 140.

4. Donald Guthrie, *New Testament Introduction*, revised edition (Downers Grove: InterVarsity Press, fourth edition, 1990), p. 811.

5. Note Guthrie's view that "such evidence leaves us with the impression that the author is the apostle Peter," p. 812.

6. Bray comments that the Church fathers came to believe that "perhaps the strongest argument in favor of the letter's authenticity was its remarkably personal style," p. 129.

7. Guthrie's summary is helpful at this point. He writes, "The choice seems to lie between two fairly well defined alternatives. Either the epistle is genuinely Petrine, in which case the main problem is the delay of its reception. Or it is pseudepigraphic, in which case the main difficulties are lack of an adequate motive and the problem of the epistle's ultimate acceptance," pp. 840–841.

8. Guthrie, *Introduction*, pp. 811–842.

9. Ibid., p. 842.

10. Ibid., p. 843.

11. The interested reader will find much help in understanding the implications of 2 Peter being interpreted as a "speech" by reviewing the arguments found in Jerome H. Neyrey, *2 Peter, Jude*, The Anchor Bible (New York: Doubleday, 1993), pp. 113–118.

12. William Klein, Craig Blomberg, and Robert Hubbard, *Introduction to Biblical Interpretation* (Dallas: Sword Publishing, 1993), pp. 270–271, will be

of particular interest for readers seeking more information. In this material, the farewell speech is defined as "an address in the first-person voice reportedly given by someone shortly before his or her death." In regard to 2 Peter, 1:12–15 leads some to consider this letter as a "farewell" speech.

13. Many "farewell speeches" are found in the Old Testament (Gen. 49:29–30; Deut. 29:2–30:20; 31:1–8; Josh. 23:1–16; 1 Sam. 12; 1 Kings 2:1–9) as well as in the New Testament (Matt. 28:16–20; Acts 1:1–11; 2 Tim. 4:6–8; 2 Pet. 1:12–15).

14. Guthrie, *Introduction*, p. 849.

OUTLINE OF 2 PETER

I. **Salutation (1:1–2)**

II. **Peter's Theme and Occasion for Writing (1:3–15)**
   A. Theme (1:3–11)
   B. Occasion (1:12–15)

III. **The Proof Section, Part I (1:16–2:10a)**
   A. Proof One (1:16–18)
   B. Proof Two (1:19–21)
   C. Proof Three (2:1–10a)

IV. **A Digression (2:10b–22)**

V. **The Proof Section, Part II (3:1–13)**
   A. Proof Four (3:1–7)
   B. Proof Five (3:8–13)

VI. **Conclusion (3:14–18)**

SALUTATION

2 Peter 1:1–2

The epistle begins with a reference to the author, **Simon Peter**. It will be recalled from the section on authorship in the Introduction to 2 Peter that this is the first of several indications of a "personal allusion" to the author. What we find here is the addition of the Jewish name Simon to the Greek name Peter. This is a strange combination.[1] Why would the compound name be used? Perhaps no special significance is to be attached; on the other hand, the two names "perhaps are meant to draw the readers' attention from the Jewish fisherman to the Christian apostle; from the old life to the new; from Simon, the name given him at his entry into the old covenant, to Peter, his distinctively Christian name."[2] Assuming this is the same Peter as the author of 1 Peter, it could be for greater emphasis and authority. The NASB notes that two early manuscripts read "Simeon" Peter, which is an older Jewish rendering of Simon. The point of authority and perhaps emphasis on his Jewish heritage could be found in this name.[3]

In his first letter, Peter referred to himself as an apostle. To this credential is added **servant** (1:1). The word also is rendered as "bond-slave." *Servant Leadership*, written by Robert Greenleaf, has popularized this biblical concept. Notice, for instance, how many kings, patriarchs, or prophets who serve as special agents of God are called servants. In the New Testament, letter senders often identify themselves as servants of God.

The recipients of this letter are identified as those who through **the righteousness of our God and Savior Jesus Christ have received a faith** (1:1). The mention of righteousness in this salutation is to be understood as identical with those references in 1 Peter (2:24; 3:12, 14, 18; 4:18) where the ethical implications of the word are emphasized. Here it means "the fairness and justice of God."[4] The word **received** carries the idea of to be given or fall to one's lot. The emphasis is that of a gift of favor, which underscores the grace of God. God has graciously given "faith." This word can carry two different meanings. It can mean a body of doctrine accepted by the early Church. It can also mean the trust that brings an individual salvation and is the God-given capacity to trust Him. Here, the second connotation is Peter's intended meaning.

This faith, Peter continues, is **as precious as ours**. The word *precious* could be translated *value*, as the NASB notes. The word also implies equally valuable, of the same kind, or of equal privilege. This precious faith is said to be "as ours." The contrast could be between Jews and Gentiles who have equal privileges, but the contrast could also be between the original apostles who had been eyewitnesses of the life of Christ (1:16) and the Christians of the second or even third generation.

Grace and peace be yours in abundance (1:2). The greetings portion of this salutation is written as an expression of a wish or desire. The same writing style was used in 1 Peter 1:2. The NASB alerts the reader to the fact that this greeting may also be worded as "grace and peace be multiplied to you." The word *abundance* means to increase, to spread, or to grow. The abundant increase comes through, or literally in, the **knowledge** of God and of Jesus our Lord. The word for "knowledge" is a compound noun. Is there any significance in Peter using a compound over the usual noun for knowledge? There are varied opinions on the question, but Michael Green quotes a writer from a century ago, J. B. Lightfoot, as saying that the compound implied "a larger and more thorough knowledge than the simple noun."[5] If Lightfoot is correct, this type of knowledge would imply recognition or knowledge directed toward a particular object, which can imply a more detailed or fuller knowledge. Another piece of evidence that Peter intends his readers to think in terms of knowledge as something more than the usual understanding of the word are the frequent references in 2 Peter to knowledge (1:2, 3, 8; 2:20; 3:18).

ENDNOTES

1.   The name Simon Peter is found in Matthew 16:16 and Luke 5:8. It is also found sixteen times in John's gospel, the first occurrence at 1:40.

2.   Michael Green, *2 Peter & Jude* (Grand Rapids: William B. Eerdmans, 2002 reprint), p. 67.

3.   Richard Bauckham, *Jude, 2 Peter* (Waco: Word Books Publishers, 1983), p. 166, observes that the form "Simeon" is the Greek transliteration of the Hebrew name. Jews of this period who bore this name normally used the Greek name Simon as its Greek equivalent. In addition to the apostle Peter, the New Testament lists nine people called Simon and two people called Simeon. It seems to have been the most common Jewish name in the period 100 B.C.–A.D. 200, no doubt partly because it was a patriarchal (and so patriotic) name that was assimilated to a common Greek name.

4.   See Green, *2 Peter & Jude,* p. 68, for further discussion of this important concept for Peter.

5.   Ibid., p. 70.

2

GROWTH IN CHRISTIAN VIRTUES

2 Peter 1:3–15

If it is the salutation and the conclusion that confirm 2 Peter as a letter, it is also true that the verses contained in 1:3–3:12 exhibit the features of an oral speech. In fact, there are four elements of a speech that are found in these verses. The first of the four elements is in this current passage. It is here that Peter's audience discovers his intention for writing. In these verses they are also made aware of the major topics to be developed in the rest of the letter. Above all else, Peter seeks to instill in his audience a sense of seriousness on their part as they reflect on what he has written to them.

As one begins this passage, a question concerning its relationship to the salutation is in order. The NASB concludes verse 2 with a semi-colon and begins verse 3 with "seeing that His divine power . . ." The NIV text concludes verse 2 with a period, which makes verse 3 begin a new section. The NIV structure makes more sense at this juncture of the letter. **His divine power has given us everything we need . . .** (1:3). Notice Peter's contrast between "need" and "want." God's divine power does not guarantee us everything we want. The contemporary Christian community, reared on their favorite television preacher, needs to hear Peter's comments. The phrase **his divine power** becomes a technical term for the name God and is the subject of **has given us**. What has God given us? He has given us everything we need **for life and godliness**. The word *godliness* implies a godly life, or godly living (2 Pet. 3:11). This godliness, or true religion, displays itself in worship and in a life of active obedience to God. How did "everything we need" come to the believers? Everything was **given** to them, which implies to bestow upon, to give as a gift, or to grant. On what basis does this gift come to Peter's audience? Everything they need comes to them **through [their] knowledge of him**. Peter's emphasis on knowledge is another reminder of the difference between knowing about God and knowing God, himself.[1]

Peter reminds his audience that it is God who called them **by his own glory and goodness.** It is this divine call that becomes the ground for His appeal for holy living. At this point perhaps Peter is reflecting on his own experience as he recalls what it was that attracted him to Jesus of Nazareth.[2] To say *by* glory and goodness suggests the means by which this call came to Peter's audience. On the other hand, as noted in the NASB, the call could be understood as *to* His glory and goodness. That would suggest that Peter's audience, due to this divine call, were given a place of special advantage. Probably the instrumental use of "by" is intended here.

God gave **through these** things **His very great and precious promises** (1:4). The tense of **has given** implies continuing results stemming from a past action. The phrase *very great* carries the idea of greatest. *Precious* means valuable, priceless, and rare. The promises from God are for a purpose, clarified by a double contrast. The positive side of this contrast is the fact that those who have the promises **may participate in the divine nature**. To become a participant means to be a partner, a sharer, or a partaker of something. The word is very similar to the word for fellowship or a close mutual relationship. One is to be a partner of a type of nature. This word *nature* means the natural condition. An individual, by birth, has a human nature. The gift of God makes it possible for humanity to be a partaker of divine nature. Peter does not mean that humanity is absorbed into deity but rather that believers, who already possess a human nature, will share in the divine nature as well. Peter echoes Paul's affirmation that "we have this treasure in earthen vessels" (2 Cor. 4:7 NASB).

Now comes the negative contrast. The promises of God serve the purpose of enabling one to **escape the corruption in the world**. To *escape* implies breaking away completely and turning our backs on something.

Also, the tense of the word *escape* denotes the decisiveness of that action.[3] Why is the world corrupt? The world is the result of God's creative action, but He did not create a corrupt world. It became so due to human disobedience as found in Genesis 3. The end result is a society alienated from God by rebellion. Currently, the world is corrupt due to **evil desires**. The idea of strong desire, lust, or passion is implied here. The basic meaning of the word denotes primarily not a sudden destruction owing to external violence, but it denotes a dissolution brought on by means of internal decay. The promises of God enable one to be a participant in the divine nature of God and escape the corruption of this world.

God's power has given us everything pertaining to life and godliness. But for an individual to live life as God intended it to be lived, a radical transformation must occur. This is only possible by God's grace and power. We believe that the natural person is born with a sinful, corrupt nature and participates in a world system that is corrupt as well. Those individuals live their lives according to their own sinful inclinations. God's grace and power seeks to change this. God's desire is for individuals to live a Christlike life and exhibit godly character. For this to happen, one must accept Christ as personal Savior. By the new birth experience, that individual has become a new creature in Christ Jesus (2 Cor. 5:17). Entire sanctification is that work of God, subsequent to conversion, in the heart of the individual whereby a sinful nature is cleansed and the Holy Spirit entirely fills the believer's heart with divine love. No wonder the hymn writer Cyrus S. Nusbaum wrote, "His power can make you what you ought to be!"

1. PETER'S LIST OF VIRTUES 1:5–11

Beginning at verse 5 and extending through verse 7, Peter employs what is known as a vice and virtue list. As mentioned earlier in 1 Peter, this common form within New Testament epistles consists of lists of qualities or actions that typify morality or immorality from a Christian perspective.[4] Sometimes the listing is simply illustrations of either vice or virtue, as in the "deeds of the flesh" in Galatians 5. On the other hand, Peter builds one virtue on the preceding virtue in the form "if A, then B," "if B, then C," "if C, then D," and so on. Peter admonishes his readers to make **every effort to add** (1:5) certain virtues. The word translated **effort** is an idiom combining the idea of earnestness or diligence with the concept of exerting or bringing alongside of. By putting these two concepts together, the idiom means to bring in every effort. In other words, we are to bring *into* this relationship, *alongside* what God has done, every ounce of determination we can muster. "The grace of God demands, as it enables, effort in man."[5] The list of virtues soon to be discussed is to be added to what you already have. The verb **to add** implies to supply, provide, or support. The word is a compound word, which gives it an accumulative force, to add further supplies. Other examples of this graphic word are found in 2 Corinthians 9:10; Galatians 3:5; Colossians 2:19; and 1 Peter 4:11.

KEY IDEAS

VIRTUES

Virtue	Definition
faith	loyal adhesion to Christian teaching
goodness	moral excellence, moral power
knowledge	knowing, understanding, or consideration
self-control	mastery, literally "holding oneself in"
perseverance	patience, steadfastness
godliness	piety, godly living
brotherly kindness	brotherly love shown by one Christian for another
love	primarily of Christian love, concern, or interest

In his commentary, Jerome Neyrey draws attention to the similarity between this list of virtues and the Ten Commandments in Exodus 20. Neyrey suggests that certain virtues in Peter's list treat human relations with God: faithfulness to, knowledge of, and self-control. Others deal with horizontal relationships among group members: piety, kinship affection, and love.[6]

If you **possess** (1:8) these qualities, good things will result. As the sense of this verse indicates, it is the possession of these qualities and their continued increase that is crucial. The tense of the verbs indicates continuous action in the present time. The idea of continuing in these virtues begins with the thought of **in increasing measure**, where the word means to abound, to increase, to become more, or to be extended. In secular writings, the word sometimes carried the idea of excess or exaggeration. In the Christian context, there can be no excess of virtues.

If these virtues are continually increasing, they will keep one from being **ineffective and unproductive**. The word **ineffective** implies useless, idle, lazy, or careless. Combined with the term **unproductive**, which means barren or unfruitful, one begins to appreciate the seriousness of Peter's argument.

On the other hand, **if anyone does not have** these qualities (1:9), there will be only negative results. The verb **have** comes with the idea of being by or being present. It will reappear in verse 12 where "truth you now have" is mentioned. If these qualities are not present, two descriptive words will characterize the situation. That individual is **nearsighted and blind**. The combination of *nearsighted* and *blind* may be an attempt to correct or limit the idea of being blind. On the other hand, the meaning may be "shutting the eyes to the truth" where the intention would be to emphasize the responsibility of the believer. With the mention of "the truth you now have" at verse 12, perhaps the latter sense is appropriate for verse 9.

But blindness is not the only problem. If these qualities are not present and increasing, the result will be that the individual will forget past blessings. This "can only mean [that he has] deliberately forgotten that he has been cleansed from his sins."[7] Therefore, due to the urgency of the situation, believers should **be all the more eager** (1:10) to make their calling and election sure. The word *eager* implies doing one's best, sparing no effort, or exerting effort. The word *eager* stresses the urgency of his plea that they should determine to live for God. To make **sure** of something carries the idea of making firm, certifying, or confirming.

What are they to confirm? They are to make firm their **calling and election**. This phrase makes this another passage that is difficult to understand. It seems to involve a paradox between God's gracious call and the individual's personal responsibility. This is the contrast between election and free will. Often it is difficult to maintain both emphases, but the New Testament makes room for both. Election comes from God alone, but our behavior is the proof or disproof of it.[8]

If you do these things, or "as long as you practice these things" (NASB), **you will never fall**. The word *fall* implies to stumble, to go wrong, or to sin.

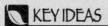

KEY IDEAS

THE NEED TO GROW IN GRACE

If believers grow in grace, two results will follow. (1) They will never fall. These Christians will be spared a disastrous coming to grief. This idea of not stumbling is a metaphor drawn from the idea of the sure-footedness of a horse (Jude 24). (2) These believers will receive a rich welcome into heaven. This is the ultimate goal of a long spiritual journey.

The negative "never" is the strongest form of negation in the Greek language. It is the combination of two negatives. In English that would make a positive. In Greek, it is the most emphatic way of indicating a negative. This combination of two negatives strongly denies even the possibility of falling. It is an assertion of the fact that "if you do these things," then you will never ever, certainly not, by no means fail. What will be the end of such a lifestyle? **You will receive a rich welcome into the eternal kingdom** (1:11). The NIV begins with "and" while the NASB begins with "for in this way." What "way" is being referred to, if one follows the NASB? The "way" is living for God, characterized by godly virtues that are ever increasing, and thus, enabling the individual to never, in any way, fall. Such a Christian lifestyle will ultimately bring eternal, heavenly rewards.

2. PETER'S SENSE OF URGENCY 1:12–15

Verse 12 begins with **so** ("therefore," or "for this reason"). It is an inferential conjunction used to draw a conclusion from a truth just stated or to indicate a result from what has preceded. This is Peter's method of underlying the relationship between verses 3–11 and 12–15. The conclusion of the matter is Peter's commitment to remind his audience of the implications of the truth discussed in the previous paragraph. **I will always remind you of these things** (1:12), Peter writes; he will do so as long as he lives. The word *always* implies constantly and suggests the prospect of frequent communication between Peter and his audience. On the one hand, Peter is determined to constantly remind his audience of certain truths. On the other hand, he acknowledges **even though** [they] **know them**. Not only does he make this concession, but he states further that they are **firmly established in the truth**. The phrase *firmly established* contains the idea of strengthened, made firm, or firmly resolved. The tense of this phrase indicates a settled state or condition based on a past action. Note that the NASB renders this phrase as "have been established." Why would one constantly remind his audience of something if they already knew the material and were established in it? The writer R. J. Bauckham suggests "there is an element of hopefulness in the description of the audience in this verse."[9]

Truth is not just something one knows; it is also something to possess. Truth can be something to know on an intellectual level that will provide a settled, firm resolve. But it can also be what **you now have**. It is the same concept found in verse 9. There, "if anyone does not have them . . ." then certain negative results are certain to follow. Here, truth is a certain, present possession. It is objective truth. It is the truth of the gospel of Jesus Christ. It is the difference between knowing about a concept and experiencing that concept itself. It is the difference of knowing about Jesus Christ and knowing Him personally.

Peter takes the responsibility of reminding the believers that they need to continue in their faith. **I think it is right to refresh your memory** (1:13). The word *refresh* means to awaken, to wake up thoroughly, or to stir up. Even truth experienced and held deeply may need, from time to time, to be stirred up. This is Peter's objective in writing this epistle. He is not presenting new material, but he is refreshing their memory of truth already believed. Peter will do this as long as he lives in **the tent of this body**.[10]

Peter is on a mission to stir up the memories of his audience. Why the urgency? Using the imagery of a tent to represent his earthly body, Peter knows he **will soon put it aside** (1:14). The word *soon* can be understood in a couple of different ways. It can mean speedily or imminent, as the NASB renders the word. This would mean that Peter is convinced that his death will take place very soon. The second meaning of the word *soon* would be swiftly. Here, the manner of his death would be the point. It won't be a slow, drawn-out event, but rather a swift demise. Either way, how does Peter know this? Jesus Christ **has made clear** this information. To make clear means to inform or to reveal. The word is sometimes used of special, private revelations, as in 1 Corinthians 3:13 and 1 Peter 1:11.

Peter could be convinced that his death is imminent because Christ, by a private revelation, has made this known. On the other hand, if Peter is talking about the manner of his death and the swift process it will entail, he may be referring back to the post-resurrection appearance of Jesus at the Sea of Galilee as recorded in John 21:18–19. Peter continues by saying that he **will make every effort** (1:15) to communicate certain concepts. Peter is speaking of making provisions for them after his death. At any time after Peter's **departure**, his audience will be able to recall these things. The word *departure* means exodus and is used to indicate physical death. Luke, writing concerning the events on the Mount of Transfiguration, reports that Moses and Elijah were speaking to Jesus concerning His departure (Luke 9:31). Peter's goal is to give information to his audience so they will always be able to recall his teaching. Thus two concepts come together: Peter is intent to make every effort to communicate ideas. His readers have the task of remembering what Peter writes.

ENDNOTES

1. One can find numerous books on the aspect of "knowing God." A good one to begin with is J. I. Packer, *Knowing God* (Downers Grove: InterVarsity Press, 1993 edition).

2. Michael Green raised the question, "What attracts a man to Jesus?" Green's answer is simply "Jesus' own unique glory and excellence. Jesus called by his moral excellence and the total impact of his Person," *2 Peter & Jude* (Grand Rapids: Eerdmans, 2002 reprint), p. 71.

3. Ibid., p. 73.

4. In addition to this text, examples from the New Testament of vice and virtue lists include Romans 1:29–31; 1 Corinthians 6:9–10; Galatians 5:19–23; and James 3:17–18.

5. Green, *2 Peter & Jude,* p. 75, distinguishes between secular philosophy and Christian ethics when he observes that Christian ethics is not the unaided product of human effort, but the fruit of our being partakers of the divine nature. Nevertheless, human effort is indispensable.

6. See Jerome Neyrey, *2 Peter & Jude*, The Anchor Bible (New York:

Doubleday, 1993), p. 155, for further discussion of his understanding of Peter's list of virtues.

7.   Green, *2 Peter & Jude*, p. 82.

8.   See Green's discussion, *2 Peter & Jude,* p. 83. Green quotes Stracham saying, "Not all who hear the Divine voice progress in Christian conduct, which is the token of election."

9.   R. J. Bauckham, *Jude, 2 Peter,* Word Biblical Commentary (Waco: Word Publishers, 1983), p. 197.

10.   Read Bauckham, *Jude, 2 Peter*, p. 198, for his interesting discussion of Peter's use of the phrase "tent of this body." Bauckham reminds us that Peter is making use of a current Greek term for the body, which is interchangeable with "tent." Paul makes use of the same term in 2 Corinthians 5:1, 4. The use of this term conveys the image of the body as a temporary dwelling place for the soul, which will be folded up and abandoned when the soul leaves it in death.

3

THE TRUE AND THE FALSE

2 Peter 1:16–2:22

This text begins a new section in this epistle, which extends to verse 2:10a. The specific purpose of this section is the proof of Peter's key points. His task is to persuade his audience of the accuracy of his position. This will entail rebutting the opponents' arguments and assertions as well as providing information to confirm his own position.

But there is a problem with this approach. The opponents are never mentioned by name nor are their own propositions ever presented. We only know the opponents' positions by reading Peter's responses. Our task will be to read Peter's responses and to read back into the text who might have said this and what exactly they might have said. This process is known as mirror-reading a text.[1] The results of this procedure will enable Peter to actually address two separate audiences. There is first of all, the individuals to whom he is writing. For them, this proof section will cause them to remember previous teaching and to stir up gospel truth deep within their hearts. The second audience will be those who are teaching false doctrine. These individuals must be addressed and their teaching must be proven to be unbiblical and unorthodox.

1. CHRIST'S GLORY AND THE PROPHETIC WORD 1:16–21

In this first paragraph, two heresies are being rebutted: that the apostles based their preaching of the Second Advent on human-made myths

(vv. 16–19), and that Old Testament prophecies were the products of human minds (vv. 20–21).

Peter asserts, **We did not follow cleverly invented stories** (1:16). The source of the stories is characterized as clever or able to reason out. The stories, or tales (NASB), refer to myths, fables, or fanciful stories. This word stood for mythical stories about gods, the creation of the world, or miraculous happenings. By using the mirror-reading approach, we can see the mockers of 2 Peter 3:3 spoke of the Christian hope of the glories to come as resting in fictitious prophecies. To **follow** after such **stories** means to obey or to depend on the stories.

The content of such stories were about **the coming of our Lord Jesus Christ**. This teaching concerning the Second Advent became the blessed hope of the Christian Church. There are three significant biblical words used in reference to the Second Advent: *Apokalupsis*, an unveiling, and (2) *phanerosis*, a showing forth, and (3) *parousia*. The word used here is *parousia*, which is literally the belief concerning Jesus' return at the end of human history. Jesus Christ will return to earth in a glorious, public, sudden, and visible manner.[2]

Peter states further that he and others (we) did not need to rely on invented stories because he and his fellow apostles were **eyewitnesses of his majesty** (1:16). The value of eyewitness reports for the early Christian Church cannot be overstated. "A stress on the apostolic eyewitness occurs when there is a need for apologetic defense of the Christian message in some way by reference to its historical basis."[3] The voice of the eyewitness has the ring of authority to it. Peter's reference to the eyewitness report centers around the account of the Transfiguration (Matt. 17:1–8; Mark 9:2–8; Luke 9:28–36). Why does Peter mention the Transfiguration? The answer is probably due to the point that the synoptic Gospels all see the Transfiguration as a foretaste of the *parousia* of Jesus, not so much His resurrection.[4] Peter especially mentions that the high point of the events on the Mount of Transfiguration was when Christ's **majesty** was revealed. Majesty is a compound word bringing together "mega" or "big" and the concept of majestic.

Thus, it becomes evident that the first false proposition—which stated that the apostles based their preaching of the Second Advent on human-made myths—is answered by Peter's eyewitness account of the activities on the Mount of Transfiguration. It was there that the majesty of the divine was revealed, and that event pointed to the Second Advent rather than to Christ's resurrection.

Near the conclusion of this paragraph, Peter introduces the second false charge stemming from the false teachers—that Old Testament prophecies were the products of human minds (1:19–21). The tie between this false charge and the previous one is that "the same God whom the apostles heard speaking in the transfiguration spoke also through the prophets."[5] It is the source of prophetic utterances that is now being addressed. Peter reminds his audience that no prophecy **came about by the prophet's own interpretation** (1:20). When Peter wrote "no prophecy," he meant that every single prophecy came about in the same way. And this way was not by an individual offering his personal explanation of something and then passing it off as prophecy. The false prophets of the Old Testament are accused of passing off personal opinion as prophecy.[6] It was the mark of a false prophet to speak from his own knowledge or interpret events on his own. What is under attack here is the very origin of prophetic Scripture.

How does Peter account for the origin of Scripture? First, in the negative: not **in the will of man** (1:21). This eliminates human thought processes as the source of Scripture. He then accounts for its origin in the positive: **men spoke from God.** When Peter's negative argument is placed alongside his positive statement, the following impression is gained: No prophecy in the Old Testament Scriptures originated from human initiative or imagination. The origin of such utterances is solely divine. The Holy Spirit inspired not only the prophets' dreams and visions, but their interpretations as well. Peter's point is clear. When the prophets spoke the prophecies recorded in the Old Testament, they were speaking for God himself.[7]

The second false accusation is finally answered. The false teachers rejected the authority of the Old Testament because they denied its divine origin. They simply thought the prophets produced their own ideas. Peter's rebuttal shows that there was common understanding among Jews, Christians, and Christ alike that the Old Testament was divine in origin. There was also the common thread of belief that when the prophets spoke the prophecies recorded in the Old Testament, they were in touch with God and acted as His spokespersons.[8]

2. THE RISE OF FALSE PROPHETS 2:1–3

This short paragraph serves as the transition between the second and third false propositions. There are two certainties for believers. First, divine truth is carried along by Holy-Spirit-inspired prophets. Second, there is also the prospect of false prophets among the believers. The term **false prophet** is a compound word that means prophets falsely named, a sham, or counterfeit. Historically, **there were also false prophets among the people** (2:1). The Old Testament contains the record of the appearance of false prophets among the children of Israel. Peter brings his readers into the present state of circumstances with this reminder that **there will be false teachers among** them as well. There is probably no intended difference to be made between prophet and teacher. From Peter's perspective, they are both false.

Peter warns that the false teachers will secretly introduce destructive heresies. The word *secretly* means to bring in under false pretenses, to bring alongside of, or to smuggle in, as in Galatians 2:4. The word *heresy* is broad enough to include division, faction, and false party or teaching. How far will these false teachers go in their destructive heresies? They will go so far as to **even [deny] the sovereign Lord**, with the term *deny* implying to disown or renounce.

The verb tense used in this short paragraph is important. While Peter begins with the historical perspective, he quickly moves into the present and future situations. False teachers **will** be among you. They **will** introduce heresies. They **will** deny. Their destruction **will** be swift. Not only is the appearance of false teachers a present danger, but Peter also warns his readers of the dangerous character of these teachers. Peter states that they deny the Lord **who bought them**. The phrase *to buy* is in the language of redemption. These false teachers were at one time believers and probably still considered themselves to be so. But they were false. It is one thing for false doctrine to come from the unbelieving world outside the Church, and it is another thing entirely when the false teaching springs from within the body of believers. Their punishment will be **swift destruction,** which is being brought on by their own actions.

False teaching cannot be tolerated. It must be dealt with, by the believers and ultimately by God. Why is the punishment of false teachers necessary? There are two reasons: (1) **Many will follow their shameful ways** (2:2). The verb *follow* contains the idea of obeying or depending on, and is the identical word used in 2 Peter 1:16. Their ways are "shameful," which suggests sensuality, indecency, and vice. The word is used in the plural, which suggests different forms of shameful ways or repeated, habitual acts of indecency. (2) Punishment for false teaching is demanded because it **will bring the way of truth into disrepute**. The term *way* refers to the teaching of the truth, the correct teaching. This expression denotes the Christian message and way of life, which are inevitably brought into discredit when their adherents identify themselves with patently immoral actions.

This paragraph concludes with Peter's word concerning the certain judgment facing the false teachers. Peter first identifies their motivation, which is **greed** (2:3). Next, he mentions their conduct, which is based on the fact that they **will exploit** others. This term carries the idea of being in business, or making profit off of. And while they may not realize it, **their condemnation** is certain. This is certain judgment because **their destruction has not been sleeping**, where *sleep* is the identical term used in the parable of the ten virgins in Matthew 25:1–13.

3. THE CERTAINTY OF DIVINE JUDGMENT 2:4–10A

The preceding paragraph (2:1–3) demonstrated to Peter's audience that false prophets have always been among the people of God and that they have also infiltrated their own body of believers. But false prophets think they are getting away with their heretical teaching because God doesn't bring immediate judgment on them (like He did to Ananias and Sapphira in Acts 5:1–11). It is at this very point that we encounter the third false proposition of the false teachers of Peter's day: "divine judgment never happens." Peter's rebuttal to this proposition is contained in the thought that biblical history tells of divine judgment on angels who sinned, the ancient world, and the cities of Sodom and Gomorrah (2 Pet. 2:4–6). Peter's rebuttal has the additional emphasis of underscoring the fact that since God has brought judgment in the past, He surely will do so again in the future.

The structure of this third rebuttal is interesting. It is built around three historical circumstances introduced by the word *if*. These are found at verses 4, 5, and 6. These occurrences of "if" statements culminate at verse 9, **if this is so, then. . . .**[9] It is also interesting to note that these historical illustrations of divine judgment are from either pre-Genesis history or the early chapters of Genesis. The point that Peter apparently wants to make is that one does not have to go far into the biblical record to find examples of divine judgment. This judgment was swift and certain. For the false teachers to teach otherwise shows they have their own agenda and have totally rejected God's Word as authoritative.

Peter's rebuttal of the proposition that divine judgment never happens begins with judgment on certain angels. **If God did not spare angels** (2:4) takes Peter back to pre-Genesis history. The fall of one-third of the angelic host coincided with the fall of Satan prior to Genesis 1 (Rev. 12:3–4 refers to this event). These angels sinned, and God did not spare or refrain from bringing judgment upon them. This identical thought is found in Jude 6. God did not spare them; He **sent them to hell**. The word translated *hell* is the word *tartarus*. This term identifies the place where the Jewish teaching of Peter's day assigned fallen angels. The hell of *tartarus* is further described as **gloomy dungeons**, or as the NASB renders this phrase, "pits of darkness." The word *dungeon* means pit or cave. The secular Greek use of *dungeon* referred to a pit used for the storage of grain, a large bin that held edible roots, or a pit made for trapping a wolf.

The second historical proof that divine judgment does occur is from the ancient world and involves the Genesis Flood episode. Noah is described as a **preacher of righteousness** (2:5), which denotes a just and upright moral behavior. He and seven others were **protected**, which points to God's activity of guarding or watching over Noah. These were protected while **ungodly people**, or godless, impious individuals, were judged. God **brought** the flood on them. Peter is clear that this devastation was not a human calamity, but rather God brought the deluge on them as an act of divine judgment.

The third example of divine judgment involves the destruction of **the cities of Sodom and Gomorrah** (2:6). This is an allusion to the circumstances found in Genesis 18:16–19:28. These two cities were **condemned**, which means God passed judgment on them. Judgment carries the idea of pronouncing a verdict against someone, to sentence to a punishment. The result of God's condemnation of Sodom and Gomorrah involved **burning them to ashes**.

If these three historical illustrations of divine judgment are true — and they are — **then** God must act accordingly (2:9). The conditional sentence is so constructed that if the "if" part of the sentence is true, then the "then" aspect of the sentence has to also be true. **The Lord knows how to rescue godly**, devout, God-fearing **men** and women. He also knows how to hold the **unrighteous for the day of judgment.** The phrase **day of judgment** implies that divine judgment may not be obvious during one's lifetime. This is why the false teachers do not believe in divine judgment. Things were going well for the false teachers. The thought of possible divine judgment never crosses their minds. However, biblical history should have taught them that divine judgment can come swiftly in this life, as the three examples show. If God does not punish immediately in this life, it must be because He has other purposes in mind.

Peter has drawn a spiritual lesson from biblical history. But his point **is especially true of those who follow the corrupt desire of the sinful nature and despise authority** (3:10). One who follows reveals the inclination to follow the flesh (Gal. 5:17). This path is characterized by pollution. *Corrupt desire* means strong desire, lust, or passion. Individuals who go after this kind of lifestyle despise authority, including godly authority. The false teachers despise the power and majesty of the Lord.

The false proposition is that divine judgment never happens. Peter's rebuttal is based on a quick review of biblical history, which proves just the opposite to be true. God takes note of wrong action, which is followed by His judgment. For the false teachers of Peter's day, if judgment does not come immediately, it may be due to the grace and mercy of God. However, the Day of Judgment is coming and divine judgment will be certain.

4. THE DENUNCIATION OF FALSE TEACHERS 2:10B–22

Peter has completed three of the five rebuttals to false teachers who reject various aspects of the orthodox teaching of the early Church. The three objections include the accusations that (1) the apostles based their preaching concerning the Church at the end of human history on human-made myths, (2) Old Testament prophecies were the products of human minds, and (3) divine judgment never happens. There will follow two more rebuttals, but now Peter turns to a direct attack on the false teachers.

KEY IDEAS

A DESCRIPTION OF FALSE TEACHERS

Descriptive Term	Intended Meaning
bold (v. 10)	daring or reckless
arrogant (v. 10)	self-willed or self-pleasing
slander celestial beings (v. 10)	can refer to angelic beings, either those heavenly beings in God's service or fallen angels; either way, mere mortals should not be so brazen to slander these beings
blaspheme in matters they do not understand (v. 12)	these individuals have no more knowledge than brute beasts would have
brute beasts (v. 12)	implies living creatures, or animal-like
creatures of instinct (v. 12)	natural, used in the sense of "mere creatures of instinct"
carouse in broad daylight (v. 13)	to take pleasure in such activity implies passion or lust; sensual gratification; debauchery in daylight was frowned upon even in degenerate Roman society
eyes full of adultery (v. 14)	unfaithful, godless people; the idea of a "loose woman" is probably intended

Descriptive Term	Intended Meaning
never stop sinning (v. 14)	unable to stop, having an insatiable appetite for sin
left the straight way (v. 15)	to leave behind, neglect, forsake, or abandon
follow the way of Balaam (v. 15)	leaving the straight way, one ends up on the wrong way—illustrated here by the path the Old Testament character Balaam took, the path of greed
springs without water (v. 17)	describes the unsatisfactory nature of the false teaching; people come to it, excited to discover a new spring, but are then disappointed to find it has no water to offer them
mists driven by a storm (v. 17)	instead of the damp mists that refresh the countryside in hot weather, they are like the haze that heralds dry weather and is quickly dispersed by a gust of wind
mouth empty boastful words (v. 18)	the word *empty* implies worthless, futile, or useless; *boastful* carries the idea of high-sounding, swollen, or inflated

What Peter does in this paragraph is classified as a digression. He interrupts his presentation of the five rebuttals to directly address his audience concerning the ultimate judgment on the false teachers. Peter's intention is to shame the opponents. This includes the denunciation of the false teachers and further amplification of their ungodliness. The chart includes a rather complete description of the false teachers. The four ethical truths serve to cast the false teachers in a bad light.

Peter concludes this chapter with a four-fold statement, declaring that what has become of the false teachers and what will be their ultimate end is simply a fulfillment of basic ethical maxims of truth. (1) False teachers promise freedom but are themselves slaves (2:19). This is true because false teachers are slaves of depravity. They continue to exist in depravity or decay in moral ruin because they are slaves to whatever has mastered them. (2) False teachers are in a worse condition now than when they first believed (2:20). Though they had once escaped the corruption of the world, they are entangled once again. The result is they are worse off now than they were prior to finding spiritual life. (3) False teachers would be better off if they had never known the way of righteousness (2:21). The false teachers had, at one time, known the way of righteousness; they turned their backs on the truth. On the Day of Judgment, it would be better for them if they had never known the truth of the gospel. (4) False teachers prove a well-known proverbial truth (2:22). This proverb refers to two disgusting images that would bring revulsion to the Jewish reader. The dog and the pig stand for all that is unclean in Jewish culture. Choosing to live like brute beasts, they become like the worst of them.

ENDNOTES

1. For the individual interested in reading more about mirror-reading as a hermeneutical tool, begin by reading John M. G. Barclay, "Mirror-Reading a Polemical Letter: Galatians as a Test Case" in the *Journal for the Study of the New Testament*, 31 (1987), pp. 73–91.

2. Find the *parousia* concept discussed in any evangelical theology text. One of the most helpful is the recent work by Thomas C. Oden, *Life in the Spirit, Systematic Theology: Volume Three* (San Francisco: Harper, 1994), pp. 409–414.

3. Richard Bauckham, *Jude, 2 Peter* (Waco: Word Books Publishing, 1983), p. 216.

4. Michael Green. *2 Peter & Jude* (Downers Grove: InterVarsity Press, 2002 reprint), p. 92.

5. Ibid., p. 101.

6. Turn to Green, *2 Peter & Jude*, p. 101, for further discussion of this common practice in the Old Testament. Green observes, "In the Old Testament, this was the characteristic of the false prophets, who 'speak visions from their own minds, not from the mouth of the Lord' (Jer. 23:16; Ezek. 13:3). But true prophecy came from God and, men as they were, the prophets were *carried along* by the Holy Spirit."

7. See Bauckham, *Jude, 2 Peter*, p. 235, for more detailed discussion of this point.

8. See Green, *2 Peter & Jude,* p. 102, for further discussion of this second rebuttal.

9. In the Greek New Testament there are four types of "if-then" sentences. The examples from 2 Peter 2 illustrate the first of the four types. This sentence type assumes the reality of the "if" part of the sentence for the sake of argument. There are over 300 examples of this type of conditional sentence in the New Testament.

4

GOD'S WORD AND CHRIST'S RETURN

2 Peter 3:1–18

1. THE CHALLENGE TO GOD'S WORD 3:1–7

With the digression completed (2:10b–22), Peter returns to his rebuttal of objections to the gospel message raised by false teachers. The current paragraph contains the fourth rebuttal. But there is something different about this one. We do not have to engage in mirror-reading with this false position. Peter includes a quote from the false teachers that summarizes their view. They say, **Where is this 'coming' he promised?** (3:4). To begin this question with *where* implies "What has become of?" This is a traditional formula for expressing skepticism. What is being doubted is the promised second coming previously mentioned in 2 Peter 1:16. The reason for the false teachers' skepticism is that **ever since our fathers died, everything goes on as it has since the beginning of creation.** In the Greek, the word *died* is the verb to fall asleep, a figure of speech to soften the concept of death. Unfortunately, some in the early Church misunderstood this use of the figure of speech and taught the concept of "soul sleep," which was interpreted to mean that the believer does not actually die but is merely asleep.

Rather than anticipating the change that will come at the end of the age, the scoffers say that **everything goes on as it has since the beginning of creation** (3:4). The phrase *goes on* carries the idea of remaining or continuing. The tense emphasizes the continual, unbroken action of whatever is going on. The argument of the scoffers is that God's promise concerning the Church at the end of human history is unreliable, and God's universe is a stable, unchanging system, where events such as the *parousia* (second coming of Christ) do not happen.

In philosophy, the universe can be understood as a closed system that operates on a cause-effect basis, and thus any sort of divine intervention is eliminated. On the other hand, a Christian philosophy would articulate a controlled system, which acknowledges a cause-effect relationship, but allows the possibility of divine intervention into the human course of events. It is a worldview that allows for the element of the supernatural. The First Advent would be an example of divine intervention. The miracles of Jesus would be another such example. The prophetic word concerning the Second Advent would be yet another example of divine intervention. The message of the false teachers in this paragraph is a direct assault on the belief of the Second Advent: life goes on as it has since the dawn of creation.

Peter counters this false accusation against God's powerful Word by reminding his readers that the scoffers **deliberately forgot** (3:5) something. The Greek phrase that is translated *deliberately forgot* carries the idea of being hidden, escaping notice, or simply ignoring. Another way of expressing this thought is to say, "They shut their eyes to this fact." Note also how the KJV suggests verse 5 should begin ". . . they are willfully ignorant of this fact, that . . ." They willfully forgot that creation happened long ago **by God's word**. The key term is the "word." It is the creative word that God spoke in Genesis 1 that resulted in the creation of our world.

Peter states that the earth was formed **out of water and by water.** Here is the positive use of water. But there is also a destructive use of water. The created world was **deluged and destroyed** (3:6) by water. Peter thus establishes a close relationship between "formed by water" and "destroyed by water." In similar fashion, the present heavens and earth are **reserved for fire** (3:7). The sense of this metaphor is to set apart for or to be destined for. The word *reserved* implies to be treasured, stored, or kept. This verb's tense emphasizes a completed state or condition. The certainty of the earth's destined destruction is based on the powerful word of God. It is being **kept** for the Day of Judgment. The concept of the world being kept carries the idea of being guarded or under the watchful eye of another.

2. THE COMING DAY OF THE LORD 3:8–13

This paragraph is the last in the main portion of 2 Peter. The main section of this letter has been identified as a proof or a series of rebuttals to the objections raised by false teachers. This fifth and final rebuttal concerns the validity of a belief in the Second Advent.

Peter begins the paragraph with an admonishment, **do not forget** (3:8). The Greek word translated "forget" is the same word used in verse 3:5, which refers to the false teachers deliberately forgetting something. But forgetfulness does not have to be a deliberate act. You can forget something by simply letting it "escape your notice" (3:8, NASB). What is it that should not escape one's notice? It is the simple fact that God is not bound by the limits of time. In Christian theology this concept is part of any discussion on the attributes of God. This particular attribute is known as the eternity of God or His infinity.[1] While it is true that God created a space-time world, He himself is not bound by its limitation of time. God is not constrained by concepts like past, present, or future. As many theologians have noted, God is the Eternal Now. Thus, to God **a day is like a thousand years, and a thousand years are like a day.**

The false teachers of whom Peter is speaking have failed to comprehend this vital attribute of God. They see themselves as creatures of a space-time world who are forced to live within the constraints of this environment. They have failed to consider the fact that God is free from such restraints. When the false teachers consider the frequently heard warnings concerning the approaching Second Advent, they understand it solely in terms of their human condition. The fact that the Second Advent has not yet occurred within their concept of time serves as proof that the idea of the *parousia* is invalid. The false teachers have not only failed to grasp the meaning of the eternity of God, but they have also failed to consider the ways of God.

Peter reminds his readers that **the Lord is not slow in keeping his promise, as some understand slowness** (3:9). The concept of slowness appears as a verb and a noun. Both carry the idea of delay or negligence. Some understand slowness from a purely human perspective, due to the fact that they are creatures of time. This understanding of slowness causes one to consider the reason for any delay. From a purely human perspective, the delay might be caused by impotence or unwillingness to perform. The false teachers think in human concepts of time. They consider the delay of Christ's return to set up His kingdom to be an indication that God cannot do what He has promised or that He has changed His mind and is no longer willing to do it.

The delay of the His coming must be understood from God's perspective. Because it is God's will that everyone be saved, God **is patient with you** (3:9). The word *patient* implies longsuffering. God is **not wanting anyone to perish**. The delay goes to the heart of what God desires for all humanity. The word *perish* implies to be lost or to be ruined. God's desire is for **everyone to come to repentance.** The word *repentance* represents one of the great themes in God's Word. It means to have a change of heart, to turn from one's sins, or to change one's ways. In Christian theology, repentance is both an act and a continuing state of being. First, it is a decisive commitment on the part of the individual to turn from sin and to serve God. We call this conversion. But it is also a declaration on that individual's part to continue in this new way. To change one's ways (the act of conversion) is accompanied by the intention to continue in this new way (the state of penitence). This is the New Testament concept of repentance. Peter speaks of individuals coming to repentance. The word *come* carries the idea of making room or having room for. Paul uses the same word in 2 Corinthians 7:2 when he pleads for the Corinthian church to make room for him in their hearts. The apparent delay is rooted in the fact that God's desire is that all would make room in their hearts for Him.

Despite what the false teachers contend, **the day of the Lord will come like a thief** (3:10). The eschatological view expressed here is that with the *parousia*, certain

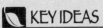

KEY IDEAS

KEY CONCEPTS OF 2 PETER 3:9

The delayed *parousia* requires some explanation. Some choose to reject the concept because it hasn't yet occurred. Others believe in this great event and use Peter's insight to explain the delay. Peter employs a sharp negation, "but," to explain the delay of the *parousia*.

Concept 1: God's promises are certain and must come to pass, *but* He is a patient God.

Concept 2: God's will is that no one would perish *but* that all would have the opportunity to "make room for God."

Concept 3: God's actions may appear to be slow, *but* the Day of the Lord will come like a thief.

events will be set in motion that are associated with God's judgment on the world. The false teachers claim that delay disproves His coming. Peter's rebuttal is centered on the fact that the false teachers do not understand God's attribute of eternity nor do they comprehend His gracious ways toward sinful humankind. Nevertheless, the Day of the Lord will come.

3. CONCLUSION 3:14–18

The final paragraph of 2 Peter is the conclusion of his argument. As a letter, this paragraph serves as a "bookend" that complements the opening paragraph (1:1–2). The final benediction in verse 3:18 returns the focus to our Lord Jesus Christ. As a speech, this paragraph serves two purposes. First, the conclusion serves as a recapitulation of both immediate (3:14–16) and all previous material in 2 Peter. The repetitions of the conclusion capture many of the dualistic expressions that are integral to the "two ways" described by Peter.[2] The two ways ultimately lead to life or death. The second purpose of the conclusion in this speech is to make a final emotional appeal to his audience.[3]

KEY IDEAS

A DESCRIPTION OF FALSE TEACHERS

The Right Way	The Wrong Way
1. They look forward to this or "these things" (NASB, 3:14a)—a clear reference to the entire sequence of events outlined for "the day of the Lord" (3:10–13).	1. Others are convinced that the delay of the *parousia* disproves the very concept of the Second Advent (3:3–5).
2. The right way involves making every effort to be found pure (3:14b)—a clear reference to Peter's concern at the beginning of his letters (1 Pet. 1:7).	2. Others, having dismissed the idea of the *parousia*, are characterized by all kinds of terms that identify the ungodly and impure (2:10b–18).
3. The right way understands that the Lord's patience leads to salvation (3:15). This is the identical message taught by Paul (Rom. 2:4; 9:22; 1 Tim. 1:16).	3. Others, who are untaught, unstable, and unprincipled, distort Peter's message as they do the rest of the Scriptures (2:1–3).

This final paragraph returns to one of Peter's main emphases throughout his writing, the theme of holiness. Two key words are found in verse 14. The first is **spotless**, which was used to describe sacrificial animals in the Old Testament and the sacrifice of Jesus Christ in the New Testament (1 Pet. 1:19). The second key word is **blameless**. This word carries with it the idea of being unblemished or of an individual who is not subject to blame in a moral or religious sense. How is this possible? Peter's response would be to tie 2 Peter with his first letter and remind his audience that they have been sprinkled with His blood and sanctified by His Spirit (1 Pet. 1:2). By God's work of grace, they are spotless and blameless.

The end result of the doctrine of Christian holiness is to enable believers to remain in their **own secure position** (3:17). This phrase carries the idea of being in a fixed position as opposed to movement. It is in direct contrast to the word unstable, which is used to describe the heretics (3:16). This verse is one of many scriptures that Wesleyans believe teach the doctrine of conditional security.[4]

By definition, conditional security teaches that God is able to keep believers from sin in this life. At the same time, we do have a free will and may neglect our spiritual lives, and in the process sin. The opposite of conditional security would be the Calvinistic teaching of unconditional security, which teaches that once an individual accepts Christ as personal Savior, there is nothing he or she can do to forfeit eternal life. Peter makes it clear that his readers are in a position of steadfastness. They are in a fixed position from which they ought not to be moved. But there is the warning: don't become careless and neglectful.

The last two verses of this epistle also contain an emotional appeal to Peter's audience. The appeal is based on his deep feeling of affection for his readers as expressed the words **dear friends** (3:1, 8, 14, 17). To clarify his affection for his audience, Peter presents a contrast between the two ways of conduct through a series of good or bad options.

Peter concludes this letter with a doxology: **To him be glory both now and forever! Amen** (3:18).

ENDNOTES

1. For a discussion of the attributes of God, see Wayne Grudem, *Systematic Theology* (Grand Rapids: Zondervan Publishing House, 1994). The author defines God's eternity by stating, "God has no beginning, end, or succession of moments in his own being, and he sees all time equally vividly, yet God sees events in time and acts in time" (p. 168).

2. The interested reader will find the commentary by Jerome Neyrey, *2 Peter, Jude*, The Anchor Bible (New York: Doubleday, 1993) helpful in understanding the structure of 2 Peter. The theme of the "two ways" is developed in this epistle in the following manner: "those who know, those who do not know; those who wait for the *parousia*, those who deny it; those who keep pure, those who are polluted; those who stand, those who fall; those who come to salvation, those who are destroyed," p. 118.

3. This will be accomplished by a contrast between negative/positive themes. Neyrey notes the negative aspect by a prediction of future heretics and a warning not to join them. The positive is seen in the exhortation to grow in grace and knowledge (Neyrey, *2 Peter, Jude*, p. 118).

4. Robert Shank, *Life in the Son* (Minneapolis: Bethany House Publishers, 1989), pp. 334–337, identifies eighty-five verses in the New Testament that teach conditional security.

SELECT BIBLIOGRAPHY FOR 1-2 PETER

1 PETER

Achtemeier, Paul J. *1 Peter*. Hermeneia. Minneapolis: Fortress Press, 1996.

Best, Ernest. *1 Peter*. New Century Bible. Greenwood: The Attic Press, 1971.

Bigg, Charles. *The Epistles of St. Peter and St. Jude*. The International Critical Commentary. Edinburgh: T&T Clark, 1975 reprint.

Bray, Gerald, ed. *James, 1–2 Peter, 1–3 John, Jude*. Vol. XI of *Ancient Christian Commentary on Scripture*. Downers Grove: InterVarsity Press, 2000.

Clowney, Edmund. *The Message of 1 Peter*. Downers Grove: InterVarsity Press, 1988.

Davids, Peter H. *The First Epistle of Peter*. The New International Commentary on the New Testament. Grand Rapids: William B. Eerdmans Publishing Company, 1996.

Elliott, John H. *1 Peter*. The Anchor Bible. New York: Doubleday, 2000.

Grudem, Wayne. *1 Peter*. The Tyndale New Testament Commentaries. Grand Rapids: William B. Eerdmans, 2002 reprint.

Lenski, R.C.H. *The Interpretation of the Epistles of St. Peter, St. John and St. Jude*. Minneapolis: Augsburg Publishing House, 1966 printing.

McNight, Scott. *1 Peter*. The NIV Application Commentary. Grand Rapids: Zondervan Publishing House, 1996.

Marshall, I. Howard. *1 Peter*. The IVP New Testament Commentary Series. Downers Grove: InterVarsity Press, 1991.

Michaels, J. Ramsey. *1 Peter*. Word Biblical Commentary. Waco: Word, Incorporated, 1988.

Perkins, Pheme. *First and Second Peter, James, and Jude,* interpretation. Louisville: John Knox Press, 1995.

Selwyn, Edward Gordon. *The First Epistle of St. Peter*. 2nd ed. Grand Rapids: Baker Book House, 1981 reprint.

2 PETER

Some of the resources listed in the bibliography for 1 Peter are used in 2 Peter as well. They have not been repeated here.

Barclay, William. *The Letters of James and Peter*. The New Daily Study Bible. Louisville: John Knox Press, 2003.

Bauckham, Richard J. *Jude, 2 Peter*. Word Biblical Commentary. Waco: Word, Incorporated, 1983.

Green. Michael. *2 Peter and Jude*, The Tyndale New Testament Commentaries. Grand Rapids: William B. Eerdmans Publishing Company, 2002.

Kistemaker, Simon J. *Peter and Jude*. New Century Commentary. Grand Rapids: Baker Book House, 1987.

Mayor, Joseph. *The Epistles of Jude and II Peter*. Grand Rapids: Baker Book House, 1979.

Moo, Douglas J. *2 Peter, Jude*. The NIV Application Commentary. Grand Rapids: Zondervan Publishing House, 1996.

Neyrey, Jerome H. *2 Peter, Jude*. The Anchor Bible. New York: Doubleday, 1993.

Sidebottom, E. M. *James, Jude, and 2 Peter*. The Century Bible. Greenwood: The Attic Press, 1967.

1 JOHN

INTRODUCTION TO
1 JOHN

The honeymoon was over and it would have been easy to panic. Two or three generations had passed since the birth of the Christian Church. It became clear that wrong ideas were being introduced to the believers that could undermine the heart of Christian faith.

The white-hot fires of faith had cooled. As each new generation of children entered the church, they became less connected with its dynamic beginnings and the original witnesses of Jesus' life and death. Everything they heard was experienced with second- or even third-hand impact. Was it possible that the whole, glorious Christian movement was slipping away?

A few of the leading minds within the early Church were rethinking all that had happened and were arriving at some very different conclusions. These ideas had begun to surface just one generation after Christ's death and resurrection. The early epistles alluded to the errant teachings, but by the end of the first century, the spurious thoughts were becoming a more formidable array of doctrines and philosophies that struck at the very heart of Christian history and teachings. What made it all so tragic was that the present danger had been given birth by those who had come from within the Church. A credible response was desperately needed.

AUTHORSHIP

Since the writer does not identify himself in the text, it requires somewhat of a patchwork quilting approach. Researching early documents, having the right perspective on the content and the historical content, as well as using discernment and a degree of subjectivity is necessary to arrive at an educated calculation on authorship. And even that does not guarantee certainty.

The majority of scholars agree that the letter was written somewhere between the years A.D. 85–100. By that time, the various errant teachings that sought to shift the focus of Christianity would have been around long enough to have been systematized and aggressively promoted. By that time, nearly all of the original apostles had died or been martyred, leaving no eyewitness from the inner circle of Christ. The one exception was the apostle John.

Earlier New Testament writings make references to errant teachings, but rarely with the specificity of 1 John. The writings of the apostle Paul are a good example of this. Colossians 2:8 reads, "See to it that no one takes you captive through hollow and deceptive philosophy, which depends on human tradition and the basic principles of this world rather than on Christ." In 1 John, the content systematically attacks the specific implications of certain teachings and teachers of that era—ideas that could have been fatal to Christianity, short of divine intervention through faithful followers. Therefore, it is very possible that the survival of the doctrine (truth) of what we call the gospel depended on God's inspired messenger speaking and writing the words that would have power to protect the integrity of the Christian message. Such a writer must have credibility among the people, as an eyewitness of Jesus' life would have had, and the authority to stand in the arenas of debate with other great thinkers and speakers of that day.

From approximately A.D. 400–1800, it was commonly accepted that the apostle John wrote all three letters carrying his name, 1, 2, and 3 John, the gospel of John, and the book of Revelation. In the last couple of centuries, however, other theories have surfaced. In addition to the apostle John, some believe the book to have been written by one referred to as "the Elder," which may refer to a respected elder in the Church at that time. Another theory considers one called "the Presbyter." Those called "presbyters" were often disciples of the apostles. Some have proposed that there was a John the Presbyter, who penned at least 1 John. And, a more recent and inventive theory credits a "writing team." We will attempt to sort out some of these possibilities.

Internal Evidence. Only 1 John and Hebrews, among New Testament epistles, give us no formal greeting, name, or title that indicates authorship. And the gospel of John is equally as vague about its author.

The early verses of 1 John indicate that the writer was one among a number of people who actually heard, saw, studied, and had physical contact with "the Word of life" (1:1–5). The overall content and context of the letter would suggest that the Word of life (1:1) is a reference to Jesus Christ. The author was personally acquainted with Christ.

The author writes as an individual. There is a dominance of references in the first person singular that would indicate so (2:1, 7, 8, 12, 13, 14, 21, 26, 5:13). The tone of the letter is urgent, emphatic, and blunt—even severe at times—yet is also pastoral and fatherly.

A very significant observation is the abundance of similarities between the gospel of John and 1 John. The traditional view is that that the same author wrote both the Gospel and the epistle. There seems to be only scattered, and not highly regarded, disagreement that the apostle John, brother of James, was the author of the Gospel.

However, one theory about the writing of the Gospel speculates that it was inspired by the Holy Spirit, fueled by the mind and memory of the apostle John, but penned by one called John the Elder. This is the "writing team" view of William Barclay,[1] as well as some other scholars.

What do we make of this anonymity? The author(s) may have simply wanted the writings to stand on their own strength and, therefore, avoided a direct identification. In that regard, the author may have been so well known that, from the outset, most locals would have known who wrote it. On the other hand, the author could have been far lesser known and figured no one would pay much attention if his or her name was attached to the letter. So, he or she may have decided to let intrigue and content make its own case. This author believes that the most likely explanation is the author wanted the writings to stand on their own. A number of scholars conjecture that "the Elder" could indeed have been the apostle John, because he would have been very elderly by the time the letters of 1, 2, and 3 John were written. Indeed, Papias, an early Church historian who was alive during the last third of the first century, refers to the apostle John as one of the elders in his *Exposition of Oracles of the Lord.*

Among nearly a dozen scholars of various persuasions regarding authorship of 1 John, little beyond surmising and personal conjecturing toward the possibility of non-apostolic authorship can be found. Evidence is lacking to turn the possibility into a probability.[2]

Therefore, let us focus our attention on the probability that the Gospel and the first letter were written by the same author. If the following observations have merit, then the arguments for the authorship of the Gospel also apply to the epistle.

John Stott notes that, "even a superficial reading of the Gospel and the first epistle reveals a striking similarity between the two in both subject-matter and syntax."[3]

Both the Gospel and the epistle demonstrate a pronounced use of opposites, or contrasts, such as light and darkness, love and hate, truth and falsehood, life and death.

Both books focus on the idea of Jesus Christ as *logos,* or "Word" from God. This is a fairly unique analogy among all New Testament writers. This reference to Christ as the Word (in the Gospel) and the Word of life (in the first epistle) demonstrates the unique thinking of its inspired originator. However, why would the writer use a different phrase in 1 John? If the Gospel and the epistle were written by the same author, why wouldn't the exact phrase be used in both? There are several possible explanations, including that the letter was written a bit later than the Gospel, the longer phrase is more specific in its description, and the dominant theme of both books is eternal life.

Another impressive comparison of the two books is the way the concept of personal salvation in Jesus Christ is developed. The approaches to salvation are virtually identical concepts presented at two times to different crowds of people. The Gospel is written to invite and convince those who still need to believe (John 3:16, 11:25, 14:6). The epistle addresses believers and seeks to confirm the true faith (5:11–13).

Yet another prominent theme is the commandment of God to love one another (John 15:1–12; 1 John 3:11, 14, 18, 23, 4:7, 11, 16, 21). The focus is amazingly similar in the two books. Besides the exceptions of Matthew 22:37–40 and Galatians 5:14, these are the only other books in the New Testament to state the sum of God's commandments this way.

Then, there is the striking combination of statements about joy and the desire for its perfection, or completion, in us and among us (John 15:11 and 1 John 1:4).

The clear and constant focus on Christ and the essential practice of believing in Him is a hallmark of both books. The Gospel is basically a presentation of the person of Jesus, with a great deal of narrative and description of His life and power, along with theological overtones. The Gospel is written to convince and invite belief. The epistle is more of a theological treatise and a defense of the faith. Its focus is to keep believers believing and pressing on to completion in faith and love.

A very striking parallel is that these are the *only* New Testament books that give succinct, descriptive phrases about the nature of God. The Gospel says that God is *spirit* (John 4:24). First John says that God is *light* (1:5) and *love* (4:8, 16). Since neither light nor love have tactile characteristics, yet are very real entities, they are useful descriptions of God as spirit.

Interestingly, the Gospel refers to Jesus as "the true light" (1:9), "the light of men" (1:4), and "the light of the world" (8:12, 9:5). Once again, these resonate strongly with the statement in the epistle that God is light. The latter statement expresses God's nature in relationship to all creation and His nature as divine being. The Gospel refers to Christ as "the light" in a way that connects Him to the Father and that Christ's role is to bring the light-nature of God to the world.

These are some of the impressive similarities of the two books. What about the *differences*? How might they affect the case for one author of both books?

A notable New Testament scholar of the mid-twentieth century, C. H. Dodd, writes that some of the terms and themes that are common to both the Gospel and the epistle are handled quite differently in each.[4] Let's explore several of the seven he mentions.

One is the distinctive descriptions of God as spirit in the Gospel and God as light and love in the epistle. This issue was addressed above in that the epistle—a later writing—is articulating the more specific nature of what "spirit" can mean, in that it includes God's nature as light and as love. This difference seems more of an expansion than a problematic contrast.

Next is the use of the Greek term which basically is translated *paraclete*. In the Gospel, *paraclete* refers to the Holy Spirit. In the epistle, it refers to Christ. In both cases the term suggests one who is counselor, comforter, and defender. In the Gospel, Jesus clearly says that He will send another comforter, and in the epistle, the writer clarifies that the comforter is none other than Jesus as a manifestation of the Holy Spirit (1 John 3:24). The apostle Paul helps clarify this as well, when he mentions in 2 Corinthians 3:17, "Now the Lord (Jesus Christ) is the Spirit, and where the Spirit of the Lord is, there is freedom."

In the introduction of the Gospel, Christ is called "the Word" (1:1). In the introduction of the epistle, the reference is to "the Word of life" (1:1). Dodd observes that the former reference is more personal, namely to Christ, whereas the latter one is more impersonal, referring to the life-giving gospel.[5] Actually, it seems that both could easily be referring to the person of Christ. While the terms are not parallel, they are certainly complimentary.[6] Both come as part of the introduction, and both imply the tangible presence of the one referenced (Jesus), which are direct responses to the Gnostic teachings of that day.

Considering the lack of impressive arguments to the contrary and the obvious and extensive internal evidence, the case for the apostle John is certainly not eclipsed by any other candidate.

External Evidence. Early Christian tradition ascribes the epistle to John the apostle. Included in that impressive list of endorsers is Tertullian, Dionysius of Alexandria, and Irenaeus (all from the early A.D. 200s). Eusebius and Jerome join the chorus of early and respected scholars who name John as the author.

Finally, it is plausible that John may have had the nickname of "the Elder." It is also an understandable theory that he may have been the mind and mouthpiece of the writing while someone else actually penned the epistle.

THE AUTHOR'S REASONS FOR WRITING 1 JOHN

The author has at least two distinct sets of reasons for writing this epistle. Multiple motives are not uncommon in human experience, but some are less beneficial to publicize. One set of reasons is stated openly. The second set is more contextual, and we are surmising a bit as to what the "between-the-lines" reasons are.

THE STATED REASONS FOR WRITING

The author explicitly states the following "outcome-based" reasons, which tend to be for the blessing and benefit of the reader.

Connection. **We proclaim . . . so that you also may have fellowship with us. And our fellowship is with the Father and with his Son, Jesus Christ** (1:3). The author wants the reader to be in healthy relationship with other believers and with Christ.

Completion and Fulfillment. **We write this to make our joy complete** (1:4). This interesting statement has a variety of potential meanings to explore regarding both the development and the delight of the believer.

Purity. **I write this to you so that you will not sin** (2:1). The author announces his case that habitual sin need not be the experience of a Christian.

Warning and Discernment. **I am writing these things to you about those who are trying to lead you astray** (2:26). The author does not want them to be unaware of the dangers they around them.

Confidence, Assurance, and Security. **I write these things . . . so that we will have confidence on the day of judgment** (4:17), and **so that you may know that you have eternal life** (5:13). There are numerous references in 1 John that relate to the confidence, assurance, and security of the believer. All are exciting themes.

CONTEXTUAL REASONS FOR WRITING

The actual content of the writing offers insight regarding reasons that lie beneath the surface of the words. Although the following reasons arise from some subjectivity of this writer, they seem to have validity.

Legacy. If 1 John was written late in the first century, then the following conditions likely existed: All of the original disciples of Jesus were now dead except for John, the son of Zebedee, brother of James. He was the only surviving witness of all that the disciples experienced in their intimate association with Jesus. Who else could better tell the story with firsthand authenticity?

Therefore, a clear, concisely written interpretation of the gospel from an eyewitness was an urgently needed gift. It would become a beautiful and powerful legacy of the lone survivor of that Upper Room experience where Jesus inaugurated what we now call the Eucharist, the Last Supper, or even more simply, Communion. A written document such as this would provide a legacy of direct linkage with Jesus.

Although John's legacy to Jesus is important, another legacy issue is even more important: the legacy of Jesus Christ himself. At a time when some were totally revising the original meaning of who Jesus was and why He did what He did, *someone* needed to speak with authority. The author of 1 John stepped up and did exactly that.

Correction. Certain individuals were gaining a hearing for their distorted views of core Christian beliefs. Such teachings either denied or distorted the classic meaning of the Incarnation, the deity of Christ, the redemptive nature of the Crucifixion, the reality of the Resurrection, and the validity the Atonement. The implications of the heretical teachings could have been sweeping in their reinterpretation of the life of Christ and subsequently the Church and Christianity.

Protection. In the process of refuting and correcting the anti-Christian teachings being circulated, the writer was providing protection for the Christians of that day and every generation to follow. Throughout the centuries, the essence of those early misinterpretations of Christ and Christianity has been repeated under various names. We will explore these as we address the text.

Affection. Even though this brief epistle is sometimes confrontational and blunt, the writer's affection for his readers shines through. The language of love and family is evident in every chapter. The writer approaches the issues as a father having a frank and important discussion with his children, whose welfare he considers paramount.

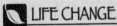

LIFE CHANGE

THE ENEMY IN THE MIRROR

In what ways does the wickedness of our world really impede the spiritual health or the growth of our congregations? Actually, the "world" is not our problem. The world is the focus of our concern! Our problems, as a Church, are almost always generated by those on the *inside*. Nearly every church failure is the result of an inside job! We have a two-fold mission as spiritual leaders: We must guide our congregations to become healthy, robust bodies, increasing in strength, love, and a sense of unity in mission. We can then better focus on those who are outside of Christ and the Church.

So, beneath the statements of purpose for his writings lie the sentiments and passions for them. Those same expressions of the author are never far from intersecting with our needs today.

PRACTICAL VALUES AND IMPORTANCE OF 1 JOHN

Can we really know where we stand with God—today? What are the clear marks of an authentic Christian? How do we detect spiritual falsehood? Can we be sure of our eternal security? Do we assume that Christians sin in thought, word, and deed every day? How is it possible to love someone we don't even like? Is purity of life even a possibility in this world? These are a few of the questions for which 1 John provides clear, concise answers.

The real beauty of this book is that it tells us clearly what God wants from us. As we consider what God wants *from* us, we discover what God wants *for* us. What a discovery!

First John is a book of optimism and hope. The writer tells us that we are called and enabled to win over sin's power in our lives; we can be winners in purity, love, and community.

This epistle was *timely*, and it is *timeless*. In the day of its writing, it just may have been used by the Holy Spirit to help save Christianity from dilution, distortion, and subsequent disregard. If the heresies of that day would have become dominant, Jesus would have been reinterpreted as being just another compassionate teacher and extraordinary person—but not the divine Son of God. In fact, what makes Christianity worth believing at all is the astounding uniqueness of Jesus as far more than just another prophet. He is the *fulfillment* of prophecy. Jesus is not the best among many; He is the only one in a category of one.

HISTORICAL CONTEXT AND CONDITIONS

ENEMY WITHIN THE GATES

In many of the other volumes of this commentary series, you will read about the influence of what was generally called Gnosticism. This was a

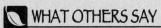

WHAT OTHERS SAY

CORRECTION OR DEPARTURE?

When the Holy Spirit convicts us of sin, wrong, or error, we must obey regardless of the cost. Sometimes that means taking a stand against wrong or walking away from those who will not change.

Luther Lee, co-founder of The Wesleyan Methodist Connection, explained that their intention was correction, not departure (from the Church): "When they commenced the discussion on the subject of slavery, they did not entertain the most distant thought of leaving the Church, they only thought of reforming the Church." They subsequently realized that the charters of the Methodist Episcopal Church indeed were written to support slavery, so their choices were to stay and fight internally or to leave and start a movement that followed their conscience. They left.

pervasive set of viewpoints prominent during the early decades and centuries of Christianity, and in recent times, these viewpoints have experienced somewhat of a revival. However, in the case of 1 John, these teachings are significantly relevant to the reason for the specific content of the epistle. This book is an all-out, though mildly veiled, attack on the Gnostic viewpoints that had corrupting effects on Christian history and truth.

Therefore, proclaiming and defending the gospel were primary concerns for writing 1 John. Because these counter-Christian views were spreading, even by some who had been a part of the Christian community (2:18–19), there was an urgent need to write the truth.

ORIGINS OF GNOSTICISM

Gnosticism is a term that represented a broad variety of viewpoints. The mixture combined some pagan views, some Jewish doctrine, and some quasi-Christian perspectives. They had a ring of truth, appealing to a wide variety of people in that day. Proponents effectively devised, developed, and disseminated an eclectic, pluralistic system of ideas.

One of the proponents of Gnostic views was Cerinthus, who was a contemporary of the Apostle John. According to historians Irenaeus and Eusebius, he and John lived in Ephesus.

Cerinthus taught that Jesus was not born of a virgin, but was the normally conceived son of Joseph and Mary, although Jesus was wiser and more holy than His contemporaries. After Jesus' baptism, the "Christ-spirit" descended on Him, represented by the dove. The newly empowered Jesus Christ proclaimed the little-known Father and performed amazing miracles. Cerinthus further taught that the "Christ" dimension of Jesus departed before the Crucifixion.

Mingled in with the Cerinthian views was an element called Docetism, which taught that Jesus the Christ only seemed to come in the flesh. This attempted to minimize the "God-with-us" nature of Christ.

Two of the assumptions of Gnostic teachings were the impurity of matter and material things and the supremacy of knowledge, especially the kind that was secretly and selectively imparted. The term *Gnostic* comes from the Greek *gnosis,* meaning to know. The Gnostic view was not merely a celebration of knowledge in general, but of a "special" knowledge.

IMPLICATIONS OF GNOSTICISM

The potential of widespread and accepted Gnostic views would have had a dismantling effect on Christianity. Following are some implications of Gnosticism for Christianity:

- God is distant and not very involved with human creation.
- A material universe could not have been created by a good God.
- The incarnation (coming in flesh) of Jesus could not be that of a holy Christ if He indeed came in flesh and blood, which is evil.
- The human body could not be considered a temple of God.
- The tangible elements of Communion could not be considered meaningful.
- Evil cannot harm the enlightened spirit. This belief results in moral indifference and moral recklessness.
- The more morally lofty versions of Gnosticism led to a kind of asceticism, or rigid self-discipline, essentially dismissing sin as a problem.
- Christ suffered on the cross only as a human, not as divine. This belief dismisses any validity of substitutionary atonement for our sins through the cross or Christ.

- The Resurrection was likely a mirage.
- Practical holiness, in behavioral terms, is not an issue of value.
- Salvation comes through special knowledge, not through Christ.

Overall, the varied thrust of Gnostic teachings was generally humanistic. They minimized the notion of a loving, engaged God. This struck at the very core of Christian teachings and truth, including the divine-human nature of Christ and His role in God's saving acts.

WESLEYAN-HOLINESS THEMES

This book beats with the great heart of Wesleyan theology. Or, it may be more appropriate to say that Wesleyan-holiness thought receives the heart of its teachings from books of the Bible like 1 John. Following are some of those themes.

SIN AND PURITY

The writer speaks strongly to the issue of sin. He does not believe that a follower of Christ needs to be dominated by it nor be doomed to habitually practice it (2:1). God's cleansing from sin is sweeping and effective (1:7). He is straightforward about the error of those who claim a life of habitual sin while having fellowship with God (1:6).

Purity is a clear expectation. It involves God's cleansing from sin and must be sustained by walking obediently in the light God gives us (1:7). Purity also includes loving one another and walking (living) like Jesus did (2:5–6), as well as living righteously (3:3–10).

FOCUS ON LOVE AND CHRISTLIKENESS

The message of this book is to love one another and to be in right relationship with God and humankind. The center of Wesley's understanding of holiness, love is also an expression of seeking to imitate God (2:29) and walking as Christ did (2:6). John offers us great insight into holiness by indicating that our love and holiness is personal but also a relational experience. Since holiness is both a corporate and individual (4:12, 17) virtue, the Church should be holy.

COMPLETION OR PERFECTION

Another great Wesleyan-holiness theme is that of Christian perfection. Rather than flawlessness, Christian perfection is transformation and maturity in faith and practice. John speaks of perfect love that drives out fear (4:18).

The theme of completeness, similar in meaning to Jesus' use of the term complete or perfect in Matthew 5:48, is addressed throughout the book (1:4, 2:5, 4:12, 17).

THE ESSENCE OF OBEDIENCE

Obedience is presented as another wonderful holiness affirmation and insight from 1 John. At first glance, obedience seems like such a dutiful, uninspiring term, but by the conclusion of our study, we will wonder why we were reluctant to fully surrender and obey God.

HOLINESS IN 1 JOHN

Regarding the issue of salvation and sanctification (holiness), theologians often separate the two into distinct categories of Christian experience. John does not. As a matter of fact, John does not even use the

LIFE CHANGE

WALKING IN THE LIGHT

One of the overlooked themes of holy living presented in Scripture is the practice and discipline of "walking in the light." It is a phrase that describes obedience or responsiveness to what we sense God has shown us or taught us. John indicates that by walking in the light, we receive cleansing from sin and all unrighteousness, which is a holiness issue.

"Walking in the light" refers to developing a discipline and a lifestyle of living according to the understanding we have received from the Holy Spirit and the Bible. There is a sense in which a person can do no better than to live consistently with the known will of God for his or her life.

terms *saved*, *salvation*, *sanctified*, or *holy*. Yet the themes of salvation and holiness are in every paragraph of 1 John.

▣ KEY IDEAS

Christ's Nature	Christ's Mission and Ministry
Divinity	Serves as the Word of life (1:1)
Jesus is eternal (1:1 and John 1:14).	Intended for fellowship with us (1:3)
Jesus is distinct from God (1:2; 1:3; 5:5).	Delivers us from sin (1:7)
He is God (5:20).	Serves as our advocate or defense attorney before God (2:1)
He is fully righteous (2:1).	Became our atoning sacrifice (2:2)
	Is our model for truth (2:8)
Humanity	Provides our gateway to God (2:23)
Jesus is tangible, touchable (1:1–2).	Demonstrated God's love to us (3:16)
He appeared in the flesh (4:2).	Reveals God's love to us (4:9–10)
He had a human existence (5:6).	Promises and provides eternal life (2:25)
	Makes possible our Christian assurance or eternal security (3:23; 5:13)
	Gives us understanding of God (5:20)
	Destroys the work of the devil (3:8)
	Laid down His life for us (3:16)
	Allows us to live through Him (4:9)
	Affords us victory over the world (5:5)

The genius of John's approach is that he calls his readers to engage in the commitments and behaviors that lead a person *to* Christ, then to live *in* Christ, and to increasingly become *like* Christ. He calls us to the discipline and devotion that leads us to holiness, the perfection of love.

THEMES IN 1 JOHN

This short epistle is an extremely well integrated letter with an enormous amount of big ideas and strong emphases, all packed into a few pages. There are many ways to organize the content of this book, but we will put it forth as follows:

I. The Christian's Creed—Getting it Right
   A. Getting it Right about Christ
   B. Getting it Right about the Creator
   C. Getting it Right about Character
II. The Christian's Credibility—Living it Right
   A. Believing Your Beliefs (Creed)
   B. Behaving Your Beliefs (Conduct)
III. The Christian's Confidence—Knowing You Have it Right
   A. Confidence by Faith
   B. Confidence through Love
   C. Confidence through Obedience
   D. Confidence through the Witness

CHRISTOLOGY—THE CROWN JEWEL OF CHRISTIANITY

John is superb in his presentation of Jesus Christ as the human/divine gift from God to all people. In only five brief chapters of content, he interlaces an amazingly complete Christology.

These passages and others offer us a rich understanding of the nature and purpose of Christ as they relate to eternity past, present-day living, and the future into eternity.

ENDNOTES

1. William Barclay, *The Gospel of John,* vol. 1 (Philadelphia: The Westminster Press, 1956), p. xi.

2. C. H. Dodd, *The Johannine Epistles* (New York: Harper & Brothers, 1946), p. 17.

3. Brooks Foss Westcott, D.D. D.C.L., *The Epistles of St. John,* Tyndale New Testament Commentaries Series (Grand Rapids: William B. Eerdmans Publishing Company, 1950), p. 17.

4. Dodd, *The Johannine Epistles*, p. 20.

5. Ibid.

6. Westcott, *The Epistles of St. John*, p. 23.

OUTLINE OF 1 JOHN

I. The Word of Life (1:1–2)

    A. The Life Revealed (1:1–2)

    B. The Life Experienced (1:1–2)

II. The Life Shared (1:3–7)

    A. John's Witness and Ours (1:3a)

    B. Our Relationships (1:3b)

    C. Joy Completed (1:4)

    D. The Light of Life (1:5)

    E. From Darkness to Light (1:6–7)

III. The Self-Deceived Life (1:8–10)

    A. The Confusion about Sin (1:8)

    B. The Confession (1:9)

    C. The Cleansing (1:9–10)

IV. Liberty and Justice for All (2:1–6)

    A. Breaking the Habit (2:1)

    B. I Think I Need an Attorney (2:2)

    C. Confidence through Compliance (2:3–6)

V. A New Commandment for an Old Problem (2:7–14)

    A. What Is Old Becomes New (2:7–8)

    B. Blinded by Darkness (2:9–11)

    C. History that Shapes Legacy (2:12–14)

VI. Lovers and Losers (2:15–29)

    A. Watch What You Love (2:15–17)

    B. Watch Whom You Trust (2:18–27)

        1. The Antichrists Are Here (2:18–23)

        2. Abide in Him (2:24–27)

    C. Security and Confidence in Christ (2:28–29)

VII. God's Child—In Name and Nature (3:1–10)

    A. Amazing Love—How Can It Be? (3:1)

    B. Living Ready (3:2–3)

    C. What Sin Is (3:4)

    D. What Grace Does (3:5)

Part One

Discovering Life—
We Are Born to Win

1 JOHN 1:1–2:6

THE WORD OF LIFE

1 John 1:1–2

The writer wastes no time launching into issues that are right at the heart of his epistle. He completely bypasses using a formal greeting or opening, as would be common in a letter. Instead, it's as though he burst through the door and breathlessly began to spill out his story.

1. THE LIFE REVEALED 1:1–2

Why then, does John use the relative pronoun "which" in his beginning statement, **That which was from the beginning, which we have heard . . ."** (1:1)? Why not say "He *who*"?

John could be referring to the whole story, and he is beginning with language that today might sound like, "Let me tell you what all has happened; my friends and I actually saw and heard firsthand." He may be giving a general reference before providing the details.

What is the meaning of the phrase *from the beginning*? Is John referring to the beginning of Christ's ministry with the disciples or some other beginning?

Verse 2 brings focus when it says the life appeared, and is then followed by the writer repeating that he had a personal encounter with "the life." His writing indicates that he means the one called Jesus. The relative pronoun, "that which," becomes a comprehensive statement about the nature, the life, and the ministry of the incarnate and eternal Jesus Christ.

The Word of life is central to the entire epistle and merits careful consideration. Some say that the phrase refers to the gospel message, which brings life. Another interpretation argues that it has a much more specific and personal meaning.

The Greek word *logos* ("word") is prominent in the early verses of John's gospel, as it is here. It is also interesting to note, as Vincent points out, that the phrase, **the Word of life**, appears only here in the New Testament.[1]

The question remains whether it is used here as an incarnate Word, as in John 1:1, or to refer to the divine revelation or message. We will come back to that issue after exploring how John so powerfully connected with his surrounding cultures—a valuable skill for our day. John wrote to engage the minds, faith, and lives of multiple cultures around him. How in the world might a person do that? Part of that strategy was his use of terms, particularly *logos*.

There is consensus among scholars that John lived in Ephesus for a number of years in his later life. There, he was surrounded by Greek culture and philosophy. John selected a term that had significant meaning not only in ancient Jewish scriptures, but also in the contemporary thinking of the Greeks. That term was *logos*.

In the opening pages of Genesis, the concept is put forth that God "spoke things into existence" (Gen. 1:3). The Hebrews developed a view of the power of words that essentially indicated that when you speak, you put something into existence that never before existed. Jesus tells us that we will be judged for every careless word (Matt. 12:36–37). The case is made with great force; the spoken word has great power for good or for evil.

LIFE CHANGE

THE WORD BRIDGE

John's use of the term "Word" or the phrase "Word of life" connected with every culture around him. His use of the words and pictures of his time is a masterful model for twenty-first century Christians. Find some connection point for the pre-Christians in your world, and use that as a bridge to introduce them to the gospel. Connection points might be in nature, sports, or other shared interests.

The root of the Greek *logos* refers to things gathered up or collected. As *logos* relates to words, it refers to those words gathered up for the purpose of presenting them in speech. It eventually came to refer to one's inner thoughts or precepts that were put in spoken form.

Philo, a Greek philosopher who was a contemporary of Jesus and John, tried to assimilate a number of the popular views of divinity from

John, tried to assimilate a number of the popular views of divinity from his day. He referred to God as the absolute being, essentially unknowable and immaterial. Since humans are matter and have always had a passion to know and experience God, Philo helped develop a mediating concept that brings God and matter into contact with one another. That concept, or bridge, was called *reason* or *the logos*.

Therefore, a primary Greek mind-set or worldview of that day used the *logos* term in a way that provided a bridge from God to humanity. The Logos, then, was, "the sum total and free exercise of the divine energies; so that God, so far as he reveals himself, is called Logos."[2]

So, both the Jewish and Greek cultures had doctrines that helped identify a bridge from God to humankind. That bridge was God's reason, thought, or divine help. And, in both cultures, as they related to the Greek language, the bridge was referred to as the Logos.

John then masterfully captured that multi-cultural term and declared that Jesus was the Logos who came to earth. The Word became flesh. We call it the Incarnation. As Barclay says, "The mind of God became a person; [Jesus] came to tell them that they need to no longer guess and grope [about God]; all that they had to do was to look at Jesus and see the Mind of God."[3]

What a powerful example John is to every Christian. He demonstrates that in order to effectively witness to a specific culture, we have to understand that culture and then find common ground that connects it to the essence of the gospel.

So, in the Gospel, the Logos is specifically referring to Christ. But, in 1 John, we have the phrase, **the Word of life**. The epistle seems to place greater focus on the practical issue of life. The very next words, beginning in verse 2, are **the life appeared**, indicating that life is the center of the author's attention for his readers. This life that appeared was the one seen, heard, and touched by the author and those original witnesses. Taking that very specific and personalized reference to "the life" and combining it with the writer's use of "the Word" in the Gospel account, it would seem that he is saying, "The unknown Mediator between God and the world, the knowledge of whom you are striving after, we have

Christianity is a message (word) of life, not death; it is a word of hope, not despair; it is a word of anticipation, not regret; it is a word that keeps us up and going, not down and out. God has given the world His Word, and His Word is sacred and trustworthy. The Word is a good word, because the Word is Christ, and Christ offers us life—abundant life. By faith, we receive the Word and truly live.

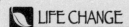

LIFE CHANGE

POSITIVE BATTLE

Differences of opinion often result in conflict and division. This happens in our marriages and families, at work, and even in the Church. The apostle John gives us a magnificent model for dealing with sensitive issues. He addresses his audience with positive and endearing terms rather than insulting or demeaning ones: "my dear children," or "dear friends." He is specific in his criticisms, rather than insulting one's intelligence or character. His remedies are constructive, emphasizing love and teamwork. He is complimentary when possible, which softens the strong admonitions. He challenges them to trust and obey God. He gives them assurance and shows them the way to security in their salvation. Using these positive battle tactics will transform the outcome of many of our differences!

In the Gospel, John makes a point of emphasizing the *divinity* of Christ. In the epistle, he places strong emphasis on the real *humanity* of Jesus because Christ's humanity is what is being challenged by the heresies of that time.

Verse 2 begins, **The life appeared; we have seen it.** In his first several sentences, the writer is establishing at least two powerful truths and combating heretical teachings at the same time.

First, he is beginning to make his case for the Incarnation of God in Christ. This truth is a centerpiece of the gospel, the good news that God loves and cares for us so personally and concretely that He came to demonstrate it in person.

Second is the marvelous reality that Christianity, unlike other world religions, was developed in the open. This is a huge difference that the critics needed to face. The beginnings of nearly every cult and major world religion had roots based on secrecy. Becoming a follower of these religions usually required taking the word of an individual concerning the secret revelations they claimed God had given them. This trust in another's revelation is immense as it relates to the credibility of a body world religion had roots based on secrecy. Becoming a follower of these religions usually required taking the word of an individual concerning the secret revelations they claimed God had given them. This trust in another's revelation is immense as it relates to the credibility of a body of religious teachings. Everything about Christianity was public domain.

Besides the positive truths mentioned above, the writer of 1 John was also combating heretical teachings contemporary to his times and ours. One such teaching was promoted by the bright and articulate Cerinthus. He taught, among other things, that when Jesus was earth, He was more of a mirage or ghost than a real and tangible presence. His view came to be known as "Docetism," a word that means to seem. Cerinthus was a proponent of a number of the Gnostic teachings of his day. Many of the Gnostics viewed all matter as fundamentally evil and only spirit to be good. If God is good, they reasoned, then He would never have worn flesh as Christianity taught. And, if Christ came at all, it certainly could not have been in the flesh, so His coming must have been less than tangible. This teaching alone would have major implications for the life and example of Christ, His death on the cross, and especially, His resurrection. All of these events would have been stripped of their legitimacy and power if Docetism was true.

So a key theme of the first two verses is that Christianity is a religion of revelation, and the revelation is tangible and credible.

2. THE LIFE EXPERIENCED 1:1–2

This section continues to focus on the first two verses, but the theme deserves separate attention. The life of Christ revealed is not

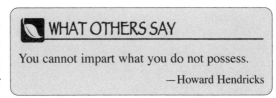

WHAT OTHERS SAY

You cannot impart what you do not possess.

— Howard Hendricks

necessarily the life of Christ experienced, and the writer makes sure that his readers catch the value of both.

The writer is reflecting back a number of years, probably sixty or seventy, yet he recalls it all like that morning: **that which we have heard . . . seen . . . looked at . . . touched** (1:1). We usually learn best what we expe-

John recalls his encounter with the Word of Life by saying, **we have heard**. Remember the stories from the Old Testament days. God "spoke" to the people occasionally through signs, wonders, the prophets, and other great leaders of that day. In Jeremiah 37:17, for example, King Zedekiah asked the prophet Jeremiah, "Is there any word from the LORD?" In every age, for those who believed God exists, there has been a deep desire to know what God was thinking, what His advice and will were, and how their lives could be better by hearing from God. Such hearing brought them confidence, security, and peace of mind.

Most of us who would be reading a commentary like this one believe that God "speaks" to us. And He does in various, easily overlooked ways. So, the writer is announcing that the one he is introducing is one whom he actually had the chance to hear—personally. And he will make the case that this "one" is none other than the Son of God in the flesh.

It is not uncommon to hear people declare that "God told me" this or that. Such a belief provides a sense of confidence and clarity for the one who heard from God. On the other hand, it can be a form of manipulation. They may imply that since God told them this or that, others should not dare suggest otherwise. Many of us are somewhere in between; we sense that God has His ways of getting through to us, but we find it difficult to know if it is God speaking.

The great announcement that the writer is in the process of making is that God has provided us with a clear, definitive,

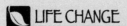

LIFE CHANGE

WAYS GOD SPEAKS

God "speaks" to us in many ways. His "voice" is heard in all of the following:

- Creation, the "thumbprint" of God (Ps. 19:1–4)
- Covenants (Old and New Testaments)
- Christ—God in flesh (2 Cor. 1:6; Heb. 1:3)
- Conscience (Rom. 1:18–21)
- Christians (1 Cor. 7:12)
- Circumstances with God's providence (Gen. 50:20)
- Counselor, Comforter, the Holy Spirit (John 16:1–15)

In which of the above ways do you sense God has "spoken" to you?

not dare suggest otherwise. Many of us are somewhere in between; we sense that God has His ways of getting through to us, but we find it difficult to know if it is God speaking.

The great announcement that the writer is in the process of making is that God has provided us with a clear, definitive, even tangible Word. We will soon see that he is saying that this Word is from the Lord God, and it is a living word that gives life.

Next, John says **we have seen with our eyes,** followed by **we have looked at.** Is he merely repeating himself for emphasis? Not at all. Let's take a closer look.

The Greek word John uses for seen is *horan*. This term basically refers to the physical experience of optical viewing, or seeing something with our eyes, without further implication.

Then, the writer expands his point by saying **we have looked at**. The Greek word used here is *theasthai*, meaning to gaze at and study something carefully until understanding breaks through. John says that he and his companions carefully studied Christ—and they understood the nature and significance of the One whom they followed.

John's careful observation of Jesus is a great example for modern-day Christians to follow. The Word of Life is indeed the supreme example for us to study intimately and to imitate carefully. He is our model for holy living.

Notice the first person plural in John's statement *we* **have seen with** *our* **eyes**. Is John using terms of humility, taking the glare off of himself by refraining from writing, "*I* saw" and "*I* heard," and "*I* touched"? Not likely, because a few sentences later, John shifts to using the first person singular term, "I," when he writes, **My dear children, I write this to you** ... (2:1). By initially using the first person plural, he is saying, "My companions and I all witnessed Jesus' amazing life." This is not what John alone saw, heard, touched, and studied; this is an experience he shared with other credible witnesses.

Keep in focus the importance of the "we" language. John was writing near the end of the first century. The other original disciples of Christ had already died or been executed. Only John remained. Inaccurate

215

APPEARING ELITIST AS WE WITNESS ABOUT OUR FAITH

John writes that he and his friends have not only seen and heard Jesus, but they **testify to it, and . . . proclaim . . . eternal life.** They are giving witness about Christ because they experienced Christ firsthand. How can we have a "relationship" with someone who is not tangibly present? This is one of the truly legitimate questions people have when they hear Christians talk about having a personal relationship with Christ.

As Christians, we tend to use insider language that leaves people in the dark. Most Christians do not intentionally try to sound like elitists, but often come across that way to those who do not share the same background or encounters with the living Christ.

Ironically, elitism is one of the very problems going on in John's day with the movement known as Gnosticism. One of the tenets of this eclectic set of views was that only those with secret knowledge or access to God were truly in the way of blessing from God. In the same way that some people in John's day felt inferior because they were not included in the elites' circles, so today people may feel excluded when Christians use elitist language. Therefore, Christians need to be very careful around pre-Christians who may get discouraged from pursuing their own faith in Christ if they think that believers possess some unattainable connection with God that they will never have.

WHAT DOES IT MEAN TO HAVE A "PERSONAL RELATIONSHIP"?

One's connection with Christ can be personal because Christ was resurrected and is alive today. The book of Hebrews says, "But because Jesus lives forever, he has a permanent priesthood. Therefore, he is able to save completely those who come to God through him, because he always lives to intercede for them" (7:24–25). Christ is alive today and able to connect with the human spirit through His Holy Spirit. Jesus said that if He left in the flesh, He would send another counselor, namely His Holy Spirit. John had firsthand knowledge of Jesus' promise and recorded it in the Gospel, chapter 14:15–21.

One's relationship with Christ becomes personal when we take it personally. He did not just die for everyone else's sins; He died for mine and able to connect with the human spirit through His Holy Spirit. Jesus said that if He left in the flesh, He would send another counselor, namely His Holy Spirit. John had firsthand knowledge of Jesus' promise and recorded it in the Gospel, chapter 14:15–21.

One's relationship with Christ becomes personal when we take it personally. He did not just die for everyone else's sins; He died for mine and for yours. When we recognize that our own sins separate us from God and that we need Christ to bring us back into fellowship with Him, then we personalize the connection. We will see that John begins to lay out that very concept of personal experience as he writes about confession.

We can experience Christ only when we make a personal appeal to Him. A personal relationship involves direct communication. Prayer is a wonderful example of personal communication with God and with Christ. Remember, the writer says that the eternal life was "with the Father" (1:2). In the Gospel, John quotes Jesus as saying that He and the Father are one (John 10:30). So, when we pray to the Father, we are praying to Jesus.

It is personal when we live out the implications of such a relationship. This relationship involves faith in Christ, trusting in Christ, and walking in the light He provides us.

Our relationship becomes intimately personal as we sense the Spirit of Christ connecting with our spirit. His Spirit offers counsel, comfort, conviction, and confidence that we are in good standing with the Lord God.

ENDNOTES

1. Marvin R. Vincent, D.D., *Word Studies in the New Testament,* vol. II (Grand Rapids: William B. Eerdmans Publishing Company, 1946), p. 306.

2. Vincent, *Word Studies in the New Testament,* p. 30.

3. William Barclay, *Gospel of John,* vol. I (Philadelphia: The Westminster Press, 1956), p. 14.

4. Vincent, *Word Studies in the New Testament,* p. 31.

THE LIFE SHARED

1 John 1:3-7

1. JOHN'S WITNESS AND OURS 1:3A

The writer is clearly enthused about sharing his experiences with his readers. This is evidenced by phrases like, **this we proclaim** (v. 1); **and testify to it** (v. 2); **we proclaim to you the eternal life** (v. 2); **and we proclaim to you what we have seen and heard** (v. 3). The first such phrase, referenced in verse 1 does not actually appear in the early manuscripts, but is implied. The writer desires to proclaim or share his story with the readers. He is testifying as a witness.

2. OUR RELATIONSHIPS 1:3B

The writer introduces one of the great New Testament terms in the last half of verse 3: *koinonia*. It is translated "fellowship" in our text. That same Greek word is used eighteen times in the New Testament. In that culture, the word's meanings included that of partnership and community, and it was even used to refer to human society. In most cases there was some binding nature to the relationship to which it was referring. With its use came the implications of responsibility, accountability, intimacy, and even generosity. The Greek culture also used the term to refer to the intimate relationship of a marriage and sometimes used it to indicate the possibility of one's relationship with the gods. The term is significant because *koinonia* is the first of the writer's five stated purposes for writing his letter:

1. To expand the fellowship of believers with God (1:3)
2. To experience the fullness of joy (1:4)

3. For deliverance from sinning (2:1)
4. To have confidence and purity before God (2:28)
5. For confidence and assurance that his readers have eternal life (5:13)

John shares with his readers what he has seen and heard in order that they **may have fellowship** with them. He is concerned that the readers experience all that is meant by the Greek word *koinonia*.

In John's use of the term *koinonia*, the common-bond fellowship clearly centers on the issue of experience and encounter with Christ and how that impacts those who share such an experience. It is more than simply human connections. **And our fellowship is with the Father and with his Son, Jesus Christ** (v. 3). As John's letter progresses, we see that he places enormous value on all aspects of our relationships with one another and the direct impact they have on our relationship with God. Conversely, he reveals how our relationship with God must impact our relationships with others.

Christian community is the context in which we demonstrate our faith and love for Christ, and it is in community that our Christian character is built.

WHAT OTHERS SAY

If love is the character, the outflowing, the communication of holiness and that which gives existence to it, and love is a quality of a person . . . something must be said about holiness that Wesley never missed, namely, that holiness has to do with *persons in relationship*.

—Mildred Bangs Wynkoop

It is not only Christian community that counts, but it is any kind of relationship we have in life. This is the classroom for developing Christlikeness and the proving ground for our genuineness as followers of Christ.

3. JOY COMPLETED 1:4

In this verse we have the second of John's five expressed purposes for his letter. He wants our joy to be complete. The Greek pronoun literally reads, "the joy of us;" it is translated "our joy" in some versions, and some versions say "your joy."

What is the meaning of the Greek term for joy, *kara*? It is a concept introduced by John in his gospel (John 3:29; 15:11; 16:24; 17:13). The writer cites statements, both by John the Baptist and Jesus, dealing with the fulfillment or completion of joy.

From the words of John the Baptist, we learn that his discovery of Jesus as the long-awaited Messiah and his honor of introducing Christ to the world brought John the fulfillment of a lifetime. Joy seems to be the internal delight of some long-sought pursuit.

Jesus makes reference to the fullness or completion of joy (John 15:11; 16:24; 17:13). In each case the joy is shared as one is in a relationship that involves loving, obeying, and abiding in Christ. Joy is a reward of right relationships.

Arndt and Gingrich indicate that this use of joy refers to the highest and best kind of joy.[1] I might add that it is a kind of ultimate fulfillment and the accompanying delight of it. And, it all revolves around our relationship to Christ and the quality of our relationships with others, especially those who also are in Christ.

One interpretation of the fulfillment of joy goes beyond this life to the fulfillment we will have in heaven. Since perfect fellowship eludes us here on earth, perfect joy will elude us until we are able to experience the ultimate fellowship with God and others in heaven.[2] It does seem consistent with John's teaching that right relationships with God and others have the power to produce life's ultimate joy.

In addition to the emphasis on joy, John provides a strong emphasis on the issue of completion, or something being fulfilled.

Jesus' use of the Greek term *telios* (translated "perfect" in the KJV) did not refer to flawlessness, rather to be developed fully in moral

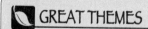

GREAT THEMES

COMPLETION, PERFECTION

Six times in 1 John the idea of completion or perfection is mentioned. Five of the six times the Greek word is from the root *teleo*, meaning "complete," "mature," or "perfect." It is the same root word used by Christ in Matthew 5:48 when we are admonished to be perfect as our Heavenly Father is perfect. The context of that perfection is love. Here, again, we have a core holiness issue being addressed: that intriguing issue of "perfect love" (2:5).

trajectory or purpose.[3] This form of perfection or completion refers to having God's view of things and pursuing His view with a passion to achieve perfection.

In each of the other cases in 1 John where some form of *teleo* or *telios* is used, the surrounding context is love, just as it is in Jesus' use of the term. From John Wesley's perspective, love is the centerpiece of holiness: love for God, oneself, and one's neighbor (Matt. 22:37–40). When love is working well in any relationship, the outcome is a deep sense of fulfillment and well-being, or as John puts it, joy completed.

More specifically, John tells us that our highest joy is the result of personal experience of Christ in our lives and being in fellowship with other believers. Believers help one another learn and practice what it means to know Christ and share Him with those who don't yet know Him.

4. THE LIGHT OF LIFE 1:5

The central thought of verse 5 is this powerful statement describing part of the nature of God: **God is light.** It is apparently something that Jesus said, and the writer is passing it on to his readers (v. 5). On one occasion in the Gospel (John 4:24) and twice in 1 John (1:5, 4:8), the writer puts before us three brief, powerful expressions of God's nature: God is spirit, God is light, and God is love. John emphasizes his point by the phrase, **in him there is no darkness at all.** He is describing a God who is pure light, all the time, without fail.

God's nature is even the measuring rod for determining what sin is. Sin includes the thoughts, words, and deeds that conflict with moral light and rightness; sin opposes what love does. Sin pollutes the spirit of humankind, blocking sensitivity and responsiveness to God's Spirit.

In the Old Testament, light was often the medium through which God revealed himself. In Genesis 1:3, we read, "And God said, 'Let there be light,' and there was light." Light represents God's presence and power. Light, in relation to God, suggests that God is a revealer, and He wants His creation to know Him. Light penetrates and helps define new horizons. The Greek term for light, *phos,* carried connotations of deliverance and delightfulness. It was a term of endearment when applied to a person; for example, "You are the light of my life."

Plants and all manner of living organisms depend on light. We are able to perceive context and color with its help. Light is conducive to life. Not only does it enrich beauty, but it also broadens our horizons. Light enhances discovery and development of all kinds.

Intellectually, light represents knowledge, truth, and revelation. It suggests learning, wisdom, and comprehension. We speak about the "enlightened mind," "seeing the light," or "the light at the end of the tunnel" representing hope and help.

Light also has a moral connotation, and this is probably the thrust of John's considerations for us and all his readers. As light, God is pure and holy. Light stands for rightness and truth; it represents holiness and purity of character. It stands for honor and integrity. Light speaks of guidance and direction, with God—Who is light—accompanying us on the journey to give us light and to be our light. Also, light exposes and lays bare that which is evil or that which is opposed to the light.

When John says that God is light, he is saying that we have a God who wants to be known, who knows all things, who is approachable, and who is willing to come to us. He is a God of righteousness and a revealer of truth about good and evil. He offers himself to go with us in life, to guide and brighten our days. Since light is essentially incorporeal, it relates to God as Spirit.

Intellectually, God is the source and essence of truth and reality. Morally, God is holy and all that is good. As a God of knowledge, wisdom, and truth, He should be the pursuit of honest minds, of all

 WHAT OTHERS SAY

The God who is light provided a startling revelation of himself. That revelation came in the person of Jesus Christ. The writer of Hebrews says it well: "The Son is the radiance of God's glory, and the exact representation of his being . . ." (1:3). And Colossians 2:9 says, "For in Christ all the fullness of the Deity lives in bodily form" (2:9). Saint Paul draws on this very symbol of light, and the truth about God in Christ, when he writes, "For God, who said, 'Let light shine out of darkness,' made his light shine in our hearts to give us the light of the knowledge of the glory of God in the face of Christ" (2 Cor. 4:6).

cultures and nations. C. S. Lewis once said that we believe that the sun has risen, not because we see it, but because by it we see everything else.[4] Likewise, since God is light, He makes it possible for us to see so much. With His light, we are no longer in darkness and need not fear. "The Lord is my light, and my salvation—whom shall I fear?" (Ps. 27:1).

5. FROM DARKNESS TO LIGHT 1:6–7

Now we approach the problem of sin and its effect on relationships. John sets darkness and sin in stark contrast to light and good. In recent decades, it seems there has been an aversion to even use the term *sin*. The word has an edge to it that makes many people uncomfortable. And, it should. John claims that we must deal with sin or face its consequences.

These two verses launch an amazing sequence of insights in which John focuses on human nature and need, human problem and divine solution, and heretical teaching and correction. It also includes one of the strongest statements in all of literature about the astounding benefits you and I receive because of Christ's crucifixion and resurrection—**the blood of Jesus, his Son, purifies us from all sin**.

Notice that verses 6 and 7 focus on the effect of darkness and sin on one's fellowship with God. John states boldly that walking in darkness and having fellowship with God cannot be done at the same time. One cancels the other. Sin separates. Sin and darkness put us on a trajectory away from God and life. They corrupt our connection (fellowship) with God—and one another. And sin, without solution, is an ongoing part of human spiritual makeup.

There were those who would **claim to have fellowship with him** (God), yet they would continue to **walk in the darkness.** The writer says that a person cannot do both at the same time.

Walking in darkness refers to an intentional, habitual lifestyle. It refers to the way one is by inner decision and outward action. As it relates to darkness, it refers to a style of life that is ungodly. The term contrasts the expressed nature of God with a life void of light. What may be happening is either delusion or denial—or both.

John describes a life that has made it a habit of living apart from godliness, and the separation from God it creates. A person becomes comfortable with the darkness and even prefers it over light.

But if we walk in the light, that is, the kind of light that reflects godliness, **as he is in the light, we have fellowship with one another.** When we

◤ TRUE LIFE ILLUSTRATIONS
FROM DARK TO LIGHT TO DARK

In World War II, the American armies came to liberate the POWs kept on a South Pacific Island. They were kept in locked huts, under guard, in total darkness. When their liberators finally secured their release, many of them slowly exited the huts, became confused and overwhelmed with the light, and returned (temporarily) to their familiar, darkened prisons!

When people come into the light of God, they may have to let their eyes adjust to the brightness, just as the prisoners had to reemerge from their darkness.

make it a habit or lifestyle to intentionally live in such a way that imitates God's ways, then even our relationships with others finds a health and wholeness that is impossible when we function in ungodly fashion.

The light of godliness includes those characteristics assigned to God, such as love and grace. First Corinthians chapter 13 reminds us what love does and does not do. It is God's nature to forgive, help, and heal. And it is God's nature to find a way to restore fellowship. The fruit of God's Spirit is love, joy, peace, patience, kindness, goodness, faithfulness, gentleness, and self-control (Gal. 5:22–23). When enemies hurled insults at the Son of God, He did not retaliate, but He entrusted himself to God's protection (1 Pet. 2:23).

The apostle Paul declares to young Timothy, one of his ministry interns, that God does not give us the spirit of intimidation, but one of power, love, and self-discipline (2 Tim. 1:7). That is living in the full light of God's gifts for us in healthy, holy, wholesome ways.

The most astounding statement of them all so far is that walking in God's light not only produces life-giving relationship, but **the blood of Jesus, his Son, purifies us from all sin.** Does this mean only forgiveness, or does it mean something more? Does it mean that we are sin-free, never to worry about sinning again? Does it suggest some kind of "eradication" of the sin tendency? Let's carefully explore the language he uses.

The first advantage of walking in the light—a lifestyle of seeking to please and imitate Jesus, who is the reflection of God—is that we have *a healthy connection* with God and our brothers and sisters in the faith. And, it should affect relationships beyond just those of the Christian circle.

The second benefit is what he calls being *purified from all sin.* Vincent notes that the Greek term for *purifies*—from which we get the word *cathartic*—is in the present tense, which denotes ongoing action, rather than a point of time or one single cleansing. So, the cleansing is present and continuous.[5] He also indicates that the meaning is beyond the mere forgiveness of sin, but it includes the removal of sin as well.

At times, some have interpreted this as teaching that God cleanses a person of the sin nature, or the inclination to sin, once and for all at a point in time. This verse is not limited to that view; however, life experience does not always validate it, nor did John Wesley.

The Greek terms and tenses would suggest the following:

- The purifying action is an ongoing process for an ongoing need.

- The cleansing process is not limited to only certain kinds of sin.

- The cleansing affects not only actions, but deals with intentions and inclinations.

- Purity is conditioned on being in right relationship with God and others.

- Being in right relationship is conditioned on walking in step with God.

Now, what is the sin from which we can be purified? The Greek term translated *sin* is *hamartia.* This term means missing the mark, transgressing against divinity, offenses against God or people, or departing from the right way.[7]

Hamartia carries a wide variety of actions, intentions, and even inclinations. These range from fairly innocently straying to intentionally doing evil or wrong. John Wesley, in his notes on the New Testament, says that the Greek term translated *sin* refers to all kinds of sin, including original (sinful nature) and actual sin. He also says that the cleansing of God includes freedom from the guilt of sin and from the power of sin but not from the possibility of sinning.[8]

The great news is that God's power to help us extends to all aspects of sin. God provides understanding, confronts us with the truth, and reveals the error of our ways. Then we have choices to make. If we

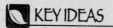

KEY IDEAS

GREEK TERMS FOR "SIN" IN 1 JOHN

Hamartia: This term carries the meaning of missing the mark or being off course. The word suggests that sin is a disposition as well as a process of becoming lost. It is used to refer to one who is experiencing delusion and deception or being misled (1 John 1:9; 3:4; 5:16–17).

Adikia: This word signifies crookedness or the bending and perverting of that which is right. Sin, then, is separation from God. When separated from Him, values are confused or reversed (1 John 1:9; 5:17).

Anomia: Used by John in 1 John 3:4, he defines it as transgression of the law. It implies rebellion, conscious disobedience, and living against the law.

follow the light, He helps us walk in the right way. If we ignore or reject the light, then we stand guilty of offense against God and others.

The purification that He desires for us is one that extends from the inside out and does not leave any waywardness untouched. God's sanctifying impact in us is comprehensive, transforming us in some ways in a moment in time, and in other ways, over a season of time.

What about the *blood of Jesus*? This phrase is widely recognized in the early Church literature to reflect on what God was doing for us through Christ's death. Jesus was the ultimate, innocent sacrifice for the all of the sins of the world.

ENDNOTES

1. William F. Arndt and F. William Gingrich, *A Greek-English Lexicon of the New Testament* (Chicago: The University of Chicago Press, 1957), p. 883.

2. Stott, J. R. W., M.A. *The Epistles of John,* Tyndale New Testament Commentaries Series (Grand Rapids: William B. Eerdmans Publishing Company, 1964), pp. 65–66.

3. Arndt and Gingrich, *A Greek-English Lexicon of the New Testament,* pp. 816–817.

4. David Jackman, *The Message of John's Letters,* The Bible Speaks Series (Downers Grove: InterVarsity Press, 1988), p. 29.

5. Marvin R. Vincent, D.D. *Word Studies in the New Testament,* vol. II (Grand Rapids: William B. Eerdmans Publishing Company, 1946), p. 317.

6. John Wesley, *A Plain Account of Christian Perfection* (Kansas City: Beacon Hill Press, 1966), p. 90.

7. Arndt and Gingrich, *A Greek-English Lexicon of the New Testament,* pp. 41–42.

8. John Wesley, *Romans–Revelation*, vol. II of *Wesley's Notes on the New Testament* (Grand Rapids: Baker Book House, 1981), p. 64.

THE SELF-DECEIVED LIFE

1 John 1:8–10

1. THE CONFUSION ABOUT SIN 1:8

In these three verses, the writer drives home his point regarding sin. Throughout history, people keep making at least one of six mistakes about sin and themselves: (1) Some think that they live above sin. (2) Others believe they have moved beyond sin. (3) Some believe that the sin nature is removed. (4) Another mistake is made by those who think they live below the dangerous threshold of sin. (5) A fifth mistake about sin is made by those who are simply blind to their own nature and behavior. (6) The sixth mistake often made is to blame God for sin. Let's look at each mistake in more detail.

LIVE ABOVE SIN

Some people believe that sin is not an issue in their life. In some sense, many Jews of John's day thought that to be the case. They believed they were free from sin and guilt before God since they were the children of Abraham. For example, some Jews did not think they needed baptism for sins, because sin was not a problem for them. That is why God spent centuries teaching them about blood sacrifices and their need to recognize their need of purification from sin. It is also amazing that the sinless Jesus submitted to baptism. It was His way of leading the people to realize that even those who think they live the best lives stand in need of repentance.

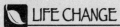

LIFE CHANGE

SIX FALSE ASSUMPTIONS PEOPLE MAKE ABOUT SIN

1. Some think they live above sin.
2. Others believe they have moved beyond sin.
3. Others believe the sin nature is gone.
4. Some think they live below the threshold of sin.
5. Some are simply blind to their own nature and behavior.
6. Others blame their sin on God.

Some of the Gnostic teachings also indicated that those who had been favored with special revelations and knowledge had no need to worry about sin. Their giftedness kept them above sin.

Even today, many have a very limited view of such; they believe that only if they have murdered, stolen, or other vices that they consider the "worst sins," they are guilty of sin.

MOVED BEYOND SIN

Some believe that though sin was a problem in their past, it is no longer an issue; they have moved beyond it. Two doctrines have contributed to this confusion about sin. First, some interpretations of the doctrine of "eternal security" would suggest that if one is predestined for heaven, then even sinning cannot thwart one's ultimate salvation. Some have become careless about sin, assuming that it is just who we are and what we do in our uncorrectable nature. Some say that God sees only Christ when He looks at us, so He does not see our sin. Such a view is totally out of touch with the teachings of 1 John, which lodges our spiritual security with the foundational virtues like faith, obedience, love, and the witness of God's Spirit.

SIN NATURE IS REMOVED

The doctrine of eradication has been taught primarily in Wesleyan circles. In its most rigid interpretation, eradication means that the tendency to sin, or the possibility of sinning, can be expunged or cleansed from a person's inner being. Some have mistakenly taught that one who is cleansed of inner sin is free from old or new temptations.

Neither Scripture nor experience sustains this view of eradication. God transforms human nature (tendency or inclination), but capacity and possibility of sinning remains (2:1); thus, we need to keep walking in the light.

LIVING BELOW THE DANGEROUS THRESHOLD OF SIN

The approach of people who believe they live below the dangerous threshold of sin is to compare with others whom they assume to be worse sinners, thereby minimizing their own culpability. Their safety and security seems to be in thinking, "At least I'm not as bad as . . ." It is as though the sins of others serve as a barrier, keeping God from seeing their own sins.

SIMPLY BLIND TO THEIR OWN NATURE AND BEHAVIOR

People who are simply blind to their own nature and behavior may lack some internal capacity of conscience or may have grown up in such depraved conditions that such living is normal to them and not considered evil or wrong. They may be victims of the human tendency to protect and preserve themselves, denying their own flaws and projecting them onto others.

BLAMING GOD FOR SIN

Some people believe if God created all things, then He must be the author of sin. If so, they reason, how can God hold us accountable for that which was of His own doing?

Many try to **claim to be without sin** (1:8), but in doing so, they deceive themselves and they are dead wrong. Sin is a power, a force, and a danger for all of us to address.

One of the challenges in this passage is the uncertainty of whether or not the writer is referring to a pre-Christian person or one who claims to be a Christian. It is difficult to know whether the first person plural, **if we claim,** is referring to any person or to followers of Christ. John is saying that nobody should avoid or deny the need to face and confess sin.

2. THE CONFESSION 1:9

What he does say is that **if we confess our sins** (1:9), or agree with God about our need, that engages a God who is both faithful and just. He will both **forgive us our sins and purify us from all unrighteousness.**

The writer is making the case that the inner tendency to sin and the practice of sinning are realities and need to be faced and admitted. Then God will respond with His transforming goodness to give us forgiveness and freedom.

3. THE CLEANSING 1:9–10

Unrighteousness is the translation of the Greek word *anomia,* which describes the state or the actions of willful lawlessness. The forgiveness mentioned would apply to all kinds of sins, including those that were unintentional. The purification from *anomia* most certainly involves addressing the will of the sinner. This implies that motives, intentions, and that willful "fist in the face of God" attitude need not continue. Transformation is available. Healing of the attitude and spirit can and does occur. The power of the resurrected Christ is the divine contribution, but the humility to confess and the discipline to live the right way both combine for a divine-human partnership or fellowship that leads us into holiness.

The Wesleyan view of cleansing draws on this

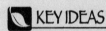

KEY IDEAS

CHRISTOLOGY IN 1 JOHN

First John offers us a terrific set of truths about Christ. This book gives us a fairly comprehensive grasp of who Jesus is. The following are from the first chapter of John:

A. Christ existed in eternity past. He is eternal (1:1–2).

B. Christ's humanity was real. He came in the flesh (1:1–2).

C. Jesus Christ is God's Son. He is divinity (1:3, 7).

D. Jesus is revelation from God (1:2).

E. Christ intended to have a relationship with us (1:3).

F. The blood of Jesus (His death) provides deliverance from sin (1:7).

verse and celebrates the power of grace to deliver us from willful inclinations to disobey God and to enable us to live the Christlike graces.

If we claim we have not sinned (1:10) is the strongest denial of all, and it has the most serious implications. John says that if we deny ever having committed a sin, then we imply that God is lying about our situation. We exclude ourselves from responding to God's truth.

These three verses (1:8–10) describe a progression of denial regarding sin. These verses also reveal the bright lights of Scripture that illuminate and uncover our condition. Best of all, they reveal the goodness of our Lord to provide a solution that is adequate for all sin. They address the inner problem and pollution of sin as well as the numerous expressions of sin in our thoughts, words, and actions.

4

LIBERTY AND JUSTICE FOR ALL

1 John 2:1-6

T he author now presents his case for authentic Christianity, although "Christianity" is not the label he uses. He sets high expectations. He identifies some of the barriers. He points to solutions from God and from within ourselves. And then, he masterfully presents the claim for liberty and justice for all and the pathway to ultimate confidence.

1. BREAKING THE HABIT 2:1

His leading phrase, **my dear children,** in verse 1, is so well placed. He has just ripped into our defenses of denial and blame regarding sin. He has shot straight and brought conviction on all who hear him. Yet he reveals his heart of love and compassion for them as he postures himself as a father having a difficult, yet constructive, conversation. He agonizes over their dilemma but is lovingly truthful with them (Eph. 4:15). He further exemplifies the nature of God and the gospel by providing the solution and the grand challenge.

One of his purposes for writing, he explains, is **so that you will not sin.** The apostle expects abstinence when it comes to sinning. The Greek verb does *not* refer to a continual practice of sinning. The impact is "to not commit a sin." He is not saying that they are incapable of sinning or that they will not sin, but that the expectation and goal are to not sin.

One of the emphases of biblical holiness addresses the practice of sin. The Wesleyan understanding of Scripture is that God's cleansing and His assistance will liberate us from the habit of sinning and transform our inclinations toward sinning. John provides a strong foundation for such teaching. He would bristle at a theology that assumes Christians will inevitably sin every day in thought, word, and deed. Conversely, this statement responds to those who believe that "sinless perfection" is their acquired position in life. In earlier verses, he declares that we all fail to some degree as it relates to sinning. John insists that the power of Christ's death and resurrection provide adequate power for our liberty from domination by sin.

2. I THINK I NEED AN ATTORNEY 2:2

However, what happens if and when we do commit sin? Have we tried in vain to be holy? Do we start all the way back at the beginning and lose the spiritual ground we've gained? Thankfully, the answer is "no." He says that **we have one who speaks to the Father in our defense — Jesus Christ, the Righteous One** (2:2).

The Greek term for that one who speaks in our defense is a word that we translate *advocate, comforter,* or *counselor.* The historical context is a courtroom where someone is on trial and the advocate pleads his or her case. An advocate is like a defense attorney. Of all the trial lawyers on the planet, can you imagine a better one than Christ to plead your case before God the Father? Knowing Christ is the best hope we could have.

In this case, Jesus Christ is not only our defense attorney, but He is also **the atoning sacrifice for our sins** (2:2). The Greek terms here leave us with a few things to sort out. Whereas the NIV uses the phrase "the atoning sacrifice," the KJV uses the term "propitiation" and the RSV uses the term "expiation." "Propitiation" connotes the idea of appeasing someone with a peace offering. Further, it has been used in some religions to suggest a way of calming God's anger, caused by our sins. "Expiation" puts less emphasis on the one being appeased and places more emphasis on the price paid to make the appeasement.

The Greek term *hilasmos,* which is variously translated as indicated above, is in apposition to "Jesus Christ, the Righteous One." That would imply that the propitiation, the expiation, or the atoning sacrifice is referring directly to the person of Jesus Christ. So, the focus is on Christ the Son, and not God the Father, in this particular statement. This would indicate that the wrath of God is not in the writer's focus; rather the focus is on the precious and costly sacrifice, Jesus. That would seem to point to God's love (John 3:16), not His wrath, in this case.

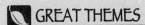

GREAT THEMES

ARE UNIVERSALISTS RIGHT?

There is a religious perspective called Universalism that believes nobody will be lost, neither in oblivion nor hell. They teach that the love of God and the death of Christ will atone for everyone. Verses such as 1 John 2:2 are used as support for this view. But Universalism is not a biblical teaching. It totally overlooks the main thrust of 1 John, which is an assurance that is based on a person believing in Christ as the Son of God and loving one another (3:21–23; 5:13).

He is not only the atoning sacrifice for the sins of a select few, **but also for the sins of the whole world.** The Greek word used for *world* is the same as in John 3:16, *cosmos*, which includes all of creation. Is this a statement declaring universalism? There is a perspective on God's love to us through Christ that teaches that such love and such a sacrifice will end in eternal life for everyone. Does John teach such a view here? It is not what he is saying.

John's statement is first and foremost about the magnificence and glory of Christ, who is the adequate sacrifice for a whole world of sins. We keep forgetting that the foundations of the gospel are all about Him, not us. The benefits reach us, but the glory is His. This is no limited atonement; it is fully adequate to save the world.

However, John's writings repeatedly project the message of human response to God as the energizing of God's grace in one's life. Those who might claim that salvation is unconditional simply have not read this apostle carefully enough. His very next sentences speak to our responsibility for our eternal security.

3. CONFIDENCE THROUGH COMPLIANCE 2:3–6

John tries to nudge us away from declaring our state or *standing* before God and keeps using terms that describe our *relationship* with God in Christ. Having said that, this book is as strong and clear as any about how each of us can have full confidence about our standing with God. We can stand secure, and that security relates to both time and eternity.

The first test is obedience. **If we obey his commands** (2:3), then that allows us the assurance that **we have come to know him.** If one's testimony is that he or she knows the Lord yet **does not do what he commands,** that person is a liar and out of touch with the truth. The reference to "lying" seems to mean less that they are trying to declare a deception, but rather they are self-deceived and empty of truth about that declaration.

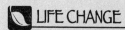

LIFE CHANGE

SALVATION—IN OTHER WORDS

Evangelical Christians tend to use a limited vocabulary when describing a person who is "right with God" in Christ. We use terms like "saved," "born again," or just "Christian." John radically expands our Christian vocabulary, using none of the above terms as he refers to one's spiritual condition.

- Have fellowship with God and Christ (1:3)
- Walk in the light (1:7)
- Have come to know Him (2:3)
- Children of God (3:1)
- Born of God (4:7)
- Have eternal life (5:13)

Vincent gives us a great insight on the meaning of "knowing him." He indicates that the Greek term means something more like *perceive* and is not suggesting the absolute, tangible knowledge of some fact, but the confidence that comes from day-to-day experience that helps us to arrive to such assurance or knowledge.[1]

John's next statement in verse 5 is a startling one: **if anyone obeys** [God's] **word, God's love is truly made complete in him.** The NIV offers an interpretation of this verse by wording it to refer to the love of God being cultivated in us, rather than suggesting that it is our love toward God that is being perfected. John focuses on the importance of love as it is mutually expressed in relationship. The preeminent relationship is ours with God. As Vincent so beautifully writes, "By our life in Christ and our love to God, we are a manifestation of God's love."[2]

This section concludes with an acid test of confidence regarding our spiritual security. In order for us to **know we are in him, we must walk as Jesus did.** In these phrases are several of the vital messages about our relationship with God and our lifestyle on earth.

The "in" concept is a truly powerful idea that is maximized by John,

LIFE CHANGE

BREAKTHROUGH!

As I sat in the seminary classroom, the professor asked us when God gave the Israelites the Ten Commandments. My attitude was, "Who cares? Just give us the answer because it will probably be on the test." Then he dropped an unforgettable insight into my life. He said, "It was after God clearly demonstrated His existence and care for them. It was after He repeatedly demonstrated His love and protection for them, watching over them like a mother over her precious little ones. Only *after* all of that did God give them the Commandments. Therefore, His message was that the Ten Commandments were a gift of love to the people."

From that day forward, every shred of inclination to resist what God wanted for my life simply dissolved, and it has never returned. What God wants from me is what's best for me! Why should I ever again resist what God wants for me?

both in this epistle and in his gospel. Its various uses in this epistle include: see that what you hear "remains in you" (2:24), "remain in the Son" (2:24), "the anointing . . . remains in you" (2:27), "remain in him" (2:27), "continue in him" (2:28), "lives in him" (3:6), "live in him, and he in them" (3:24), "he lives in us" (3:24), and "God lives in us and his love is made complete in us" (4:12).

Being in Christ or God, and He in us is a major issue to John as well as for us. The phrase refers to intimacy of relationship, an ongoing dynamic, a constancy and closeness of fellowship in the lives of those engaged and committed. It is the human spirit and the Holy Spirit being so mended together that it becomes increasingly difficult to differentiate one from the other.

To those who believed the heresies of John's day, God was quite distant, and from that distance He bestowed grace on a few select persons. But the verses we have just studied in this chapter refute the idea that God

WHAT OTHERS SAY

What God looks for in His search for spiritual maturity [is] relationship to him and to people. If our Bible study does not show up in a life that looks increasingly like Jesus' (captured by His heart for people), it is merely a head trip, a point of pride, and an idolatrous substitute for genuine spirituality.

—Reggie McNeal, *The Present Future*

selects and chooses who is eligible for His grace.

John Wesley's insight on this set of verses is helpful. He said, "To 'know him,' to be 'in him,' to 'abide in him' are nearly synonymous terms, only with a graduation: knowledge, communion, constancy."[3] This kind of connection with God is made possible in Christ. Such relationship requires thinking about and communicating with our Lord. It requires that He have a central place in our lives, in all we are and do. It would suggest that there is nothing in our lives that we leave untouched by the light and influence of Christ.

 WHAT OTHERS SAY

"He that followeth after me shall not walk in darkness" (John 8:12). These are the words of Christ, and they teach us how far we must imitate His life and character. . . . Let it be our most earnest study, therefore, to dwell upon the life of Jesus Christ. . . . He . . . that will fully and with true wisdom understand the words of Christ, let him strive to conform his whole life to that mind of Christ.

—Thomas à Kempis, *The Imitation of Christ*

Finally, verse 6 tells us that if we are going to talk the talk, we must walk the walk. **Whoever claims to live in him must walk as Jesus did.** Those who claim intimacy with Christ must demonstrate a lifestyle that complements Jesus. This is the essence of holy living.

ENDNOTES

1. Marvin R. Vincent, D.D., *Word Studies in the New Testament*, vol. II (Grand Rapids: William B. Eerdmans Publishing Company, 1946), p. 326.

2. Vincent, *Word Studies in the New Testament*, p. 328.

3. John Wesley, *Romans–Revelation*, vol. II of *Wesley's Notes on the New Testament* (Grand Rapids: Baker Book House, 1981), p. 65.

Part Two

The Optimism of Grace

1 JOHN 2:7–3:24

5

A NEW COMMANDMENT FOR AN OLD PROBLEM

1 John 2:7–14

God's commandments and will for us have not changed; however, He has given new meaning and beauty to their truth. This section begins to help us understand why obeying God's commandments is the smartest and best thing we could ever do for ourselves and others.

1. WHAT IS OLD BECOMES NEW 2:7–8

When the writer says, **I am not writing you a new command but an old one** (2:7), he sounds either confused, confusing, or both. But he clarifies it when he goes on to say that the commandment about which he speaks is that **which you have had since the beginning . . . the message you have (already) heard.** He is speaking of the collected commandments of God, such as the Ten Commandments, which were and had been a part of their teachings for centuries. But because of Christ's life, death, and resurrection, it is new in two powerful ways.

First, every generation must discover the faith for themselves. We must personally accept faith in order for it to be our own. The gospel makes specific appeals for personal faith. The classic description of a Christian is one who has "a personal relationship with Christ." John highlights our need for firsthand faith in verses 12–14.

The second sense in which the commandment is new is in its new expression, since **its truth is seen in him** (Christ) **and you, because the**

darkness is passing and the true light is already shining. In the first chapter of the Gospel, John says of Jesus, "The true light that gives light to every man was coming into the world" (1:9). God's truth, as expressed in the commandments, has been revealed in Jesus Christ. In Matthew, Jesus identifies the consummate commandment as the command to love God, oneself and one's neighbor (Matt. 22:37–40).

The heart of God's truth centers on His will for us: His commandment to love. Christ is the embodiment of that truth and of God's love for us (John 3:16; 1 John 4:10). Further, our response to Christ is the clearest and best way to return that love to God the Father.

2. BLINDED BY DARKNESS 2:9–11

John rivets our attention by exposing the self-deception of **anyone who claims to be in the light but hates his brother** as one who **is still in the darkness** (2:9). This is serious. Many Christians suggest that sin only affects our fellowship with God. John suggests that it breaks the flow of Christ's redeeming blood in our lives as well as breaks our fellowship with God. And John says that such fellowship with God is indeed the fabric of our lifeline to God—thus salvation. Too often we speak of the time we "got saved." John speaks in terms of "being saved" and *remaining* in a saving relationship.

LIFE CHANGE

SALVATION—IN OTHER WORDS 2

The following are more terms and phrases from 1 John that stretch our vocabulary to describe one's relationship with God or Christ beyond our fairly standard terms like "saved," "born again," and "Christian."

- Fellowship with Him (1:6)
- Live by the truth (1:6)
- In Him (2:3)
- Passed from death to life (3:14)

John warns his readers that whoever remains in hatred or **walks around in the darkness** is lost and confused **because the darkness has blinded him** (2:11). This is a powerful statement because, in all cases where the word *darkness* (in the Greek, *skotia*) "is not used of physical darkness, it means moral insensitivity to the divine light."[1] In other words, being in darkness is being in deep trouble of soul, and in deep trouble with God.

This set of verses is vital for all who claim and believe that they are in good spiritual standing or that they are walking with God. Hatred is darkness, and God is light. Any form of sin leads us into darkness. The one who has already been cleansed still has full capacity to wander into darkness of some kind. Even though we are in Christ, we are still at risk.

3. HISTORY THAT SHAPES LEGACY 2:12–14

John takes a brief detour in something of a poetic or rhythmic form. Each phrase begins with **I write to you** and occurs six times in the short span of the three verses. But, there is a distinction. The first three times, the verb is in the Greek present tense, having the effect of "I am writing." In the second set of three, the verb is in the Greek aorist, or past tense, having the effect of, "I wrote," or "I have written." What could this mean? Various opinions include the thought that the past tense usage refers to a previously written letter, such as the Gospel. Some say, as the NIV translates, that there is essentially no difference at all.

Another interpretation is that the present tense describes his current act of writing the epistle, and the past tense places John in the reader's place, as though he is right with them as they read his letter.[2] Barclay thinks that both verb tenses refer to John's process of writing this letter.[3] He is guiding them through it, in advance, as he helps them reflect on what he has already written, what he is writing, and what is yet to come in the letter—all for the sake of reminding the Christians of who they are and what God has done for them.

Now, to whom is he writing? Are these two or three separate groups? Are they different generations, or are they Christians at different maturity levels in their lives—or both?

First, the phrases that are interpreted either "dear children" or "dear friends" are used at least fourteen times in this letter. It would seem that such phrases refer, in general, to John's reading audience and that he is acting as the aging, loving parent or grandparent figure. However, in verse 12 the Greek word translated *children* is *teknia*, while in verse 14 the Greek word is *paidia*. The first term tends to refer to a child who is young in age, and the second term implies a child young in experience. If that is the case, he may be covering his bases by referring to all who are young both in age and in experience. John appears to be addressing all of his reading audience, whether they are young in age or young in the faith.

His message to those readers is **your sins have been forgiven on account of his name** (2:12). This message is the essence of the gospel. It is the great commission that Jesus gave His earliest disciples, including John. That message was to preach repentance and the forgiveness of sins in the name of Jesus (Luke 24:47). That message is relevant people of any age or maturity.

He writes in verse 13 that they have **known the Father.** This message is similar to the one he writes to the fathers, which appears twice, identical both times, which says, **you have known him who is from the beginning** (2:13, 14).

His message to the young men is **you have overcome the evil one** (2:13), which is repeated in verse 14, and **you are strong and the word of God lives in you** (2:14). The message to the older, and possibly more mature, readers is that they have had experience in their knowledge of God and His Son. They have the perspective, the peace, and determination that come with weathering the storms and stresses.

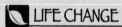

LIFE CHANGE

SALVATION—IN OTHER WORDS 3

The following are more of the terms and phrases John uses to describe a believer's relationship with God or Christ:

- Live in Him (2:6)
- Lives in the light (2:10)
- The word of God lives in you (2:14)
- Belong to the truth (3:19)

He reminds the younger men to brace for battles of the soul that would throw them off the race they are running in Christ. He reminds them that they have overcome the evil one before, and they can continue to do so— and they must. He offers messages of reflection and gratitude, as well as signals of hope and perseverance. In all of that, the not-so-subtle message is that all believers are in this life of faith together. They must help one another. He reminds them that they all have a history that will help them leave a legacy. Some of us do, too, and we must build well on such foundations—as we lay them for those who will come after us.

ENDNOTES

1. Marvin R. Vincent, D.D., *Word Studies in the New Testament,* vol. II (Grand Rapids: William B. Eerdmans Publishing Company, 1946), p. 331.

2. Vincent, *Word Studies in the New Testament,* p. 334.

3. William Barclay, *The Gospel of John,* vol. 1 (Philadelphia: The Westminster Press, 1956), p. 60.

6

LOVERS AND LOSERS

1 John 2:15-29

This section contains dramatic predictions, stern warnings, shocking revelations, curious compliments, and surprising unveilings. It is not easy to claim certain interpretation on some of these issues, but they really get the mind and heart racing to comprehend the implications and applications of what John says.

1. WATCH WHAT YOU LOVE 2:15-17

In the next three verses, John describes the love that loses, the love that leaves, and the love that lives forever.

The command to **not love the world or anything in the world** (2:15) is direct and seems to rule out a lot of things to love. You wonder if John is saying that our love should be "out of this world." Or is that exactly what he is saying?

It seems confusing when John tells us not to love the world when he penned one of the grandest lines in all of history in the Gospel: "For God so loved the world" (3:16). Is he giving us mixed messages or suggesting that God does something we should not? First, let's take a look at his use of the

 WHAT OTHERS SAY

Oh how quickly passeth the glory of the world away! . . . How many perish through empty learning in this world, who care little for serving God. And because they love to be great more than to be humble, therefore they have become vain in their imaginations. He only is truly great, who hath great charity (love).

—Thomas à Kempis
The Imitation of Christ

term *world*, which here is the Greek *kosmon*. The range of meanings for this term extends from reference to the physical planet to the total of humanity to a system of ethical issues such as "the ways of the world."

John uses the term numerous times. He sometimes means the universe (John 1:10); sometimes the sum total of humanity (John 3:16); at times he references "life of earth" (1 John 4:17); and at times, he refers to a "moral order" (1 John 2:15). More often than not, he is referring to "the life of human society organized under the power of evil" (Dodd) or "the order of finite being regarded as apart from God" (Westcott), both cited by Stott.[1] We will encounter other shades of use as we move through this epistle.

Fortunately, John helps us understand his intended meaning of world **or anything in the world** with the phrases, **the cravings of sinful man, the lust of his eyes and the boasting of what he has and does** (2:16). This is a dynamic revelation for us, and we need to clearly grapple with its meaning and our personal responses to these forces of spiritual calamity. It is so important that if we fall prey to them, then **the love of the Father is not in** [us].

Let's explore each segment of this "trinity of trouble."

THE CRAVINGS OF SINFUL PEOPLE

The RSV uses the phrase "the lust of the flesh." We often limit the meaning of this phrase to mean sexual sins. It has, however, a much wider field of reference. The meaning extends to a life being driven by the physical senses and a determination to satisfy them apart from consideration of God's will. This trio of trouble is in James' mind as he writes that we ask God for things and do not receive them because we want to selfishly satisfy our passions (James 4:3). John's phrase refers to those who want to gratify their physical desires, regardless of the well-being of others and apart from consideration of what God wants. Life abandoned to lust of the flesh is a life lived with ourselves at the center.

LUST OF THE EYES

Lusting with our eyes is having a particular inclination to want the things we can see. It is a focus on material mongering. The progression is "I see it," "I like it," "I want it." Then, ultimately "I must have it," and "Here's how I will get it." This approach to life gives little value to the unseen treasures in this life or the next. People who have this approach to life have their values anchored in tangible things. They are consumers of things bought with a price or stolen from others. A person driven by sinful cravings and lusting eyes will have great difficulty loving God or even other people. The central object of this person's affection is self.

THE PRIDE OF LIFE

Using the phrase **the boasting of what he has and does** (2:16), the NIV offers an interpretive wording in this verse. This describes a person who likes to trumpet his own "non-existent importance."[2] Barclay further reminds us of the vivid Greek word used here, which is *alazoneia*. This term describes people who brag of accomplishments and possessions that are not even rightfully theirs, just so they will look good in the eyes of others. These people feed their sense of importance and try to build themselves up so others notice. All of this is done to achieve a sense of value that, in the end, is a bankrupt account. Jesus refers to such a person in His graphic description of those who sound the trumpets and make a big public deal as they prepare to give their pathetic little gifts to the poor (Matt. 6:1–4).

The world and its desires pass away (2:17), John writes. He reminds us that because the object of love is not permanent, love for it fades, and the effort made to love it is not finally fulfilling. Then he finishes the grand contrast by saying, **but the man who does the will of God lives forever.**

This is a core verse in the epistle. He puts the case directly before us. Those who invest their affections and resources primarily in worldly pursuits, to the point of crowding out a life of love and service to Christ, will meet with devastating disappointment as well as ultimate emptiness and loss. On the other side is a life spent doing the will of God, which is all about faith and love. Our highest honor is to invest our faith, worship, and allegiance to the One who will never disappoint and will guide us into fullness of life and eternity.

2. WATCH WHOM YOU TRUST 2:18–27

Talk about a sense of urgency! John follows one dramatic admonition with a daunting assessment of current reality. Did he mean that the coming of Christ was imminent? Was the end of time about to arrive? Had the Antichrist come? His comments are clear, strong, and direct to the mind and heart: **this is the last hour** (2:18).

We are reminded that the Old Testament has numerous references to "the last days" (Isa. 2:2; Hos. 3:5; Mic. 4:1).[3] The Jews of that day tended to see time in two great periods: the present age, dominated by evil, and the age to come, during which God will rule and reign.

The specific phrase, *the last hour*, is used only by John in the New Testament.[4] He is not likely referring to the end of the world, but to a period of time preceding a crisis or a time of testing as the Church labored to advance the cause of Christ in the world. This is alluded to, in part, by his announcement that many antichrists have come. It is because of these antichrists' arrival that they **know it is the last hour** (2:18).

It is Barclay who reminds us that in a very real sense, every hour is the last hour for somebody, someplace.[5] This is true not only in terms of death, but also in terms of facing choices that involve aiding the cause of Christ, giving this concept an ever-current relevance.

THE ANTICHRISTS ARE HERE

Once again, John keeps our attention as he makes a shocking revelation: **the antichrist is coming, even now many antichrists have come.** This sounds more like the "end times" than a mere transition time.

John is the only New Testament author to use the particular term *antichrist*.[6] The term occurs in this verse, 2:22, 4:3, and 2 John 7. Many have looked for a single personage of evil — a Christ-substitute — but John reveals there are many other enemies in the camp.

Later, in verse 4:3, John indicates that "the spirit of antichrist . . . is already in the world." Is Barclay correct in determining that "antichrist" is more often a principle than a person?[7]

Some scholars claim that "anti" means one who is *instead of* rather than *against* Christ. John does not use the term for false Christ, which is used in Matthew 24:24 and Mark 13:22. According to Plummer, a number of commentators interpreted these terms to refer to one or ones who were adversaries of Christ, opposing, denying, or even counterfeiting Christ.[8] This kind of description could apply to many anti-Christian teachings or movements that intentionally or unintentionally taught things which became a Christ substitute or denial of His rightful identity.

Wesley says that "under the term antichrist, or the spirit of antichrist, he includes all false teachers, and enemies of the truth; yea whatever doctrines or men are contrary to Christ."[9] He goes on to say that even though the apostle Paul mentions "the man of sin" (2 Thess. 2:3), John's use of the term tends to refer to being anti-Christian rather than one specific person.

Finally, the reference of "the antichrist" could have been to Cerinthus whose teachings undermined belief in the divine-human nature of Jesus. He was a strong opponent of Christianity.

In verse 22, the writer offers what may be the best definition of his own term when he asks, **Who is the liar? It is the man who denies that Jesus is the Christ. Such a man is the antichrist—he denies the Father and the Son.**

His comment that **you have an anointing from the Holy One** (2:20) is interesting. The term *anointing* is used four times in the short space of several verses; then does not appear again in this epistle. The term is the Greek word *chrisma,* which is the same root word used for Christ. This term is used other places in the New Testament and three times in verse 27.[10] Since Jesus Christ was the Anointed One from God and we become joint heirs with Christ (Rom. 8:17), all followers of Christ are anointed ones.

Although the Spirit is not specifically designated here, "the Holy One" could refer to any one of the Trinity. In context, the "anointing" seems to relate to our exposure to and belief in the truth about Christ; hence, **and all of you know the truth.** All of this points to a case for the Christians being charged to remain faithful to the truth in Christ that they had been taught. That truth was being challenged by those who taught concepts that would undo (or disprove) who Christ was, is, and what He did. John was encouraging the believers to resist such lies as well as remain true to the truth and touch of Christ in their lives.

ABIDE IN HIM

The writer presents believers two safeguards against deception. First, they are to make sure that the apostolic teachings about Christ **remain in** [them] (2:24). If they (and we) stick to the original teachings of the gospel, they will **remain in the Son and in the Father.** In other words, keeping the truth alive in us keeps us alive in the Father and in Christ. This can be a battle for the mind because there are **those who are trying to lead** [us] **astray** (2:26). So the first safeguard is to embrace and live by the original teachings of the gospel, rejecting new philosophies and theologies that might appear to enhance the original truth.

The second safeguard is **the anointing** [we] **received from him,** because **his anointing teaches** [us] **about all things,** and **that anointing is real** (2:27). Again, we see his emphasis on "the anointing." As we think again about his meaning of anointing, we reflect back on Jesus' teachings recorded in the Gospel's chapters 14, 15, and 16. They are rich in some of the very same terms and phrases. At the center of most of it is Jesus' teaching about the work of the Holy Spirit in the lives of the believers.

John records that the Holy Spirit is the Spirit of truth (15:26). He writes that the Spirit will be with them forever (14:16). The Holy Spirit will guide them into all truth (16:13). In chapter 15, Jesus repeatedly mentions the importance of remaining in Him and remaining in His love. He also says He will remain in them. Other translations use the term "abiding," but the meaning is to remain firmly in faith and communion with Christ. As we remain in Him, He will remain in us. In light of all of this, it would seem that the "anointing" is the empowerment we receive from the Spirit of Christ as we remain committed in faith to Him.

3. SECURITY AND CONFIDENCE IN CHRIST 2:28-29

John assures us that as we continue or persevere in Christ, **we may be confident and unashamed before him at his coming** (2:28). Our security does not need to rest in a hope that He "has our number" or that we are one of "the elect." We can live with spiritual confidence and have security for eternity as we sustain our trust in Christ and continue to walk in His light.

John then uses an interesting play on words when he says that if we **know that** [Jesus] **is righteous,** [we] **know that everyone who does what is right has been born of him** (2:29). The use of the terms *righteous* and *right* are from the same Greek root word. Therefore, John is saying that as we seek to live the way Christ lived, we have confidence that we are His spiritual offspring. Here again is a theme at the heart of holiness. Christlike living is one of the foundations of our security.

ENDNOTES

1. J. R. W. Stott, M.A., *The Epistles of John,* Tyndale New Testament Commentaries Series (Grand Rapids: William B. Eerdmans Publishing Company, 1964), p. 99.

2. William Barclay, *The Gospel of John,* vol. 1 (Philadelphia: The Westminster Press, 1956), p. 69.

3. Barclay, *The Gospel of John,* pp. 70–71.

4. Marvin R. Vincent, D.D., *Word Studies in the New Testament,* vol. II (Grand Rapids: William B. Eerdmans Publishing Company, 1946), p. 337.

5. Barclay, *The Gospel of John,* p. 72.

6. Vincent, *Word Studies in the New Testament,* p. 337.

7. Barclay, *The Gospel of John,* p. 7.

8. J. R. W. Stott, M.A., *The Epistles of John,* Tyndale New Testament Commentaries Series (Grand Rapids: William B. Eerdmans Publishing Company, 1964), p. 104.

9. Wesley, John. *Wesley's Notes on the New Testament* (Grand Rapids: Baker Book House, online at http://www.ccel.org/ccel/wesley/notes.pdf), p. 437.

10. Vincent, *Word Studies in the New Testament,* p. 338.

7

GOD'S CHILD—IN NAME AND NATURE

1 John 3:1–10

The following are some of the questions this portion addresses: Is every person a child of God? Whatever happened to sin? What is sin? Is it possible for me to be able to not sin? What is love? In what way is obeying God's command what we all want?

🍃 WHAT OTHERS SAY

1 John: Values of Our Connection and Faith in Christ

Chapter 1	Incarnation	Jesus is the life-giving Word (1:1).
Chapter 2	Atonement	Jesus is our defense attorney (2:1).
Chapter 3	Example	We shall be like Him (3:2).
Chapter 4	Bridge to God	Christ is our bridge to God (4:2).
Chapter 5	Eternal Life	Believing in Jesus gives us new birth from God (5:1).

1. AMAZING LOVE—HOW CAN IT BE? 3:1

John is overwhelmed by the great love God **has lavished on us** (3:1). The Greek term describing love has prompted many interpretations: "Behold, what manner of love" (NKJV). "What marvelous love the Father has extended to us. Just look at it" (The Message). "See how very much . . . " (NLT). It is a term that suggested something foreign, as if coming from another country, beyond their experience, or out of this world

This old man of the gospel is still aglow about the amazing love that God has bestowed on us. What amazes John is that God's love has prompted Him to suggest that **we should be called children of God! And that is what we are!** The writer is amazed that we would even have the title of God's children, much less actually *be* His children.

Some might ask, "But aren't we all God's children?" We are His children by creation. In John's writings, however, he makes a distinction when he uses phrases like "born of God" and "born again." He quotes Jesus in His conversation with Nicodemus (John 3), then he develops variations of the same phrase to refer to a spiritual birth that is distinct from one's natural birth.

John admits that, in a sense, **the world does not know us** because **it did not know him.** This is not a "victim's complex" coming through, as it might be with some. This is the reality for Christians of that day and, to varying degrees, to followers of Christ in our day. If the world did not recognize Christ for what and who He was, we may experience some of the same response.

John may also be taking a swipe at the Gnostic crowd who trumpeted their spirituality on the basis of special knowledge, yet did not recognize the Almighty in their presence.

2. LIVING READY 3:2-3

John raises some fascinating issues when he makes statements like, **But we know that when he appears, we shall be like him, for we shall see him as he is** (3:2). His mind is on the future and what it will be like for the spiritual children of God. The phrase **when he appears** seems to refer to the second coming of Christ. John was in that select group who saw Jesus ascend from the earth (Acts 1:6–11). John has bridged the discussion into eschatology, the issues of "last things" such as death, resurrection, and immortality. Among those issues of theology is the teaching of the second coming of Christ. Clearly, the disciples believed Jesus when He said He would return, and most of them assumed that Christ's return would come in their lifetime.

John intrigues all of his readers when he writes that when Christ comes, **we shall be like him, for we shall see him as he is**. What could this mean? Here are several possibilities:

He could mean that we will finally achieve the moral qualities that make us like Christ, holy from the inside out. He could be referring to our physical-become-spiritual bodies. People are understandably curious about the *form* we will have then. It may mean that we will see Jesus in more of the heavenly nature He possessed before He came to earth and after He returned to heaven. The glory of Christ will have a transforming effect on us.

LIFE CHANGE

LIVE READY

There is the wonderful biblical teaching of Christ's return to earth, called the Second Advent. For centuries, and particularly in the first century, believers thought Christ would return in their lifetime. Of course, God's timing is not always what we want or expect. The conservative, evangelical churches of the twentieth century taught that Jesus was coming soon. Some even dared to predict when He would return. They were, of course, wrong.

We need to quit predicting and start proclaiming the motto "Live ready." That way, whenever Christ returns, we will share the glory! That's our second coming theology: First, He *will* return. Second, live *ready*.

Whatever John has in mind with those statements, and whenever Christ returns, this phrase forms the theology of a Christian who anticipates the coming of Christ.

John's statement that **we shall be like him** is another of the many components in this book that add up to a strong transformational theology. It is reflected in this verse again with his challenge that **everyone who has this hope in him purifies himself, just as he is pure** (3:3). In that regard, he holds before us a hope that motivates purity in our lives. It would be something like the passion homeowners have to keep their house looking its very best when important company is coming.

3. WHAT SIN IS 3:4

John says that **sin is lawlessness** (3:4). In this one statement, the writer uses two Greek terms, *hamartia* and *anomia,* to describe aspects of sin. This statement helps us discuss and deal with sin because it gives a clear understanding of what John meant by "sin" or *hamartia.* For John, sin did not include mistakes and human blunders. It is true that some of the Greek words translated "sin" suggest a wide scope of weaknesses, misdirection, and wrongdoing—but not in this epistle. When the writer references the term most often used for sin, that is *hamartia,* he is writing about lawlessness. For him, the sin of greatest concern is the inclination, the attitude, the conscious, rebellious determination to do what is wrong.

This rebellious sin is the kind for which there is clear and full deliverance in this life. A person does not need to live a lifetime with the heart of a rebel. In the partnership of consecration and cleansing, where we come together with God, a person can become brand new in intention, attitude, and behavior. Our consecration or full surrender to God (Rom. 12:1) is the beginning of a whole new journey with God in sanctification. We can forever leave behind that "in your face" attitude and replace it with a deep and abiding desire for what God wants for our lives. This is the way to live. The cleansing of the sin nature is a portion of the great theology of holiness.

In his widely read and appreciated book, *The Divine Conspiracy*, Dallas Willard observes that American evangelicals have too often settled for a Christianity that minimizes the power of repentance and transformation, settling instead for a "ticket to heaven."[1] The cheap grace preoccupation with imputed righteousness has caused many to neglect the Holy Spirit's actual impartation of holiness in the believer, leaving us powerless to bring about true Christian discipleship.

4. WHAT GRACE DOES 3:5

The entire gospel concept is built around the awesome realization that God's love and grace sent Christ, and **he appeared so that he might take away our sins. And in him is no sin** (3:5). Here again is the gospel truth in simple yet profound terms. God's amazing grace sent His one and only

Son, who was sinless, that He might address our sins and the internal sin problem we have. He did, and He does. People everywhere need to hear and comprehend the awesome beauty and strength of this truth, which will transform their lives and let them live in joy and hope in the Lord.

5. AN OXYMORON: SINNING CHRISTIANS 3:6

The *Random House College Dictionary* defines an oxymoron as a figure of speech that combines contradictions, such as "jumbo-shrimp."[2] Many Christians, including some outstanding scholars, use an oxymoron when they refer to "sinning Christians." This would be considered by John as a very unfortunate and not a humorous oxymoron. He writes, **No one who lives in him keeps on sinning** (3:6). The Greek verb form for "sin" in this statement is the present tense, which has the implication so well identified in the NIV as a *habit* of sinning.

There has been a teaching among Christians of the Calvinist theological persuasion that Christians sin in thought, word, and deed every day. John would not agree and neither does a Wesleyan understanding of Scripture and life. The cessation of habitual sinning is one of the themes of this epistle.

John reinforces his statement by insisting, **No one who continues to sin has either seen him or known him.** Whatever else the writer is saying, or whatever our various theologies say, John stresses that there is a fundamental incompatibility with knowing God and living an ungodly life. He is appealing for obedience, discipline, and consistency. We must walk in the light God gives us. If we claim to be His child, we must demonstrate Christlike character. Our belief and our behavior need to agree with each another. It is human nature to want it both ways at the same time. John addresses at least three errors. He is clearly addressing the Gnostics of his day who taught that sin does not really have much to do with a person's relationship with God. He is also addressing the person who believes that a lifestyle of sin is essentially to be expected, but that it is not a problem because the merits of Christ's death "cover us" so that when God looks at us He really sees Christ. He is also letting the reader know the wonderful fact that none of us needs to be enslaved to a life of sin, particularly as he has defined it in this very context.

6. RIGHTEOUS IS WHAT RIGHTEOUS DOES 3:7

Character and nature are revealed by behavior. The writer of this epistle says **he who does what is right is righteous** (3:7).

It seems that people continue to create an either/or discussion when discussing faith and works in the life of a Christian. John and his old friend James indicate that we should not have one without the other. Is our salvation about faith or works? The answer is "Yes."

7. OUR COMMON ENEMY 3:8

This is John's first reference, in this epistle, to the devil as a personification of evil. He says, **He who does what is sinful is of the devil, because the devil has been sinning from the beginning** (3:8). In this reference, John does not say that the devil makes us do wrong things, but he states that we identify with the devil when we do sinful things. Vincent quotes Augustine as saying, "The devil made no one, he begot no one, he created no one, but whosoever imitates the devil is, as it were, a child of the devil, through imitating him, though not being born of him."[3]

Once again, the first phrase in this verse, **do not let anyone lead you astray**, indicates that there are those who taught that sinning has no ill effect on one's godliness or redemptive connection with God.

The second half of verse 8 states that the **reason the Son of God appeared was to destroy the devil's work.** In this passage, John introduces some unique terms. For one thing, this is the first time in this epistle that the specific title **Son of God** is used. This is one more piece of the Christology that appears in 1 John. He announces that Jesus Christ is the long-awaited Son of the Most High. It is an emphatic response to the false teachers of the day and a strong affirmation of the divinity of Christ.

The phrase, **to destroy the devil's work**, is a strong statement. The devil's work, from the beginning, has been rebellion against God's law and will. The devil hoped to replace God or at least usurp God's power over creation. Sin is lawlessness, a rebel's spirit. So, the devil's work is sin. Christ came to break the power and pollution of sin. This refers to the whole scheme of redemption that liberates those caught up in the devil's influence. It suggests the hope of righteousness or holiness, which is a clear goal for all of us. One of the best ways to destroy the work of the devil is to convert those who have been doing the devil's work.

8. THE ULTIMATE DNA TEST 3:9

This is one of the strongest statements in all of Scripture about sin. It is not a mere slip of the quill either. John intentionally writes, **No one who is born of God will continue to sin** (3:9). This is a very inclusive statement, indicating a norm for all of us who have been born of God.

Key phrases in 3:9 are **born of God, God's seed,** and **cannot go on sinning.** If we can unlock their meaning and how they connect with one another, we have identified a major piece of doctrine on holiness, sin, and the follower of Christ. Otherwise, this verse and some surrounding it could be misused as a radical overstatement about eradication of sin and even its possibility in the life of the believer. Or it may be dismissed as totally impossible to achieve, causing us all to miss the freedom we are being offered.

BORN OF GOD

The phrase *born of God* and its nearly identical statement *born of him* are used at least six times in this epistle. John seems to be using symbolism that he heard from Jesus. In the third chapter of the Gospel, Jesus says

LIFE CHANGE

SALVATION—IN OTHER WORDS 4

The following are more phrases used by John to describe the follower of Christ's connection with God:

- Does the will of God (2:17)
- Remain in the Son and in the Father (2:24, 27)
- Continue in Him (2:28)
- Has been given eternal life (5:11)

to Nicodemus, "You must be born again" (3:7). A few phrases later, Jesus brings more light to that phrase when He speaks of those "born of the Spirit" (3:8). He distinguishes this kind of birth from "flesh giving birth to flesh" and "Spirit giving birth to spirit" (3:6). So, John is clearly referring to a spiritual birth.

One fascinating innuendo that John brings into this verse is that God is assigned both the male and the female role in spiritual birth. One is "born" of a woman, but the genesis is a man's seed. God is the source of our spiritual birth, and it is "God's seed" that remains in us.

This phrase *born of God* is at the heart of the meaning of spiritual regeneration. It means that a person has come alive to God. This has come to pass for all those who receive Him and who believe in His name. He gives us the right to become "children of God—children born not of natural descent, nor of human decision or a husband's will, but born of God" (John 1:12–13). This is the first use of the exact phrase *born of God* by the author. God responds to our specific belief in Christ and brings to pass a whole new relationship and life. We now live with God's DNA, so to speak, rather than with our own or our human parents.

GOD'S SEED

Now, what about the phrase, **God's seed**? John Stott cites references from the ancient writings by Philo and some Gnostic thinkers that indicate they used the phrase *sperma Theou,* meaning *God's seed*, during the time of the apostle John. So John may again be borrowing a term already used by those outside the Church, but he gives it new meaning as he did with *logos* and *chrisma.*[4]

It makes good sense that God's seed may be related to God's Word or His truth. When Jesus tells the parable of the sower and the soils, the Matthew 13 account refers to the seed as "the message about the kingdom" (13:19). When the same story appears in Mark 4, the seed is "the word" (4:14), and in Luke 8, the interpretation reported that Jesus gave of the seed is "the word of God" (8:11). Therefore, it would seem that God's seed is His Word, the gospel of the Kingdom, or Kingdom truth. Whether speaking of human birth or of crops on the farm, the seed is a germinating force and determines the nature of what grows. Besides whatever else John is saying, he says that God meets with us in such a way that His essence becomes a part of who we are, and that has a transforming effect on us, even on our behavior.

One surprising insight is helpful. Vincent informs us that the grammatical form of born is the perfect participle, indicating one who has been born of God and remains His child—an active, ongoing relationship.[5]

CANNOT SIN

This imposing thought is now before us. In the NIV, the phrase is somewhat interpreted for us as it says, **cannot go on sinning.** Does John suggest that one born of God is no longer capable of sinning because of some eradication of that nature? Or is he suggesting that one is not permitted to sin, such as a parent would say, "You cannot cross the street by yourself"?

The following are several interpretations of this phrase:

1. Some say that it refers to only the most awful of sins, such as criminal offenses and the truly dastardly offenses against love that one may visit upon another.

2. Others argue that the Christian cannot sin because what is sin in the life of an unbeliever is not so regarded by God in the life of a believer.[6] This interpretation seems like sleight-of-hand with words.

3. A fairly popular idea is that John is describing an ideal that will only be reached in the next life, rather than a reality for this world. That would not be a Wesleyan interpretation.

4. Others, including Wesleyans, have taught that it refers to "sinless perfection." John does not teach that (1:7–9), nor does Wesley.

5. The viewpoint that fits the most accurately with John's earlier definition of sin as lawlessness or the spirit of rebellion says that what a Christian cannot do is willfully and deliberately sin.

The Greek tenses help us understand that John is not talking about one specific instance of sinning, but the present tense indicates that he is speaking about the cessation of willful, habitual sinning.

John teaches us that one born of God who continues to abide in Him loses the spirit of rebellion. Obedience to God's Word and the presence of His Spirit within us provide the power to overcome sinning. Those who are following Christ will be, with the Spirit's help, victorious over the practice of sin.

It is not that sinning is no longer *possible*; it is no longer *acceptable*. Sin cannot continue, if one is to remain in the Lord. We are still susceptible to it, but victorious over it. That is freedom. The writer gives us a strong instruction in holy living. We must get our attitude right before God, which includes a total commitment of intention and God's gift of faith. Then, as we exercise that faith and obedience, as well as love, walking in His light and loving our brothers and sisters, life takes a radical turn toward Christlikeness.

9. DOING DEFINES BEING 3:10

John now gives us a way to determine whose child we are: **Anyone who does not do what is right is not a child of God; nor is anyone who does not love his brother** (3:10).

GAP THEOLOGY

Christians need a well-developed theology of "the Gap." For some, "the Gap" is best recognized as a popular clothing store for the stylish. From a spiritual standpoint, the gap is the distance that separates the faith one claims from the reality of practicing it in life.

The gap is normally easy to spot in someone else. When we observe it, we call that person inconsistent, a hypocrite, or a phony. The wider the gap, the worse a witness for Christ one becomes. Frankly, nobody likes a phony whether regarding Christianity or something else.

If we wear the title of "Christian," then we need to become as much like Christ as possible. With the Lord's help, we close the gap between what we claim and how we live.

A SUMMARY OF JOHN'S TEACHING ON SIN AND SOLUTION

- We all have a problem with the power and practice of sin in our lives (1:8, 10).

- Sin is any kind of wrongdoing, especially willful violations of God's law and the inclination to do so (2:16; 3:4; 5:17).

- God's goal for us is total abstinence from sinning. We are born to win over sin (2:1, 13–14; 3:6–7; 4:4; 5:4–5, 11).

- God has provided, in Christ, the ultimate solution for the power and practice of sin (1:7, 9; 2:1–2, 12; 3:3–8; 4:10).

- If we are tempted and fall, Christ is our defense attorney (2:1–2).

- The unchecked practice of sinning is not compatible with the Christian life and fellowship with God (1:6; 2:1; 3:3–6; 5:18).

- Continuing the practice of unchecked sinning would indicate that a person is not truly born of God (3:9–10).

- The power of faith, righteousness, and love at work in our lives helps us eliminate sin (2:1).

- Some sins are fatal in this life and some are not (5:16–17).

- Victory over sin is not possible on our own—we need the help of the Holy Spirit and others (1:9; 2:2; 4:10–12).

ENDNOTES

1. Dallas Willard, *The Divine Conspiracy: Rediscovering Our Hidden Life in God* (San Francisco: Harper Collins Publishers, 1998), pp. 5–60.

2. *Random House College Dictionary* (New York: Random House, Inc., 1988), p. 951.

3. Marvin R. Vincent, D.D., *Word Studies in the New Testament,* vol. II (Grand Rapids: William B. Eerdmans Publishing Company, 1946), p. 348.

4. J. R. W. Stott, *The Epistles of John,* Tyndale New Testament Commentaries Series (Grand Rapids: William B. Eerdmans Publishing Company, 1964), p. 129.

5. Vincent, *Word Studies in the New Testament,* p. 349.

6. Stott, *The Epistles of John,* p. 131.

DOING WHAT LOVE DOES

1 John 3:11–18

U p to this point, John has demonstrated, instructed, testified, admonished, informed, refuted, rebuked, encouraged, and clarified that God is light. The writer now shifts the focus more directly to reflect the God who is love. The core agent of transformation is love. The objective of human transformation is love. Simply put, to love is to live and give life.

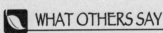

WHAT OTHERS SAY

LOVE'S EXPERIENCE

John lifts up the highest outworking of faith and obedience, which is the experience of love.

1. LOVE TO LIVE 3:11–15

This is the message you heard from the beginning (3:11), John tells his readers. It is not new, but for many it remains undiscovered. For even those who have discovered the message, it still may not be experienced. And, for those who have experienced it, there remain struggles and failures as well as the need for restoration. The message is and always has been that **we should love one another.**

Love is the reason God sent His Son. Love is why Christ died for our sins. Love is the best way to imitate Christ. Love is the central message of Christianity, and it is the core dynamic of holiness. In this passage (1 John 3:11–15) John offers several more of his characteristic contrasts: love and hatred, life and death, self-sacrifice and murder, confidence and uncertainty. The determining factor, time and time again, is love.

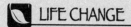

LIFE CHANGE

HOW LOVE GROWS

Philippians 1:9–11 offers amazing insight on how love grows. The apostle Paul prays that the Philippians' love will grow "more and more" (v. 9). This gives us the cue that indeed love *can* grow! And he suggests that such growth is not beyond our control; it is not some mystical experience.

Even if you are struggling with someone in a relationship and the "feelings of love" are not doing well, your love for that person can still be growing. It will grow as long as you keep figuring out what he or she needs and doing what is best for that person, in a way that glorifies God, benefits him or her, and demonstrates the results of righteousness!

Next, John cites one of history's saddest chapters, the murder of Abel by Cain. **Do not be like Cain** (3:12) seems so obvious that one wonders why he would bother to address it. He writes that **Cain . . . belonged to the evil one and murdered his brother.** The Hebrew word describing that first homicide is a term that was often used to refer to the butchering of cattle or cutting the throat of an animal about to be used as a sacrifice for sin. So Abel's murder was a sacrifice *because* of sin; Jesus Christ is a sacrifice *for* our sins.

Looking into the text of Genesis 4, we begin to understand the motives for this murder. Ironically, the murder occurred over an act of worship. God looked with favor on Abel's offering but not on Cain's, whose offering was flawed more by his attitude than by anything else.

Apparently Cain was dealing with some deep-seated resentment. God gave him the perfect opportunity to regroup, confess his pain and anguish, and find favor with God. But Cain refused the counsel and rejected the opportunity to address his own jealous and prideful nature, and he deliberately and maliciously slaughtered his own brother. He is a prototype of the worst in human nature. The direct reason John gives for the murder was that Cain's **actions were evil and his brother's were righteous.**

The reason John indicates as motive for the murder reveals that evil and goodness are poles apart and will generate animosity. The saddest part of the truth John gives us is that attitudes of anger and hatred kill the one who holds such attitudes. Therefore, we should **not be surprised . . . if the world hates** [us] (3:13). Here, again, John's use of the term *world* refers to the system of ungodliness that exists as a force to be reckoned with by the people of God.

2. WHAT LOVE IS 3:16–18

People may be willing to admit that there is a need for love in their lives and that they stand convicted about some of their attitudes. Even though they want it, they may simply not understand what love is. This is a common problem and deserves a worthy solution.

John's instruction and insight becomes rich and practical at this point. The author helps us understand **how we know what love is: Jesus Christ laid down his life for us. And we ought to lay down our lives for our brothers** (3:16).

Our model is Jesus Christ. He is our inspiration and our source for love. Jesus is God's love gift to each of us—the demonstration of the extent of God's love. We can risk loving others because we can know that we are loved by God. At the heart of the gospel is the awesome truth that Christ laid down His life, willingly, on a cross for you, me, and the whole world (2:2).

LOVING AS CHRIST LOVED THE CHURCH

John holds Christ up for us all as the model and supreme example of *agape,* or love, that is intended to motivate our lives. How has Christ loved us, and what can we learn from His love?

It Was and Is an Initiative-Taking Love. John's message is that God first loved us and gave for our sake. Love takes the initiative to make the right kind of difference. Such love seeks to understand and discern the needs of the ones we are seeking to love, and it acts in love whether or not we are receiving the same from other people.

It Was a Sacrificial Love. The love of Christ took appalling human abuse. He was willing to suffer and die for our sake, for our sins.

His Love Was a Purifying Love. The apostle Paul reminds us that Christ "gave himself up for her to make her holy" (Eph. 5:25–26). I heard a woman say that she was a better person because of the love of her husband. That's what Christlike love does; it generates improvement in the object of such love.

Christ's Love Is an Understanding Love. Once again, the apostle Paul reminds us in his writings to the Philippians that godly love seeks to gain understanding, discernment, and knowledge (Phil. 19–11). God will help us love others in a way that keeps the love growing.

His Love Is an Overlooking Love. When sinners were brought before Jesus, He did not ignore their sin, but He looked beyond it to see their need and respond appropriately. He does not ignore our sins, but offers grace to forgive and cleanse us and help us with our deepest needs.

In verse 17, John shows yet another dimension of God's love in Christ: **If anyone has material possessions and sees his brother in need but has no pity on him, how can the love of God be in him?**

Jesus gives us a glimpse into the issue of compassion and generosity when He teaches about the sheep and the goats. He says that God honors acts of kindness and that others should say of us, "I was hungry and you gave me something to eat, I was thirsty and you gave me something to drink, I was a stranger and you invited me in, I needed clothes and you clothed me, I was sick and you

GREAT THEMES

THE WESLEYAN DNA

The Wesleyan Church came out of Methodism in the 1840s. The primary issue was slavery. Certain Methodists finally refused to continue tolerating the lack of a stand in The Methodist Episcopal Church regarding slavery. In the words of one of the founders, Luther Lee, "Slavery was the first and great issue." The early Wesleyans were directly involved in the abolitionist cause. Under the church where Luther Lee was pastor, in Syracuse, New York, the tunnels still exist where runaway slaves were hidden on their way to Canada and other destinations! The early Wesleyans demonstrated a love that had compassion on their black brothers and sisters. And, not far from Syracuse, in Seneca Falls, New York, the first women's rights convention ever held in America was convened in a Wesleyan chapel in 1858!

looked after me, I was in prison and you came to visit me" (Matt. 25:35–36).

If we Christians stand indicted on any deficits of our ways, it would be that our faith has not expressed itself in the love that includes compassion and social justice. Such ministries may be the best bridges of love we can build to the world in the name of Christ. Ask God to give us eyes and hearts to see and respond to needs that exist. Evangelism would be given multitudes of open doors through such acts of kindness, compassion, and generosity.

John's words are convicting and deserve response. When we respond with such love, as that which he describes, then **we set our hearts at rest in his presence.**

9

HOW TO HAVE ETERNAL SECURITY

1 John 3:19-24

In this segment, John tells us how to possess deep and abiding confidence about our standing before God. He gives insight into the psychology of Christian faith and doubt. He offers a formula for hope, refutes key heresies, and presents a liberating view of obedience to God.

This section of verses begins and ends with the statement, **This then is how we know ...** (3:19, 24). It is the centerpiece statement on a core issue in John's epistle: Christian assurance.

1. CONFIDENCE AND SELF-CONDEMNATION 3:19-20

It is not unusual to encounter personal doubt and self-condemnation. The doubts may be part of one's spiritual struggle in relation to God or the struggle may be self-doubt. The context for verses 19–20 is captured in the words **whenever our hearts condemn us** (3:20). The writer *expects* those inner attacks to occur. Some people spend enormous amounts of their lives being consumed by feelings of self-condemnation. Such feelings adversely transform our perspective, alter our moods, and can incline us to under-respond and over-react. But God understands. God also provides help in such times of need. God's Word and Spirit offer healing and hope. We need that healing and hope, and we need to offer it to others.

John's instructions are extremely practical. He informs us **how we know that we belong to the truth, and how we set our hearts at rest**

in his presence. He guides us toward God's desires for us in the areas of confidence and comfort. He wants us to be positive about ourselves as well as at peace with God and ourselves.

The term *know* is a core term in this epistle and in the Gospel as well. The Greek word that John uses has the various meanings of being persuaded, assured, quieted, or certain. The term is used again in verse 24 in reference to Christian assurance.

We return to **how we set our hearts at rest in his presence whenever our hearts condemn us.** It is not uncommon for devout Christians to feel like they have failed in some aspect of their service to Christ. Actually, the more committed we are, the more vulnerable we are to a sense of defeat. In earlier days of our lives, maybe even before committing to Christ, our conscience was not as sensitive to some things. We may have used lies to get out of difficult situations, freely gossiped about others, or given in to various temptations. The common rationale was that "everybody does it," so we accepted it as a way of life.

But as we grow in our understanding of Scripture and the pursuit and practice of holiness, we see things differently. Right and wrong—and even "debatable" things—take on new meaning. We realize that Christ offers us a high calling, not the least of which is godly character and integrity in every area of life.

So, some of the self-condemnation we experience is because we sense that we are falling short of our high calling in Christ. In many people, the sense of self-condemnation has been preconditioned from early-life relationships. It has become normal for some to feel lowly and guilty.

Sometimes our guilt is real, and sometimes it is false. One of life's projects is to learn the difference between the two (2 Cor. 7:8–10). When we labor under false guilt or the undeserved kind, we need release and deliverance. We need a radically new perspective and healthier criteria for recognizing the way to freedom from false guilt. However, some people are insensitive to their sins and failures, so they could use a good dose of conscience. A serious desire to follow Christ and imitate Him can help bring the needed changes in sensitivity.

When the guilt is "deserved," we need to deal with the causes. Asking for forgiveness can be a cheap way to feel absolved if it is done without the intention to change. Repentance is needed. To repent means to look at the way things have been, determine that change is needed, and set about going in new directions. Notice what happens when we add John's sentence, **For God is greater than our hearts, and he knows everything** (3:20). That sounds like a good news-bad news statement. What could it mean?

On one hand, God's omniscience (knowing everything) could suggest that He would be even harder on us than

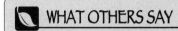

WHAT OTHERS SAY

The perfect knowledge that belongs to God, and to God alone, is not our terror, but our hope.

—William Barclay

we are on ourselves. For some, that will be true. But in the context of this portion of scripture, the meaning seems to be much more comforting.

2. GETTING WHAT YOU WANT 3:21–22

Now the author looks at the brighter side of the picture: **if our hearts do not condemn us, we have confidence before God** (3:21). Once again, John is holding forth the great experience of confidence and assurance we can have as we stand before God. That confidence comes **because we obey his commands and do what pleases him** (2:22). And, as a result of such living, we **receive from him anything we ask.** Though it sounds like God pampers His children by providing whatever we want, this is not what John is saying.

The fuller explanation is in the immediate context. When we obey God's commands and do what pleases Him, we want what God wants. His will is our will. We declare, "Thy will be done, Father." What we ask will be in the scope of what God wants for us anyway. This interpretation seems to be supported by the writer's statement in 5:14, "This is the confidence we have in approaching God: that if we ask anything according to his will, he hears us." In this verse, there is no guarantee of receiving—just of being heard.

There are many people who struggle with the notions of obedience and commands. They may have endured a childhood with overbearing parents and were forced to live under very controlling circumstances. The very mention of *obey* or *command* brings back horrible memories. Wise instruction can bring a wonderful liberty to those so enslaved. When we come to realize that God's commandments are a clear statement of His love and care for us, a light comes on. We realize that anything God expects of us or commands us to do will be for our best interest. So the very best thing we can do for ourselves is respond gladly to what God wants from us. That is spiritual liberty. The battle to obey is over. Our desire is to know and do His will.

3. ETERNAL SECURITY 3:23–24

Verses 23 and 24 are centerpiece statements in John's epistle. For the Christian, everything comes to this statement and proceeds from it. Verse 23 continues where verse 22 left off regarding obedience. John moves from the plural "commandments" to the singular, "command," in which the others are summarized. **And this is his command: to believe in the name of his Son, Jesus Christ, and to love one another as he commanded us** (3:23). Beginning with the last phrase first, John is likely referring to statements like Matt. 22:37–40, where Jesus' summary of the commandments is to love God with our whole being and to love our neighbor as ourselves.

The command has two parts: to believe and to love. In this expression of the core of Christianity, John brings together the revelations of the God who is light and love. The phrase **to believe in the name** is where we will begin. The verb form for the Greek term regarding belief is a dative form of the aorist tense.[2] This has the force of a decisive and completed act. Just do it. Decide to believe. Choose to believe who Jesus is. At other times, the author uses forms that call us to "believe in" or "believe on" Jesus.[3]

Vincent informs us that believing "in" or "on" one suggests that we rest upon, trust in practical matters, or draw upon all that is offered by the one in whom we believe.[4] So, by bringing the various uses of the terms together, John teaches us to make a decision, once and for all, to trust or believe that Jesus is the Son of God. We are to choose to believe the truth about Christ, and continue to believe in Him as a way of life. When it comes to our view of Christ, we are to turn the corner and keep on going—to make a commitment of a lifetime to trust in Him, and then take the rest of our lives to live out that trust.

The verb forms of "believe" appear over one hundred times in John's gospel. So, we know that active believing is a major teaching of this saint's writings and life. Now, merely **believ**[ing] **in the name of his Son** could sound a little "light duty." Why just the name? In John's day, to reference one's name was to include their character and nature. John states it this way for exactly that reason. Some of the heretics of John's day did not deny that the person Jesus lived. What they refuted was that His nature was divine as well as human. So, calling us to believe in the name of Jesus is to have us believe in the Jesus who is God's only Son, the sinless and sacrificial Lamb of God who has provided atonement for the sins of the world. That's why John uses "name." He calls us to believe in the historical Jesus who is the eternal Christ. As Barclay reminds us, "To believe in the name of Jesus Christ is to accept Jesus Christ for what He really is."[5] Jesus is Lord.

Next is the other half of the command: **to love one another.** There is nothing new here. We will focus on more insights on love as we approach chapter 4.

In light of our innate needs and desires, the writer tells us what God commands. And what God commands or wants from us is exactly what we crave anyway—something to believe in, as well as to love and be loved. **Love one another**, he writes. What a compelling case for the Christian way. So, to respond to what God expects from us will provide for us exactly what we need and enjoy.

John Wesley beautifully summarizes verse 23 this way: "This is the greatest and most important command that ever issued from the throne of glory. If this be neglected, no other can be kept: if this be observed, all others are easy."[6]

John then describes a faith that has intimacy. **Those who obey his commands live in him and he in them** (3:24). It would seem that he is recalling the words of Jesus, "If anyone loves me, he will obey my teaching. My Father will love him, and we will come to him and make our home with him" (John 14:23).

As with the previous verse, John seems to be gathering the various themes he has been bringing to us on fellowship (1:3, 6–7), remaining in

Christ (2:24–28), obeying His commands (2:3–8), loving, and believing in and on Christ. John is proving the case that a person can have a true, personal, and intimate relationship with our Lord.

He concludes by returning to the theme of Christian assurance as he writes, **this is how we know that he lives in us: We know it by the Spirit he gave us.** This is the first mention of the Spirit in this epistle. Also, the term is never found with "holy" in John's epistles or the Apocalypse.[7]

This verse serves as a bridge into the next chapter, which addresses the vital issue of spiritual discernment. It also places the final touch on a powerful biblical doctrine: Christian assurance. Some forms of Christian doctrine teach what is called "eternal security." That doctrine is based on the belief that God has predestined each and every person for either heaven or hell. Whichever destiny God has decreed for each of us, Calvinism teaches, is exactly what we will experience. In its most brittle interpretation, it would suggest that human beings are essentially playing out God's prewritten script. This doctrine leaves virtually no room for God-given free will.

On the other hand, the Wesleyan view is that God, in His sovereignty, has given us the capacity to respond (response-ability), which includes the capacity to evaluate and choose. It is a dangerous freedom, but an essential one if love is to be part of the divine-human relationship.

Words in 1 John that are translated *know* or *known* are found thirty-nine times. This book is straightforward with truth and totally infiltrated with the message that we can live with certainty about the truth itself and our relationship to the truth. Confidence exudes from John's writings, and he wants that same confidence to be the possession and life-long experience of every committed follower of Jesus Christ.

The Bible offers us an essentially irrefutable "formula" that affords us confidence or assurance about our standing with God and eternal life. There are four pillars of assurance. They are, as presented in 1 John:

1. **Faith** or the act of believing in Christ (3:23; 5:1, 4–5, 13).
2. **Love** that is toward God and others (3:23; 4:16–21; 5:1–2).
3. **Obedience** to God's commands, which are to believe and to love (3:21–23).
4. **Witness** of the Spirit who lives in us (3:24; 4:13).

The first letters of these four dynamic activities spell "FLOW." Together they build a platform of assurance in the life of one who takes them seriously. Rather than basing our security with God on human ideas, we should base it on the undisputable teachings of the Bible.

ENDNOTES

1. Marvin R. Vincent, D.D., *Word Studies in the New Testament,* vol. II (Grand Rapids: William B. Eerdmans Publishing Company, 1946), p. 352.

2. J. R. W. Stott, *The Epistles of John,* Tyndale New Testament Commentaries Series (Grand Rapids: William B. Eerdmans Publishing Company, 1964), p. 150.

3. David Jackman, *The Message of John's Letters,* The Bible Speaks Series (Downers Grove: InterVarsity Press, 1988), p. 107.

4. Vincent, *Word Studies in the New Testament*, p. 49.

5. Barclay, William, *The Letters of St. John and Jude* (Philadelphia: The Westminster Press, 1958), p. 104.

6. Wesley, John, *Romans–Revelation,* vol. II of *Wesley's Notes on the New Testament* (Grand Rapids: Baker Book House, 1981), p. 58.

7. Vincent, *Word Studies in the New Testament*, p. 354.

Part Three

Perfect Love and
Blessed Assurance

1 JOHN 4:1–5:21

10

DISCERNING THE SPIRITS

1 John 4:1-6

According to the prevailing worldview of John's day, the world was filled with a variety of spirits and spiritual activity. How was one to discern which spirits and teachings to follow? The writer takes the very tests he has just announced, namely belief and love, and puts them forward as the tests of spiritual truth and Christian integrity.

John picks up from the statement he made in 3:24 about the Spirit of God (the Holy Spirit) given to us. As the apostle Paul records in 1 Corinthians 12 and 14, in the Church were demonstrations of prophecy and speaking in tongues, as well as various manifestations of the Spirit. There were many reasons for confusion concerning the spirits behind the spiritual experiences, encounters, and professions.

1. TEST THE SPIRITS 4:1-2

There are so many religions and even variations of Christianity and spirituality. Everyone has his or her favorite truth, and if truth is not the issue, then they debate various ways of experiencing religion. Even various Christian groups think they have found some divine nugget of vital truth that everyone else has overlooked. We tend to respond to spirituality in one of three ways: (1) we lock in on one "brand" and defend it to the end; (2) we walk away in confusion or disgust; or (3) we join some group but spend a fair amount of time faking what we believe.

John offers a solution for those trying to sort through this myriad of teachings and truths. **Do not believe every spirit, but test the spirits to see whether they are from God** (4:1). Now, keep in mind that in John's day, "All the world believed in a universe, not only peopled, but thronged with demons and spirits and spiritual powers . . . It was a haunted world."[1]

We really cannot be sure how intense the activity might be in that "other" world of the spirits. Some of us are inclined to dismiss the activity of the world we cannot see or feel. Yet we have learned that there is a world of microscopic life that exists among us. The human eye simply cannot see many of those creatures.

The writer helps us better understand his use of the term *spirits* when he adds, **because many false prophets have gone out into the world.** He is not simply referring to the mystical world of intangible, bodiless spirits. He is specifically referring to teachers, some of whom were teachers of false religion.

A prophet was the mouthpiece of some spirit. True prophets were the mouthpieces of God, who in verse 6 is called "the Spirit of truth."[2] John tells the people to pay attention to the spirits that are embodied in the form of spiritual teachers.

There are many kinds of spirits: the human spirit, evil spirits, teaching spirits, and the Holy Spirit. And we are to test the spirits. How? John writes, **This is how you can recognize the Spirit of God:** Every spirit (teacher and teaching) **that acknowledges that Jesus Christ has come in the flesh is from God, but every spirit that does not acknowledge Jesus is not from God** (4:2–3). The first test John recommends is theological. It is the test of specific content in the teaching. John says that we can know if the teaching spirits are inspired by the Spirit of God if they say that Jesus Christ has come in the flesh. By giving this clear criterion for discernment, John addresses three important issues.

First, he addresses the Gnostic teaching that a truly divine Son of God could not possibly come in the flesh because a holy God would never inhabit sinful flesh. John destroys that argument.

Second, he points to one of the hallmarks of the Christian gospel: God is light, and He does not hide His truth from us. He shines a light on His truth and sends that truth in the human manifestation of Jesus Christ. We refer to this act as the Incarnation.

Openness and lack of secrecy is a premier uniqueness of Christianity; the gospel is not truth that emerged from some secret cave after supposedly being divinely transmitted to a human messenger who proclaimed he was "the favored one." God himself came, in human form, to reveal himself to us and become the solution for our most devastating problems. It was all predicted, verified as it happened, and substantiated in the form of compassion, truth-telling, and signs and wonders for all to see. Christ's resurrection was the culminating verification of who He was. Jesus returned from death to life and brought us from darkness to light. Christianity is the religion of light, accomplished by light, and bent on bringing light to a dark world.

Third, John helps us learn that we must choose to believe. Life is full of choices. It was back then, and it is today. Ours is a world of options and choices. The writer of Hebrews says that when it comes to believing in God, "we must believe that he exists and that he rewards those who earnestly seek him" (11:6).

This is a brilliant instruction. No person is smart enough, educated

 GREAT THEMES

RELIGION OF LIGHT

One of the overlooked, yet powerful, testimonies to the uniqueness of Christianity is its contrast with the mysterious origin of nearly every other world religion. They inevitably require followers to believe the teachings or experiences of a human leader whose revelations were "discovered" in secret or in private with no witnesses. In awesome contrast, the heart of Christian truth is that which unfolded in full view of the people of that era. God spoke through His prophets; Jesus lived among the people. God, who is light, reveals himself and His will for us. Christianity is a "religion of light" in more ways than one! For this reason, and many others, it has no equal.

enough, or has traveled the universe enough to dig up final evidence to declare that God exists. That is beyond our capacity. What the biblical writers say is that we have a wealth of "clues" and some tangible acts of God in history. Then there is the superior declaration in Jesus Christ. Since we have all of this, we can choose to believe that God exists and that He is a good God who responds to those who sincerely pursue Him. Believing is an act of the will.

2. THE SPIRIT OF THE ANTICHRIST 4:3–4

John says that **every spirit that does not acknowledge Jesus is not from God** (4:3). This is a negative restatement of what he wrote in verse 2. *Spirit* seems to be related to the teachings and purported truths that were going around, not just to some spiritual force or being.

Next he gives us a helpful view of the term *antichrist*. He indicates that the person who does not acknowledge Jesus as being from God **is the spirit of the antichrist, which you have heard is coming and even now is already in the world.** Contemporary Christianity has tended to focus on the coming of *the* Antichrist. Although such a person is spoken of in this epistle (2:18), he gives us the view of a clear and present danger: those among us who have the spirit of antichrist. These are people who either oppose Christ or those who teach that Jesus is not the Christ, the divine Son of God. That is a much broader understanding of what antichrist means.

It is important, however, that we do not demonize those who do not yet believe in Christ. Many have simply not processed or comprehended the astounding claims the Bible makes about Jesus. The writer is referring more to the overt opponents of the divine Christ rather than those simply unconnected or uncommitted. We must be liberal with grace whenever possible and carefully discern when judgment is appropriate.

The important thing is that we are in Christ **and have overcome them** [antichrists], **because the one who is in [us] is greater than the one who is in the world** (4:4). John encourages us by reminding us that the Spirit of truth is in all believers and provides protection from the spirit of falsehood and evil.

In a sense, the human spirit is a battlefield. When we are trusting in Christ, His Spirit of truth protects and guides us. There is no spiritual force in the universe that can overpower the forces of God within us. We must claim victory before the battle and pursue the victory during the battle. Then we will be able to celebrate victory after the battle has passed. We must learn to test the spirits.

3. TRUST HIS SPIRIT 4:5–6

Once again, John is offering a practical way to discern the spirits. He concludes by stating, **This is how we recognize the Spirit of truth and the spirit of falsehood** (4:6). He has already cited the theological, or content, test. Now, he reveals the worldview test.

It is human nature to align with those who share our worldview or our specific perspectives. It is similar to political alliances. We get passionate about the candidates whose viewpoints we share. And those who don't share our viewpoints are essentially "the enemy." John says that people who are open to or who share the gospel viewpoint will respect and appreciate it when they hear it. Those who oppose our message, or are resistant to it, will be inclined not to listen.

As followers of Christ, we need to mature to the point where we do not allow the opinions of those around us to negatively shape our own convictions or behaviors. Christians are called to look to Christ, not to the crowd, for their cues. Pilate is the classic example of one who failed this test, demonstrating for us how *not* to determine what we do with Jesus. He asked the mob outside his palace, "What shall I do, then, with Jesus who is called Christ?" (Matt. 27:22). The question is a powerful one. How we answer it determines our eternal destiny.

ENDNOTES

1. William Barclay, *The Letters of St. John and Jude* (Philadelphia: The Westminster Press, 1958), p. 106.

2. J. R. W. Stott, *The Epistles of John,* Tyndale New Testament Commentaries Series, (Grand Rapids: William B. Eerdmans Publishing Company, 1964), p. 153.

11

LOVE TO LIVE

1 John 4:7–16a

This portion of John's epistle offers insights into the theology and practice of the Christian life. His thoughts on the perfection of love are priceless. His proactive approach to the prevailing heresies of his day is an example to us to stay focused, strong, and positive. John demonstrates that even if we sometimes feel defensive, we don't have to act like it; we can maintain a positive and gracious attitude even in times of conflict.

John also raises some penetrating questions, including, how is it possible that a non-believer is often better at loving others than a Christian? He also presses us to come to a more accurate understanding about the nature and practice of love.

1. GOD IS LOVE 4:7–8

The dominant statement in this section is **God is love** (4:8). This is one of the companion statements by John that describes God's nature. He is spirit (John 4:24), He is light (1 John 1:5), and He is love (4:8). The Greek term that is used for love, *agape,* is a word to which the Bible gives new meaning for the benefit of the world. *Agape* is given definition in passages of the Bible like 1 Corinthians 13:1–13; Galatians 5:22–23; Ephesians 4:20–5:33; and Philippians 1:9–11. This understanding of love is infinitely higher and more life-giving than any concept of love that the poets and scholars of the world have put forward.

Again, John places before us another test of genuine Christianity. It is the love test, and it is stated in terms of a love triangle of sorts:

Let us love one another, for love comes from God (4:7). The implication here, and the clearer statement later, is that God loves us, and He is the source of love that needs to extend beyond us. Since each of us is loved by God, He exhorts us to share that love with one another. Whether or not we love others becomes a test of whether we have been **born of God.**

John has used the phrase *born of God* fairly often, and it is reminiscent of Jesus' statement that we need to be born again (John 3:3). To possess God's characteristics, or DNA, is to validate that we are His spiritual offspring. It is the love test.

 WHAT OTHERS SAY

Regarding verse 8, John Wesley said, "This little sentence brought St. John more sweetness, even in the time he was writing it, than the whole world can bring. God is often styled holy, righteous, wise; but not holiness, righteousness, or wisdom in the abstract, as he is said to be love; intimating that this is his darling, his reigning attribute, the attribute that sheds an amiable glory on all his other perfections."

John notes the fuller context of who is born of God: **Everyone who loves has been born of God and knows God. Whoever does not love does not know God.** Has it ever troubled you that some strong believers in Christ are less gracious, compassionate, loving, polite, or kind than some unbelievers? John's statement causes us to wonder if love is more or less important than faith.

Once again, John's inspiration and his wisdom combine to help us with this issue. He has just told us that it is not one or the other, but both faith and love that God expects of us (3:23). We must believe and love. Grace makes love a reality, and truth calls for belief. God is light (truth to believe), and God is love.

2. THE LOVE TRIANGLE 4:9–12

When John begins with **this is how** (4:9), we are reminded of what a wonderful coach and mentor he is to his readers. He gives us "handles" for understanding and applying his teachings. This is the mark of a good teacher and a person of experience.

John writes, **This is how God showed his love among us: He sent his one and only Son into the world that we might live through him.** What a fabulous statement! Let's explore some of its meaning.

First, the phrase **among us** reinforces the truth of God as a revealer. The gospel truth unfolded before the very eyes of the public, not in clandestine secrecy for a limited few. This is a distinctive of Christianity among world religions.

Second, this verse is a reflection of John 3:16. God did not merely talk about love, but acted out His love to us. God's love is demonstrated through Christ for our benefit.

Third, it helps us understand that God's love takes the initiative. This was mentioned earlier, but it bears repeating. That point is clarified when he says, **This is love: not that we loved God, but that he loved us and sent his Son as an atoning sacrifice for our sins** (4:10).

Fourth, it reveals that God's love takes action at great sacrifice. These verses remind us that Jesus was the one and only Son of God.

Fifth, we are informed that we can have life through Christ. As John will later tell us, there is life in the Son.

Sixth, the Son became an atoning sacrifice for our sins. He paid our debt before God. He paid the price for our eternal freedom. As Charles Wesley wrote, "Amazing love! How can it be that Thou, my God, shouldst die for me?"

Seventh, the "among us" translation gives the strong impression that community and relationships are very important in the whole understanding of the gospel. One of John's original reasons for writing was that his readers would experience fellowship (1:3). The issue of love is a work of God within us, between us, and among us. This will be more fully explored in the commentary on subsequent verses.

Verses 9 and 10 present a succinct presentation of the heart of the gospel. This is the root of Christianity: God's love expressed in Christ's incarnation, death, and resurrection, leading to our deliverance and life. John has just given us the heart of Christian theology.

He makes his case for the love triangle. In verse 11, he says that **since God so loved us, we also ought to love one another.** Whereas the gospel statement offers eternal life to the individual, this passage suggests that those who receive love and life should share the love and, therefore, the life with others.

John goes on to write **no one has ever seen God . . . if we love one another, God lives in us and his love is made complete in us.** This statement gives rise to several great insights.

The first one is that the spirit world and spiritual life are given credibility and vitality in tangible actions and relationships, namely in loving one another. A second observation is that John again mentions the completion, finishing, or perfecting of something in us. God desires that we achieve some important goals and that we arrive at desired destinations. Loving one another is one of these achievements or destinations.

Finally, we notice the author restating the love triangle concept: God's sacrificial love, which has been poured out to us, must find its way from us to the lives of others. Otherwise, there is reason to doubt that God lives in us. This is a most serious consideration. John calls for us to demonstrate what we claim to believe by the way we treat others.

Jesus taught the same principle of the relationship triangle when He taught the disciples to pray (Matt. 6:12–15). There, Jesus indicated that forgiveness is received as forgiveness is offered. He even clarified His statement by saying, "If you forgive those who sin against you, your heavenly Father will forgive you. But if you refuse to forgive others, your Father will not forgive your sins" (6:14–15, NLT).

John Stott summarizes this section beautifully when he says, "God's love, which originates in himself (7, 8), and was manifested in his Son (9, 10), is perfected in His people" (12).[1]

LIKING AND LOVING

How is it possible to love people that we don't like—let alone our enemies, as Jesus tells us to do? It helps to realize that "liking" is not simply a lesser degree of "loving." It's not a matter of degree but direction. Liking is all about our reaction to external stimuli. For example: "I did not like what he said to me." We are the receivers, as it relates to liking or disliking.

Loving has little to do with what comes *at* us and is all about what goes *from* us to others. When we do not like what others are saying or doing to us, we can control what goes from us to them. The supreme example is Christ offering forgiveness to His executioners.

3. THE CONFIDENCE IN LOVE 4:13–16

Once again, John stresses the "assurance" theme. He writes, **We know that we live in him and he in us, because he has given us of his Spirit** (4:13). The phrase **live in him and him in us** is related to Jesus' statements about abiding in Him (John 15). There is a sense in which such terms of intimacy must be at least the equivalent of the more common term *saved*. John broadens our vocabulary with his many phrases that suggest spiritual well-being—or its opposite.

The focus of this confidence is our possession of the Holy Spirit. Once again, the elements of our Christian assurance taught in this epistle are faith, or believing; love of God and our brothers and sisters; obedience to God's commandment, which is to believe and to love; and the witness of His Spirit.

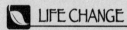

LIFE CHANGE

SALVATION—IN OTHER WORDS 5

We continue with terms and phrases John uses instead of "saved," "born again," or "Christian," even though the term "Christian" had been coined by that time (Acts 11:26):

- From God (4:4)
- Live in Him, and He in them (3:24)
- Knows God (4:6)
- Born of Him (2:29)

Jesus promised His disciples that if they loved Him and kept His commands, He would ask the Father, and He would send "another Counselor" to be with them—"the Spirit of truth" (John 14:16–17). He then said that unless He left, the Counselor would not come. He promised to send the Spirit of truth when He left (John 16:7).

The apostle Peter told the people on the day of Pentecost that they could receive the gift of the Holy Spirit if they would repent and be baptized (Acts 2:38). The apostle Paul says in Romans 8:9 that "if anyone does not have the Spirit of Christ, he does not belong to Christ." Then, we are instructed in Ephesians 5:18 that we are to continue being filled with the Holy Spirit. Again, in Romans 8:16, the Holy Spirit bears witness with our spirit that we are children of God.

It is easy to miss the magnitude of this biblical insight. When we are in Christ, we do not need to lack confidence about our standing before God. We can live with a deep sense of security. That security is within our reach and is the result of responding to God in ways that He even helps us to do. We need not fall victim to the multitudes of spirits that might inhabit the universe. There is no force of evil that can overpower Christ and get to us—if we abide in our Lord. His Spirit within is also our sufficient protection from the self-deception of our own spirit.

John then offers his personal experience as testimony **that the Father has sent his Son to be the Savior of the world** (4:14). This is a central teaching of 1 John. We are blessed to have a God of love, whose love reached out to us through the giving of His only Son, Jesus. The road to becoming the Savior of the world was the road to the cross, crucifixion, and death, followed by His resurrection.

The phrase *Savior of the world* is used by John only here and in John 4:42. In fact, it is not often used in the New Testament. In the history of other religions of that day, there were some that used the savior language about some of their gods.[2]

John writes, **If anyone acknowledges that Jesus is the Son of God, God lives in him and he in them** (4:15). The term *acknowledges* has the meaning of speaking out or admitting that something is true. He is essentially talking about our testimony or witness to our relationship with God in Christ. So the witness related to our assurance is not only the Spirit within, but is related to our spoken acknowledgement of our belief in Jesus.

Verse 16 provides more emphasis on our confidence in Christ, only this time John's focus is on our confidence in God's love for us, personally. He says, **we know and rely on the love God has for us.** We can allow this love to have amazing power in our lives. Besides the inner peace and confidence it offers, we can overcome the obstacles that exist in trying to love someone else, especially those who have injured us or those who are hard for us to like. This kind of power is what everyone in the world needs.

John repeats that **God is love. Whoever loves lives in God, and God in him.** Besides whatever else all of this means, it is clear that John has been inspired to tell us that loving others is the most significant demonstration of our faith that we could possibly express.

ENDNOTES

1. J. R. W. Stott, *The Epistles of John,* Tyndale New Testament Commentaries Series (Grand Rapids: William B. Eerdmans Publishing Company, 1964), p. 164.

2. Marvin R. Vincent, D.D., *Word Studies in the New Testament,* vol. II (Grand Rapids: William B. Eerdmans Publishing Company, 1946), p. 358.

12

PERFECTING LOVE

1 John 4:16b–21

We have in this section a mini-clinic on perfect love, which is a central teaching of Wesleyanism. Many are not aware of the purposes for which John Wesley raised up the movement of people called Methodists One of those reasons was to proclaim the doctrine of "Christian Perfection," or "Perfect Love," which Wesley called the "Grand Depositum" of Methodism.[1]

The very term *perfect* tends to create confusion in the minds of those who hear us teach it—and who also know our weaknesses. In this chapter, we will try to clarify what John the apostle and John Wesley meant when they referred to the business of perfecting love.

1. GOD IS PERFECT LOVE 4:16

For the second time, John exclaims that **God is love** (4:16). The first mention is in verse 4:8 and is a sort of test of one's "God connection or experience." John uses the phrase in similar fashion here, indicating that **whoever lives in love, lives in God and God in him.** If we are going to claim that we are people of God, John says that it is essential that we love others as a way of life.

Love would almost seem to be a test of one's salvation, yet can that be true? If we were to do a New Testament survey on this issue, the dominant conclusion would be that we are saved by God's grace and energized through our God-given capacity to believe in Christ. Wesleyans subscribe to the theology of salvation by faith. Yet we are saved to grow and serve in grace. We are called to the discipline of obedience, or "walking in the light," as John puts it. The companion of faith must soon become love in action.

We are not called to merely love, but to perfect or complete that love (4:17–18). The term, *perfect* is often misunderstood when it comes to human development in love.

Only the love of God is absolutely perfect. Compared to Him, we will only begin to be an imitation of Him in His love (see Eph. 5:1–2). As impossible as it seems, God knows we can pursue such a goal and make progress. The question is, can we arrive? Jesus seemed to say we can when He said, "Be perfect, therefore, as your heavenly Father is perfect" (Matt. 5:48).

 WHAT OTHERS SAY

If you preach doctrine only, the people will become antinomians; and if you preach experience only, they will become enthusiasts; and if you preach practice only, they will become Pharisees. But, if you preach all these and do not enforce discipline, Methodism will become like a highly cultivated garden without a fence, exposed to the ravages of the wild boar of the forest.

—Nicholson Square Church
Edinburgh, Scotland

In the meantime, let us take great comfort in the fact that God is perfect love. His love is exactly what we need. Think of the humility, yet the confidence, such love can inspire. The only hope we have of attaining any degree of such perfection is based on our pursuit of God and our surrender to His Spirit, who assists us in grace's transformation (Eph. 4:22–24).

2. PERFECT LOVE 4:17–19

One of John's dazzling phrases is **love is made complete among us so that we will have confidence on the day of judgment, because in this world we are like him** (4:17).

He prefaces the above statement with the phrase, **in this way.** Which way? The way of living in God and God in us, allowing love to be made complete among us. The Greek for *completed* in verse 17 is the same term used in verse 19 that is translated *perfected*. The same Greek word is also used in verse 12.

Remember, as we address the issue of completed or perfect love, we are not implying love that is either flawless or faultless. Here are several of John's insights on "perfect" love.

LOVE IS PERFECTED IN RELATIONSHIPS

What is love? As we have discussed in earlier chapters, love is fundamentally the intentions and actions of goodwill toward others. It is the communication to others of our affection or care for them. Also, love often includes really liking another person.

Love is not experienced in isolation. That experience takes place in relationships or community. Bible passages that relate to love focus on what love *does* or *does not do* (1 Cor. 13:4–6; Gal. 5:22–23; Phil. 1:9–11).

In all fairness to the true nature of love, there is an individual, internal side to it. As a matter of fact, that internal part is essential in expressing love. Love begins *within* us. Jesus stressed the internal aspect of almost every sin and virtue in His Sermon on the Mount, Matthew 5–7. Love's roots are the motives, attitudes, and intentions we hold regarding others in general.

Jesus brought up an issue concerning relationships when He said that we are to love God and love our neighbor as ourselves (Matt. 22:37–39).

The fact is, we cannot complete, perfect, or mature our love apart from others. John says that **love is made complete among us.** This insight is consistent with the Apostle Paul's concept of the Church as a body of believers, all needing each other for completeness (1 Cor. 12:12–27).

LOVE REPLACES ANXIETY WITH CONFIDENCE

This wonderful reality of love being made complete among the body of Christ is driven home by John's reason for doing so—having **confidence on the day of judgment**—as well as his statement, **There is no fear in love** (4:18). Many of us have struggled with fears of losing a loved one to another. Or, we have allowed jealousy to become a monster that can ruin a good relationship with someone we love. In what ways can love eliminate these fears and give us confidence?

For one thing, the immediate context of this verse is focused on our relationship with God and our assurance before Him regarding judgment. John writes, **But perfect love drives out fear, because fear has to do with punishment.** When we know that our focus is to love God and others, we take it by faith that such obedience will deliver us. We need not live in fear of God, or in anxiety about our destiny.

But what about the fear we experience in other love relationships? Cultural clichés say that we tend to "hurt the one we love" and that "it is better to have loved and lost, than to never have loved at all." And there are times when we can feel consumed with fears of losing what or whom we love. But John says, **The one who fears is not made perfect in love.**

We must remember that love includes decisions and discipline. There is wisdom and truth in recognizing that love is a choice. Love requires discipline. Doing what love does will call for effort, discipline, fortitude, and even sacrifice.

The good news is that as love grows and matures, it eliminates that which contaminates and includes that which purifies the other person and the relationship. When love refuses to be dominated by the winds of emotion or past failures, it gains the strength and health that minimizes fear and anxiety while it maximizes fulfillment and joy. As we learn to forgive, sacrifice, and dream, everyone thrives.

LOVE IS A GIFT THAT MUST BE SHARED

John informs us of the highest motive and rationale for loving others when he writes, **We love because he first loved us** (4:19). God is the original lover. Being loved is a life-giving, life-saving gift from God. God is love, and He cannot help but love us. We must embrace His love and pass it on. He will help us.

Maybe it would be better to think of it this way: rather than us loving others, we need to think of God loving others through us. As time passes, maybe we can learn to do a bit more of it as God coaches us along. Increasingly, then, **in this world we are like him** (4:17).

We are to let God's love become our motive to return love. Regarding this verse, John Wesley writes, "This is the sum of all religion, the genuine model for all Christianity. None can say more: why should anyone say less, or less intelligibly?"[2]

3. LOVE WITH INTEGRITY 4:20–21

John returns to a familiar theme: love's integrity and consistency. One of the most frequent reasons that the nonbeliever cries, "Hypocrite," is due to this issue Most likely we all know someone who talks a lot about loving God but clearly does not love others well. He claims, **"I love God," yet hates his brother** (4:20). John says that if one does not love his brother, **whom he has seen,** then he **cannot love God, whom he has not seen.** It's often easy to think we love people in another land, though we have no contact with them. The people who are present—and in our face—are sometimes the most difficult people to love. Loving others who are among us is one way that we love God. As we do that, we are in the process of perfecting our love. And we live with no fear before God, as well as with a lot less fear before everyone else.

John wraps up this amazing chapter with a command and challenge: **Whoever loves God must also love his brother** (4:21). No further commentary is needed. Just do it.

ENDNOTES

1. Steve Harper, *John Wesley's Message for Today* (Grand Rapids: Zondervan Publishing House, 1983), p. 91.

2. John Wesley, *Romans–Revelation*, vol. II of *Wesley's Notes on the New Testament* (Grand Rapids: Baker Book House, 1981), pp. 58–59.

LIFE IN THE SON

1 John 5:1–13

Moving from the discussion of loving God, chapter 5 begins with a description of one who believes in Christ Jesus. Genuine Christianity practices believing *and* loving. The theology of believing is very specific: that Jesus is the Christ, born of God (5:1) and that Jesus is the Son of God (5:5). The loving we are called to do is directed toward both God and others.

John coaches his readers toward Christian truth and practice of victorious, holy living in Christ. At the same time, he wages an apologetics campaign against the heretics of his day.

If it is possible for a book to have three key verses, this one does. They are in sequence and are in progressive order:

 KEY IDEAS

A COMPOSITE CHRISTOLOGY IN 1 JOHN

Jesus is God's Word of life (1:1).

Jesus is the eternal Christ (1:1).

Jesus is God in flesh—God with us, incarnate (1:2, 5:6–7; 5:20).

Jesus is God's Son, therefore divine (1:3; 2:23; 3:23; 4:14–15; 5:5).

Jesus' crucifixion provided atonement for our sin (1:7; 2:2; 3:5–6; 3:16; 4:10).

Jesus is the righteous, sinless one; He is holy (2:1; 3:5).

Jesus is our example (2:6).

Jesus is God's Word in flesh (1:1–2).

Christ makes all forgiveness available and meaningful (2:2).

Jesus is the Christ, the Messiah, our deliverer (2:22). *continued*

"And this is the testimony: God has given us eternal life, and this life is in his Son."

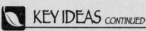

KEY IDEAS *CONTINUED*

A COMPOSITE CHRISTOLOGY IN 1 JOHN

Eternal life is in the Son (5:11–13).

We can have a relationship with Christ (1:3)

Christ is our Savior from sin and gives us life (3:5; 4:14; 5:11).

Christ destroyed the works of Satan (3:8).

Jesus is gift of love from God (4:9).

Christ is the primary object of Christian faith (3:23–24; 5:1, 10–11).

Christ is our security and assurance before God (5:13).

"He who has the Son has life; he who does not have the Son of God does not have life."

"I write these things to you who believe in the name of the Son of God, so that you may know that you have eternal life" (5:11–13).

It all begins with God giving us life, which is in His Son. After we take hold of this gift of life, we can live with certainty that we have eternal life, as we continue to believe.

TERMS OF ENDEARMENT

We can learn from the apostle John when it comes to terminology. He was not constrained to a few pet terms to describe a follower of Christ. We tend to limit ourselves to the terms *saved*, *born again*, or *Christian*. John used an impressive array of words and phrases to speak about the person who was "in Him."

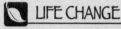

LIFE CHANGE

SALVATION—IN OTHER WORDS 6

Here are seven more of the different terms and phrases that John uses in this epistle to describe those in right relationship with God.

- Live by the truth (1:6)
- Walk in the light (1:7)
- Have come to know Him (2:3)
- He who does what is right is righteous (3:7)
- God lives in him and he in God (4:15)
- He who has the Son has life (5:12)
- Is in Him who is true (5:20)

Maybe we would do well to move beyond pet words and phrases to describe a healthy, holy, and growing follower of Jesus. It makes good sense to use terms that connect with the cultures in which we live. The term *perfect* is laden with specific connotations that can sometimes get in the way of a clear under-standing of holiness. Certainly *love* is a term that remains relevant, as long as it is properly understood. What is important is to understand the meaning of the words we use and to use words that convey accurate meaning to those we seek to reach and teach.

1. LOVING GOD 5:1–5

The author launches this section with the two requirements for one who is **born of God**, a phrase that seems to be a favorite of John's. That person **believes that Jesus is the Christ,** and shows love for God by **obey**[ing] **his commandments.**

John continues to build on his "three tests of genuine Christianity," as John Stott calls them. The author of this commentary considers them the "pillars of assurance" that allow us to live in confidence before God, rather than in appre-hension or fear. Those pillars, or tests, are obedience, love, and belief, all included in chapter 2. In chapter 3 he addresses only obedience (2:28–3:10) and love (3:11–18). Then chapter 4 places focus on belief (4:1–6) and love (4:7–12). Now, in chapter 5 we are reminded of all three again.[1]

LOVE

The comfort of certainty and security emerges as he writes, **This is how we know that we love the children of God** (5:2). One of the curious things about John's emphasis on love is that the love seems to be directed to the brothers and sisters of the faith. For example, in verses 2:9–11 he writes in terms of loving or hating one's brothers and sisters. In 3:10 he says that anyone who does not love his brothers and sisters is not a child of God. He then gives the example of Cain, who killed his brother, Abel, out of envy and anger. Then, in 3:15, he indicates that anyone who hates his brother or sister is a murderer and does not have eternal life in him.

In chapter 4, the language is a bit more general, in that he calls his readers "dear friends" and admonishes them to love one another. However, by the end of that chapter in verses 4:19–21, he returns to the very specific language of loving or hating one's brothers and sisters. Now, in chapter 5, the context is once again the family of God.

Is John suggesting, by omission, that it is less important to love someone who has not been born of God? Is he recommending a preferential love? There are several possible responses to this problematic question:

He May See All of Humanity as the Family of God. We know that in his gospel, John was reaching to a far wider audience than were Matthew, Mark, and Luke. John's gospel was written to make a case for Christ as the Son of God, Savior of the world. The first sentences of this epistle seem to be to a wide audience that he hopes to include in the fellowship of believers (1:3).

He May Be Saying that the Priority Is on Loving Other Believers. In his gospel, John makes a strong case for our Christian witness. He quotes Jesus saying that Christian unity is a witness to the world (John 17:23). When the world observes Christians in conflict with each other, it is a horrible witness for Christ and Christianity.

John Must Have in Mind the Inclusive Love of Christ Whenever He Speaks about Love. John quotes Jesus saying that God loved the world so much that He gave His Son (John 3:16). John would not have forgotten Jesus' teachings about loving one's enemies (Matt. 5:44).

John Is Saying that Love Must Begin "at Home." Home refers to our birth family and our "born again" family. If we are not able to love those we interact with on a regular basis or those of our own bloodline, how can we genuinely love those outside of that inner circle?

The above rationale is implied when John says that **everyone who loves the father loves his child as well** (5:2). In real life, that may not always be the case, but John is presenting a logical case here. It make sense that if we love another person who is a father, we would naturally be inclined to love that person's children as well. That, he says, is how it should be.

OBEDIENCE

He continues that same line of thought when he says, **This is how we know that we love the children of God: by loving God and carrying out his commands** (5:2). In our human existence, we disconnect love and obedience. A child will sometimes be obedient out of fear. There is also obedience that is motivated by a desire to please. Plenty of obedience in this life is motivated by reasons other than love.

Obeying God's commands is the best thing we can do for ourselves and for those around us because it leads to healthy living and life lived to the fullest. Obeying Him shows our love for Him. **This is love for God: to obey his commands. And his commands are not burdensome.** What He expects may be difficult and challenging, but God's commands build us up and energize us. Believe and love; those are His commands. Faith gives energy, quality, and hope to our lives and all those we touch. Then, there is love. When it is done well, love is transforming.

John then tells us how enormous is the power of faith when he writes, **This is the victory that has overcome the world, even our faith** (5:4). We are born to be winners.

There are two rare finds in that phrase. First, is the term *victory*. That term is used only here in the New Testament.[2] It is commonly assumed that this is a reference to one's faith in Christ, which provides salvation from sin and gives us power to live above the temptations of the world, referenced in 1 John 2. We overcome the world by being brought into union with Christ. John remembers Jesus declaring that He had overcome the world (John 16:33).

It is difficult to know exactly what is involved in overcoming the world, but it is clear what it is that brings such victory: our faith. God, through Christ, makes us more than conquerors. (Rom. 8:37–39). **Who is it that overcomes the world: Only he who believes that Jesus is the Son of God** (5:5).

2. THE TRIPLE TESTIMONY 5:6–10

John is once again responding to the teachings of the Gnostics when he writes, **This is the one who came by water and blood—Jesus Christ** (5:6). The terms *water* and *blood* are the objects of discussion and debate regarding their specific meaning. Barclay indicates that this is one of the most perplexing passages not only in 1 John, but in all of the New Testament.[3]

The reference to Jesus coming by water could refer to His human birth, His baptism, or both. The Gnostic teachers of that day taught that an incarnation of God was impossible. Also, they taught that Jesus was only human until His baptism. At His baptism the divine Spirit came upon Him, but departed before the Crucifixion..

The impact of that teaching would strip the gospel of God's direct involvement in the Incarnation, the Crucifixion, and even the Resurrection. What would be left? Not much.

The reference to water witnesses to the fact that Jesus, the Son of God, took on human form and identified with the human condition. His blood represents life sacrificed for sin—the atoning death.[4]

John continues by adding the third witness to the messiahship of Christ: **And it is the Spirit who testifies, because the Spirit is the truth.**

 KEY IDEAS

THE WITNESS OF THE HOLY SPIRIT TO CHRIST

The Scriptures give us a fascinating glimpse into the witness of the Spirit to Christ:

1. *The Spirit gave witness at Jesus' baptism.* There was a voice from heaven, affirming the identity of Jesus as the Son of God (Matt. 3:16–17; Mark 1:9–11; Luke 3:21–22; John 1:32–34).

2. *The Spirit baptizes men and women.* John the Baptist baptized with water, but Jesus came to baptize people with the Spirit (Matt. 3:11; Mark 1:8; Luke 3:16; Acts 1:5).

3. *The Spirit gave witness at Pentecost.* The birth of the Christian movement, or Church, was inaugurated and empowered by the Holy Spirit (Acts 2:4).

4. *The Spirit bears witness with our human spirit that we are children of God.* The Scriptures are clear that God's Spirit energizes the work of Christ in our lives and responds to our faith as God's force for holiness within us (Rom. 8:16).

John seems to summarize his comments by saying that **there are three that testify: the Spirit, the water and the blood; and the three are in agreement** (5:8). There were some words added in the KJV that say, "There are three that bear record in heaven, the Father, the Word, and the Holy Ghost: and these three are one." These words do not appear in any of the credible manuscripts found before the sixteenth century. However, we do not need such a statement to support the teaching of the Trinity. We have plenty of other biblical indicators.

It is usually difficult to get three witnesses of the same event to agree to anything. Thankfully, in this case, they do. They all give witness to the real humanity and the divinity of Christ. And they speak of His atoning death for us. John is adamant about preserving and perpetuating the purity and power of the gospel truth. Each generation of Christ's followers must discern how to do the very same thing.

Humans may give testimony to a fact, but human testimony cannot compare with God's testimony. **We accept man's testimony, but God's testimony is greater because it is the testimony of God . . . about his Son** (5:9). This phrase states the obvious: it is nice to hear human testimony about Christ and His divine mission, but God's testimony is the one we need.

This is true in our own lives. People give us advice, encouragement, criticism, and all manner of "testimony" about life and about us. Yet our ultimate assurance comes from the forms of testimony that directly come from God. Believing, loving, and obeying are the actions we can take. The direct witness of His Spirit has no substitute. We must learn to discern the intimate voice of the Spirit as witness to our hearts, convicting and confirming us. John recalls some of Jesus' great teaching on the work of the Spirit in our lives (John 16:5–15).

The contrast is stark. John says that one who **believes in the Son of God has this testimony in his heart. Anyone who does not believe God has made him out to be a liar, because he has not believed the testimony God has given about his Son** (5:10). This is a strong statement. It seems as if John is giving us a warning not to deny the inner voice of God when He speaks into our lives.

John states the danger of "making God a liar" in 1:10 as it relates to denying that we have ever sinned and that sin is not an issue for us. In the light God gives us, such denials are not merely mistakes; they are sins. It is wrong and dangerous to disregard the light and truth God brings to us in a wide variety of ways.

John views the existence of the witnesses as extremely important. In his gospel, we find a variety of witnesses confirming Jesus as the Christ: John the Baptist (John 1:15, 32–34; 5:33); Jesus' deeds (John 5:36); the Scriptures (John 5:39); God the Father (John 5:30–32, 37; 8:10); and the

Spirit (John 15:26). John is convinced that the evidence is there for anyone open to receiving it.

3. THE SON OF LIFE 5:11–13

John is now beginning to summarize and sharpen the focus of his message: **And this is the testimony** (5:11). Here it is. All of his life and teaching, all of the sacrifice and the suffering, all of the inspiration and perspiration are about this: **God has given us eternal life, and this life is in his Son.** In a sense, verses 11–13 really conclude this epistle. They are the top of the grand staircase that John has helped us to ascend. After this astonishing paragraph, his comments seem like a postscript.

That passage is the heart of the gospel. There be may be no words of truth more magnificent in the Bible. They are the near equivalent of John 3:16 in terms of importance and centrality. They teach us several lessons.

ETERNAL LIFE IS A GIFT FROM GOD

Eternal life is not available for purchase nor can it be earned. It is the gift of God to those who believe. What is eternal life? It has been a grand fascination of humankind in virtually every culture over the centuries. It is often thought of in terms of its duration or in terms of "forever." Endless time, as we know time, is not the whole concern of eternal life.

It certainly must be more than simply existing forever. Such an existence, for some, would be considered a curse, not a gift.[5] Since time and space are empty vessels, the real question is, what might eternal life be filled with to make it so desirable?

For one thing, when we think of eternity and heaven, we connect them with God. It would seem that God and His nature help describe eternal life. Think of every limitation and weakness of this life, and then think of the pure possibilities if all limitations vanished. Consider the goodness of achieving a great goal, the love of family, and the joy of being with loved ones. What are the pure imaginations of your mind as you consider the vast universe? What are the lingering mysteries? What about final justice and the injustice suffered here on earth? How will God resolve that in eternity?

After all of the wild imaginations of your mind have been exhausted, consider that you have not even scratched the surface of what awaits those who trust Christ for such life. And the good news is that we do not have to wait for it all to begin. The verb tenses in verse 11 indicate that God has already given us eternal life, and this life is in His Son. Eternal life begins with Jesus and is not interrupted by death. God will take care of us even through death.

THIS ETERNAL LIFE IS IN HIS SON, JESUS CHRIST

One of the good news/bad news messages the Bible presents is that eternal life is found only in Christ. He is the only way to life that God has provided. John writes, **He who has the Son has life; he who does not have the Son of God does not have life** (5:12).

The good news is, of course, that there is eternal life in Christ, so if we are in Christ, we have that life. The bad news is the declaration that the one who does not have Christ does not have life. John does not suggest that if one misses the gift of life, that the alternative is automatically hell. He simply does not address that issue, so we need to go to other scriptures for teachings on the ultimate residence of those who do not receive the gift of eternal life.

What we are sure of is that nobody will receive eternal life apart from the provisions Christ has made for us all. His atonement was big enough and good enough to cover "the sins of the whole world" (2:2). We are called to respond by faith to His sufficient atonement (1 John 3:23) and then to be His witnesses.

Because it expresses John's grand purpose for writing this letter, verse 13 is the third of three key verses: **I write these things to you who believe in the name of the Son of God, so that you may know that you have eternal life** (5:13).

John wants no one to be left behind. He wants every reader to have Christ and have eternal life. And He wants us to live with total confidence about the security of that relationship and the certainty of where we stand "in the Lord."

This is the way to live.

ENDNOTES

1. J. R. W. Stott, *The Epistles of John,* Tyndale New Testament Commentaries Series (Grand Rapids: William B. Eerdmans Publishing Company, 1964), p. 171.

2. Marvin R. Vincent, D.D., *Word Studies in the New Testament,* vol. II (Grand Rapids: William B. Eerdmans Publishing Company, 1946), p. 127.

3. William Barclay, *The Letters of St. John and Jude* (Philadelphia: The Westminster Press, 1958), p. 127.

4. R. Duane Thompson, *Commentary on Jude*, vol. VI of *The Wesleyan Bible Commentary* (Grand Rapids: William B. Eerdmans Publishing Company, 1966), p. 358.

5. Barclay, *The Letters of St. John and Jude,* p. 134.

14

FINAL ASSURANCE

1 John 5:14-21

The first few comments of this passage sound like an overstatement concerning boldness when making requests of God. Then follows a series of comments about sin and its consequences. He seems to say that certain sins are punished with greater severity than others. In addition to those confusing comments, John seems to say that there is a point at which we might as well give up on praying for some people. He concludes with his familiar and wonderful "assurance and certainty" theme. Then, he gives one final warning.

1. A TEST OF WILLS 5:14-15

John describes for us **the confidence we have in approaching God** (5:14). His often repeated theme of assurance and confidence is about to be taken to a new level. He speaks not merely about the final judgment in terms of where and when God will finalize all decisions about personal destinies; instead, he speaks about the courage to face God, here and now. John says that if **we ask anything according to his will, he hears us.** And then he goes on to make a very interesting statement: **And if we know that he hears us—whatever we ask—we know that we have what we asked of him** (5:15). What a declaration!

This could be interpreted as John saying that God is our heavenly servant, which could lead some to abuse both God and prayer. There are two key phrases that help us understand the meaning of this verse. The first phrase is *he hears us.* John says that we can have confidence that we will receive whatever we ask, if we are sure that God hears us. The confidence that He hears

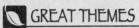

GREAT THEMES

CHRISTIAN ASSURANCE

TEACHING OF 1 JOHN

Pillar One: Faith—"I write these things to you who believe in the name of the Son of God so that you may know that you have eternal life" (1 John 5:13).

A. Specific Faith (4:9–10; John 3:16)

B. Spoken Faith (4:15)

C. Sustained Faith (5:1, 10–13).

Pillar Two: Love—"And so we know and rely on the love God has for us. God is love. Whoever lives in love lives in God, and God in him. In this way, love is made complete among us so that we will have confidence on the day of judgment, because in this world we are like him" (1 John 4:16–17).

A. Sacrificial Love (3:16)

B. Compassionate Love (3:17)

C. Love in Action (3:18)

Pillar Three: Obedience—"We know that we have come to know him if we obey his commands" (1 John 2:3).

A. The Command (3:23)

B. The Faith in Christ (3:23)

C. Love One Another (3:24)

Pillar Four: Witness (of the spirits)—". . . And it is the Spirit who testifies, because the Spirit is the truth" (1 John 5:6).

A. The Human Spirit (3:21)

B. The Holy Spirit (3:24; Rom. 8:16)

us is in the phrase *according to his will*. This provides a bright light of understanding about the prayer that God answers.

Sometimes, our relationship with the Lord becomes a test of the wills: His and ours. One of the greatest decisions we can ever make is a deep-level, once-and-for-all commitment to agree to whatever we sense is God's will for us. Some refer to this as the "lordship" commitment. Some refer to this as the consecration of one who seeks holiness. It is as if God gives us a blank sheet of paper and asks us to sign our name to it, agreeing in advance to whatever He wants to fill in.

What God wants is what we want. We have now settled the question. The test of wills has been resolved. When we pray, what we pray for is God's will to be done "on earth as it is in heaven" (Matt. 6:10).

2. TO INTERCEDE OR NOT? 5:16–17

There are eye-popping phrases in this section: **a sin that does not lead to death; a sin that leads to death;** and **I am not saying that he should pray about that** (5:16). For one thing, it seems foreign to read that sins are simply divided into two categories; however, who would put lying to save a life in the same category as murder? It is easy to drift toward categorizing sins, but it is truly difficult to think of God assigning the exact same degree of wrongness to them all. It would have been helpful if John would have distinguished for us the nature of sins that lead to death and those that do not.

Verse 16 opens with the admonition to pray, or intercede, for a

 **LIFE CHANGE**

DO YOU WANT WHAT GOD WANTS?

The will of God has been a subject of mixed emotions for many followers of Christ. For one thing, we tend to think that whatever we want, God will not, and we fear that whatever God wants will be the very thing we don't. However, a study of 1 John and other scriptures will confirm that the following is more true to the essence of God's will for our lives:

1. God's will is liberating and positive (2:17; 3:23).

2. God's will may take us out of our comfort zones (loving people who are hard to like, Matt. 5:43–44).

3. God's will is more relational than directional (faith in Christ; loving others, Matt. 22:37–39).

4. God's will is more about character than career (3:2–3).

5. God's will for our lives, in one word: Jesus! (3:23).

believer who commits a non-lethal sin. This assumes that the phrase *he should pray* refers to the non-sinning brother and the statement "give him life" refers to the sinning believer. The Greek sentence structure does actually affirm this interpretation.

What is very interesting is that the phrase, *pray and God*, is not in the Greek text. This could raise the question of whether or not the asking is a prayer or a direct confrontation with the brother, much like Galatians 6:1, which says, "Dear brothers and sisters, if another Christian is overcome by some sin, you who are godly should gently and humbly help that person back onto the right path. And be careful not to fall into the same temptation yourself" (NLT). John's text does read that if anyone **sees his brother**, as the Greek text in verse 16 says, "sinning a sin," then the context commands he should appeal to God for such a believer.

The following is the essence of Barclay's excellent comments on the issue of the two categories of sin:

- The sin unto death is not a deadly sin, like murder; it is a sin that, if continued, is leading the person toward death.

- This sin is being committed by a person who is knowingly and intentionally defying judgment for his or her sin, or unconcerned about such judgment.

- This is the sin of a person who believes this sin to be as good as it is bad, and has so rationalized the sin that he or she has no intention of repenting; therefore, no forgiveness; therefore, death.[1]

One view is that a sin that leads to death refers to physical death. This interpretation could be supported by the comment that a brother should pray for one whose sin did not lead to death, since praying for a living sinner is intercession with hope. The author does not encourage prayer for the person who has committed a sin that led to his death. Probably it is too late for the prayer to have redemptive effect.

Another approach to this passage is that John is speaking less about a particular type of sin and more about a deadly trajectory of sin that will lead to death—physical and/or spiritual. This interpretation gives us reason to be warned about concrete actions in our lives that are taking us on a course of destruction.

A third consideration is that he is referring to the unpardonable sin of blasphemy against the Holy Spirit—a sustained resistance to conviction and repentance. That is a deadly pathway. It is difficult to tell what was on John's mind when he penned these words. We can be sure, however, that the consistent and repeated teaching of Scripture is that God responds to the contrite heart. When a person repents of sin, there is forgiveness. That is the good news.

The final point of confusion is over the statement, **I am not saying that he should pray about that.** Once again, the usual Greek term for prayer does not appear in the Greek text. A Greek term that is better translated *inquire* appears in the text. John is challenging us to pray for those whom we know are sinning. However, he would also encourage us to challenge the person to be praying and inquiring of God for forgiveness and life (1:9–10). Repentance and confession of any sin is always the most certain way to life.

3. KNOWING HIM 5:18–21

It seems that verse 18 is closely related to several of the previous verses since the sin theme continues. However, John shifts to the bright subject of assurance once again.

We are reminded that **anyone born of God does not continue to sin** (5:18). John strongly made that case in 3:9. When God gives us new life, that life does not tolerate a pattern or lifestyle of sin or lawlessness (3:4).

The next statement, however, seems strange: **the one who was born of God keeps him safe, and the evil one cannot harm him.** Of whom does he speak when he mentions the one who *was* born of God? In every other such reference, he speaks of the one who *is* (present tense) born of God. Vincent believes that this likely refers to Christ, the only begotten of God, taking us back to where John began: **That which was from the beginning . . . the Word of life** (1:1).

Next, John quickly contrasts the condition of the children of God with that of the rest of the world, which **is under the control of the evil one** (5:19). Our hope and our help is in the Lord. He **has come and has given us understanding, so that we may know him who is true.**

The simple phrase, *that we may know him*, is the *magnum opus* of John's final appeal. It is parallel to the apostle Paul's testimony near his life's end, "I want to know Christ, and the power of his resurrection" (Phil. 3:10). This phrase, *so that we may know him*, is the grand challenge that John's apostolic brother Peter also gave: "But grow in the grace and knowledge of our Lord and Savior Jesus Christ" (2 Pet. 3:18).

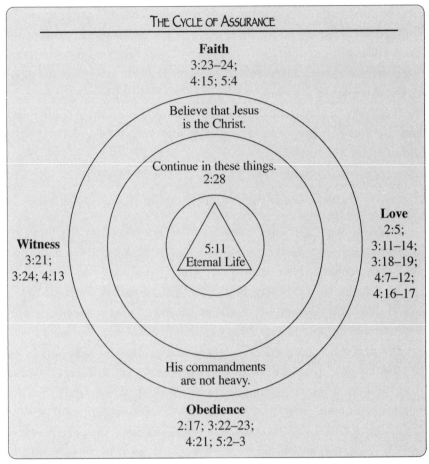

THE CYCLE OF ASSURANCE

Faith
3:23–24;
4:15; 5:4

Believe that Jesus
is the Christ.

Continue in these things.
2:28

5:11
Eternal Life

Witness
3:21;
3:24; 4:13

Love
2:5;
3:11–14;
3:18–19;
4:7–12;
4:16–17

His commandments
are not heavy.

Obedience
2:17; 3:22–23;
4:21; 5:2–3

John writes, **He is the true God and eternal life** (5:20). Then, with the following concluding statement, he warns them not to ruin such an opportunity and privilege by messing around with lesser gods: **Dear children, keep yourselves from idols** (5:21).

There it is. We have been given a magnificent set of instructions, warnings, and assurances in just a few pages of sacred Scripture. When people near life's end, their words often become fewer and to the point. Such an approach describes 1 John. May we also learn to choose our words carefully, and speak the truth in love, with passion, as our John has done for us.

ENDNOTES

1. William Barclay, *The Letters of St. John and Jude* (Philadelphia: The Westminster Press, 1958), pp. 142–143.

2 AND 3 JOHN

INTRODUCTION TO
2 AND 3 JOHN

We are about to study the two briefest books in the New Testament. Both begin with a personal greeting and gesture of goodwill, continue with the main message, and conclude with a collective greeting from others, a stated desire to see one another face-to-face, and final words.

Second John is a bit more doctrinal in its orientation, but both of these letters eventually address the same practical issue and give advice based on the situation being addressed.

AUTHORSHIP

Both of these letters begin with the same opening: **The elder.** It seems to be the general consensus of scholars that one author wrote both letters. But who was the elder? The three most commonly suggested candidates are the apostle John, a disciple of the apostle John, and a respected presbyter of the early Church.

Beginning with the last suggestion first: there is virtually no support for a "mystery author" who was not directly connected with the apostolic elders. There were those who were disciples of the apostles, and one of them living in Ephesus was reputedly named John. It is apparent that the author of the second and the third letters of "John" made the assumption that his recipient(s) knew him; otherwise, he was wasting his authoritative advice. This would indicate that the author was probably a known and trusted apostle or the disciple of one.

The Greek word translated *elder* is *presbyteros*. That term meant an old man, but it also came to be used to refer to an official title of respect and leadership in the Church. Various scholars site some of the early Church fathers and writers who claim that there were two elderly, respected disciples of Christ named John who lived and died in Ephesus.[1] Barclay takes the position that it was not John the apostle who wrote the two letters, but a different John—the elder.[2] This elder could have been a respected leader whose mentor was the apostle John.

The debate over which "old" John wrote the second and third epistles is not a recent debate. Gerald Bray reminds us that it was a matter of controversy in the early Church.[3]

The Muratorian Canon contained a fragmentary list of New Testament books accepted as biblical. The canon, known in Rome since A.D. 200, includes the first two epistles, but not the third. Church fathers Irenaeus, Eusebius, Jerome, and Papias subscribed to the theory of two different writers: one for 1 John and another for the other two letters.[4] C. H. Dodd believes that all three epistles were written by John the presbyter, not John the apostle.[5]

There is no convincing evidence that John the elder and John the apostle were two different men. Scholars do seem to agree that whoever wrote 2 John also wrote 3 John. This agreement of one author for the two epistles brings us to an interesting observation.

The theological concerns of the second letter mirror several thoughts expressed in the first epistle. This is true with the command to love one another not being a new command (v. 5), the importance of acknowledging Jesus as the Christ who has come in the flesh (v. 7), watching out for the deceivers and the antichrist (v. 7), and the concept of "walking in" something. In 1 John, it is light (1:7); in 2 John it is walking in truth, love, and obedience (v. 4, 6).

There is significant reason and evidence to attach the two shorter letters to the author of 1 John. And that writer most likely was the aged apostle John, original disciple of Jesus Christ.

RECIPIENTS

Second John is directed to **the chosen lady and her children** (v. 1). Is this referring to an individual and her children, or to a congregation? Here is a summary of possibilities:

First, the letter may have been written to a woman, possibly named Electa. Second is the theory that the letter was written to a specific congregation or Christian society. Third, the letter may have been addressed to the Church in general.

Third John is directed to **my dear friend Gaius** (v. 1). Gaius was a very common name in that day. Since that was the case, and since the threat of persecution was increasing, it is possible that both the second and third letters used code names to prevent enemies of the faith from actually identifying any one person connected with the letters.

Aside from the above theory, every indication is that 3 John was directed to a person known by the author. Though the letter may have been personal,

 WHAT OTHERS SAY

FIRST-CENTURY LETTER

Irenaeus to Apolinarius his brother, my greetings. Continually I pray that you may be in health, even as I myself am in health. I wish you to know that I arrived at land on the sixth of the month Epeiph, and I finished unloading my ship on the eighteenth of the same month, and went up to Rome on the twenty-fifth of the same month, and the place welcomed us, as God willed. Daily we are waiting for our discharge, so that up till today no one of us in the corn service has been allowed to go. I greet your wife much, and Serenus, and all who love you, by name. Goodbye.

its concerns and principles were transferable and applicable to a more general audience.

Barclay reminds us that in the New Testament there are three references to a person or persons named Gaius (Acts 19:29; 20:4; Rom. 16:23).[6] The Gaius referred to by John is not necessarily any of the above mentioned. However, the Gaius that is referred to by John was apparently a man with an open mind, an open heart, and an open door to his house.

THE OCCASION FOR WRITING

It appears that in the early years of the Church, there came to be a number of itinerate teachers. They were traveling teachers, preachers, and philosophers, and some were even miracle workers. Since the beginning of Jesus' ministry, there were several kinds of traveling ministries.

First, there were the original apostles of Jesus. They were called by Christ to follow Him. There have been none like them since those first days.

Next, there were the prophets. The writings of *The Didache* tell us something about them.[7] They were a special order of servants who traveled to prophesy in the in the name of the Lord. They went where the Spirit led them and said what God inspired them to say. As time went along, the numbers of wandering preachers grew, as well as the scope of their message.

Third, there were the elders. Their role was to remain in a town or community, usually to work with a specific congregation of believers. They were originally appointed by ones like the apostle Paul to give guidance and pastoral care to the local communities of Christians.

In the case of the letter to the elect lady, there appeared to be problems that had developed with some of the wandering preachers or prophets. They were becoming deceivers (2 John 7) in that they would not **acknowledge Jesus Christ as coming in the flesh.** The first letter of John describes the same kind of problem (2:22).

The traveling evangelists or prophets typically relied on those to whom they spoke to host them and care for their needs while on the road. This, in itself, led to all kinds of abuses. As a result, the hospitality they offered the prophets became an entry for heresy within the Church.

 WHAT OTHERS SAY

REGARDING VISITORS

Let everyone that cometh in the name of the Lord be received, and then, when ye have proved him, ye shall know, for ye shall have understanding to distinguish between the right hand and the left. If he that cometh is a passer-by, succor him as far as ye can; but he shall not stay with you longer than two or three days, unless there be necessity. But, if he be minded to settle among you, and be a craftsman, let him work and eat. But, if he hath no trade, according to your understanding, provide that he shall not live idle among you, being a Christian. But, if he will not do this, he is a Christmonger: of such men beware.

—*The Didache*

If the original recipients of this second letter were a lady with children, then John may have offered his counsel in order to protect her from unscrupulous wanderers posing as prophets of God. More specifically, if there were those who did not teach the truth as the people had been taught about Christ, John says that their homes should not be open to such persons.

In the third letter, the problem is similar yet

different. Again, the issue is hospitality, but the advice John gives is the opposite of that which he gives in 2 John. This letter addresses the problem of a self-centered church boss who wants to reject the "good guys." Whereas John identifies for the elect lady those who are not to be trusted and taken in, he identifies those whom the church pillar is rejecting as men of God who should be graciously received.

Both of these letters offer sound teaching that relates to issues in our day.

ENDNOTES

1. J. R. W. Stott, *The Epistles of John,* Tyndale New Testament Commentaries Series (Grand Rapids: William B. Eerdmans Publishing Company, 1964), p. 198.

2. William Barclay, *The Letters of St. John and Jude* (Philadelphia: The Westminster Press, 1958), p. 150.

3. Gerald Bray, ed. *Ancient Christian Commentary on Scripture*, vol. XI (Downers Grove: InterVarsity Press, 2000), p. 231.

4. David Jackman, *The Message of John's Letters,* The Bible Speaks Series (Downers Grove: InterVarsity Press, 1988), pp. 174–175.

5. Stott, *The Epistles of John,* p. 37.

6. Barclay, *The Letters of St. John and Jude,* p. 172.

7. Ibid., p. 155.

OUTLINE OF 2 JOHN

I. Truth: The Best Foundation for Any Relationship (1–3)

II. The Christian Walk: Truth, Love, and Obedience (4–6)

III. Virtues that Safeguard Victory (7–11)

IV. Face-to-Face (12–13)

THE CHRISTIAN WALK

2 John 1–13

Who indeed is **the chosen lady and her children** (v. 1)? As was mentioned in the introduction, there is debate over the recipients of John's second letter. Is this a woman and her children, or is it a church? Warren Wiersbe has an interesting view of who the lady and her children are. He acknowledges that by John's use of the plural in several parts of the letter, it seems that he is speaking to a group (vv. 6, 8, 10, 12). And yet, in several verses, he speaks to an individual (vv. 1, 4–5, 13). Possibly, John is writing to a house church that meets at the home of the "chosen lady," and he has both the family and the congregation in mind.[1]

Vincent says that the phrase **whom I love in the truth** actually has the impact of truly or really.[2] If that is the case, it does not have the same meaning as the forms of *truth* used in verse 2. Does *truth* in verse 1 refer to a body of true information or doctrine? Does it refer to Christ, the Truth sent from God? In 1 John 5:6, John says that the Holy Spirit is the truth. In his gospel, John quotes Jesus as saying that He is "the way, the truth, and the life" (John 14:6), and John says that Jesus came into the world, full of grace and truth (John 1:14). As a matter of fact, John speaks about truth as much as any other contributing author of Scripture. When he speaks of "truth," it may be the truth about God, the truth from God, or the truth incarnate — but **because of the truth**, we have life and liberty, and since it **lives in us and will be with us forever** (v. 2), we have security regarding eternity.

John warms our hearts and excites our minds as he says, **Grace, mercy and peace from God the Father and from Jesus Christ, the Father's Son, will be with us in truth and love** (v. 3). Grace is the

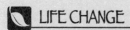

LIFE CHANGE

TRUTH IN LOVE

John is strong in his emphasis on truth and love, which are the core of Christian living and the heart of holiness. John said in his gospel that Jesus came "full of grace and truth" (John 1:14). Truth brings liberty. People who fancy themselves as big on truth can be very lean on grace or on the softer side of love. Truth can be used as a weapon in a relationship—and often is. The apostle Paul helps us by using truth and love in just the right mixture when he writes that we should speak the truth *in love* (Eph. 4:15). Speaking the truth in love helps us to monitor *what* we say, *when* we say it, *how* it is said, and *why* we say it. Handle the strength of truth with the grace of love.

unearned and undeserved favor of God, mercy is the release from deserved punishment, and peace is what God gives those who trust in Him. John affirms the Lord's identity as **Jesus Christ, the Father's Son.** This is not only building the Christ-centered nature of Christian theology but also taking a swat at the heresies that minimized the divinity of Jesus.

Despite whatever else we might think comes from the hand of God, John delivers the point that we can depend on grace, mercy, and peace from Him.

1. TRUTH: THE BEST FOUNDATION FOR ANY RELATIONSHIP 1–3

The dominate term in the first three verses of 2 John is *truth*. The truth is apparently the gospel truth about Jesus Christ (1 John 3:23–24). The beauty of John's letter is that he does not simply hang the truth in mid-air as an object to gaze upon, but he describes three actions that we should take in regard to the truth.

LOVE IN THE TRUTH

John writes, **whom I love in the truth,** referring to the **chosen lady and her children**. Some say that truth is used as an adverb, meaning "truly love." That could well be true. John cites Jesus making similar statement about being sanctified in the truth (John 17:17).

There are several related meanings that this phrase offers. It means that the love for the "chosen lady and her children" is in the context of the shared gospel of Christ, which creates a bond of mutual care, interaction, affection, and protection—all of which are acts of love. Christians share common bonds of appreciation and mutual affection in Christ in the truth.

A second insight and healthy practice is viewing truth and love as having an inseparable relationship. The apostle Paul reminds us that we "must put off falsehood and speak truthfully to [our] neighbor, for we are all members of one body" (Eph. 4:25). Deception is not consistent with love. He also cautions us to use the truth "in love" (Eph. 4:15). The truth can become a weapon if not used for the right reasons. Even the truth of the gospel can be abused if not expressed in love.

LEARN THE TRUTH

John indicates that it is not only he who loves those to whom he is writing, **but also all who know the truth**. Know is in the Greek perfect tense and has the effect of "to learn to know."[3] Gathering truth into our lives is not like taking a spelling test by rote memory or by simply remembering that two plus two always equals four. Truth that is foundational is also comprehensive, meaning it takes time and experience to grasp and internalize it. It has many implications for our lives and many applications in our lives. We really never stop getting to know and understand the truth.

LIVE THE TRUTH

This is what gives credibility to our Christianity. It is the heart of integrity for Christians: this **truth, which lives in us and will be with us forever.**

As was mentioned earlier, it is one thing to comprehend the truth; it is something else to live like we really embrace and believe in that truth. This is why John keeps attaching behavior to belief (1 John 3:23–24).

"The Gap" theory focuses on the gap that exists between what we say we believe and how we believe, which becomes either confirmation or contradiction of our stated beliefs. John is passionate about Christians closing the gap. First John 2:4 launches the attack on the gap. It continues in 1 John 2:9 and builds to a crescendo in 1 John 3:18, "Dear children, let us not love with words or tongue, but with actions and in truth." This, John writes, is what allows us a clear conscience and gives integrity to our witness. God reveals himself in Jesus *through* truth and love (John 1:14, 17), leading believers *into* truth and love. It is as Christians grow in truth and love that they go on to experience the fullness of God's blessing.[4]

Verse 3, which begins **Grace, mercy and peace from God the Father** contains several terms that are more reminiscent of Paul than John (1 Tim. 1:2; 2 Tim. 1:2). John rarely mentions grace, and this is the only time he refers to mercy; however, John does occasionally write about the theme of peace (John 14:27; 16:33).

Barclay notes that when the apostles Paul, Peter, or Jude refer to some combination of grace, mercy, and peace, they are doing so in the form of a hope or a prayer. John, however, states that these three blessings will be with us.[5] He is confident that God bestows these great gifts upon us—that they are truly gifts from God, not things we can earn. However, they can only be **with us in truth and love**.

> ## GREAT THEMES
>
> ### LIVING LETTERS
>
> Our lives are living letters "read" by others. They speak volumes as people watch and listen. The content needs to reflect what we claim to believe as Christians. Too often the gap between our profession of faith and our practice of the faith is huge—so wide that our witness for Christ has little credibility. Second Corinthians 3:3 says, "You show that you are a letter from Christ, the result of our ministry, written not with ink but with the Spirit of the living God. . . ."

There is power in Christian truth and in Christian love. It is the love demonstrated by **Jesus Christ, the Father's son**. Christ's love endures; it always seeks the highest good of the one being loved. It is a dedicated, disciplined, and determined love. It is the love to which we aspire.

2. THE CHRISTIAN WALK: TRUTH, OBEDIENCE, AND LOVE 4–6

John has capitalized on the phrase *walking in* certain aspects of Christian life. In 1 John, he calls us to walk in the light (1 John 1:7), which indicates that some are walking in the darkness (1 John 1:6). He then says that believers "must walk as Jesus did" (1 John 2:6).

In 2 John 4–6, he adds three more walking exercises for a follower of Christ.

WALK IN THE TRUTH

In verse 4 John says that he experienced **great joy to find some of** [the chosen lady's] **children walking in the truth.** To walk in something refers to lifestyle or behavior, to the principles and practices by which we

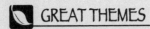

GREAT THEMES

TAKE A WALK

John's use of the term *walk* is so practical. He is referring to our lifestyle or behavior. If we walk in mud and dirt, we get soiled. If we walk through fire, we get burned. If we walk in the rain, we will get wet. John challenges us to walk in the light (1 John 1:7) and in the truth. In so doing, we are covered with the truth. Then truth is what people get when they are touched by our lives. Truth has the power to liberate us and those who are influenced by the truth. God's truth is transforming. Our daily lives might not always seem to be making an impact; however, over time and through circumstances, people see how we live and talk. They will observe how we react to the ups and downs of life. Our walk is our witness!

live. The essence of the gospel teachings comprises "the truth." He then repeats a common theme in his writings by calling them to obey the command that is not new, but an old one that they have had **from the beginning**—the command to love.

WALK IN OBEDIENCE

The specific obedience required is **to** [God's] **commands.** Even the word "obey" strikes some of us negatively. Many children grow up with parents who are harsh and demanding. When these children grow up, they respond to religion in one of two ways: they either react strongly against any religion that requires obedience, or they look for a demanding style of religion because it's what they know from their home life. It is actually a "comfort zone" for them.

Others come from homes and families that were light on expectations and obedience. Once again, their reaction can be one of resistance and repulsion or one of welcome oversight.

The great news is that God's commands are always safe and good to obey because they issue from His love for us. The essence of every commandment of God is incredibly healthy for us to follow.

WALK IN LOVE

Notice the way John connects the amazing relationship between love, obedience, and commands: **And this is love: that we walk in obedience to his commands** (v. 6). Then he writes that **his command is that** [we] **walk in love**. It all begins—and ends—with love. Everything God calls us to be and do orbits around His love for us and His desire that we love Him and love one another. First John 3:23–24 lays out the core belief and behavior of Christians: correct belief about Christ plus correct attitude and behavior toward one another.

 WHAT OTHERS SAY

It [is] well you should be thoroughly sensible of this, "The heaven of heavens is love." There is nothing higher in religion; there is, in effect, nothing else; if you look for anything more than love, you are looking wide of the mark, you are getting out of the royal way, and when you are asking others, "Have you received this or that blessing?" if you mean anything but more love, you mean wrong; you are leading them out of the way, and putting them upon a false scent. Settle it then in your heart, that from the moment God has saved you from all sin, you are to aim at nothing more, but more of that love described in the thirteenth of the Corinthians. You can go no higher than this, till you are carried into Abraham's bosom.

—John Wesley

The very heart of John Wesley's theology was holiness driven by love. Purity of intention and action is paramount in Wesleyan theology.

3. VIRTUES THAT SAFEGUARD VICTORY 7–11

Now we arrive at the concern John bears for the church and the families he is addressing in this letter. The false teachers had departed from early orthodoxy (1 John 2:19), but they were apparently getting into the believers' fellowships and striking at close range those who would offer them hospitality.

John warns the believers that **the deceivers . . . and the antichrist** do **not acknowledge Jesus Christ as coming in the flesh** (v. 7). This deception seems as though it comes from some of the Gnostic teachings, especially those of Cerinthus (see the Introduction of 1 John).

John's battle for the purity of the faith is a strategic one. It appears that various heresies were now gaining influence, and John is the remaining link directly to Christ. Therefore, no one else could write with the credibility or the authority of the apostle John. So, John delineates virtues for Christian victory to the chosen lady and her children, as well as to us and our children.

DISCERNMENT

John warns us that we should be alert to the variations of the truth once delivered to the Church—especially heretical teachings about Jesus Christ (v. 7). The incarnation of Christ is essential Christian truth.

DISCIPLINE

John also warns that we should be care that we **do not lose what** [we] **have worked for**, so we will be able to **be rewarded fully.** He says to be careful not to run ahead and to continue in the teaching of Christ (v. 9). Some tried to detach Jesus from God, therefore denying Christ's relationship with the Father and denying Christ of His divine nature.

DENIAL

There is a time to deny hospitality and fellowship. When heresy is being advocated, John does not recommend taking the "enemy of truth" into our own homes and churches. Rather, he says, **do not take him into your house or welcome him** (v. 10). Anyone who makes such a mistake in the name of kindness or hospitality **shares in his wicked work** (v. 11). He says we become an accomplice in evil. We should never let falsehood enter our homes.

4. FACE TO FACE 12–13

Having challenged his readers with the way to walk in Christ, and after warning them against receiving false teachers, he then pens, **I have much to write to you**, but that he prefers to talk to them in person—**face to face** (v. 12). Why? He tells them.

ANTICIPATION OF FELLOWSHIP

Both Paul and John placed incredible value on being with their students and partners in the faith. The times of worship, study, counsel, and enjoying friendships were priceless to them. Times of fellowship in our churches are often fun times, but may lack depth. This is not a criticism; it is hard for any of us to get into a deep conversation at the typical church supper or party. The fact is depth of conversation requires a format and intention that is conducive to meaningful study, sharing, learning, and worship.

GREAT THEMES

THE BIG IDEA OF SMALL GROUPS

Jesus launched His ministry on earth with what we would call a small group. Such a group is able to develop accountability, intimacy, bonds of respect, and has the opportunity for accelerated learning. In every field of endeavor, the use of groups has proven effective in problem solving, conflict resolution, learning, and bonding of all kinds. John Wesley's great genius, according to many scholars today, was his ability to mobilize groups for the sake of discipleship development. The Church today would do well to consider how to mobilize groups for the sake of accomplishing our mission.

FULLNESS OF JOY

Once again the concept of completion enters John's letter as he states he desires that his **joy be complete** (v. 12). This time, however, it does not relate to perfection, but experience. It is the difference of two loved ones standing on opposite sides of a glass door with hands and faces touching the glass, only a fourth of an inch away from one another, separated by so little distance—able to perfectly see one another—but oh, so far away when compared to physical touch. Writing is fine, but face-to-face is so much better.

THE CHILDREN SAY "HI"

To conclude his letter, John writes, **The children of your chosen sister send their greetings** (v. 13) **The children of your chosen sister** (v. 13) is a strange phrase. The fact that it is the children who send their greetings would tend to confirm the interpretation that the "chosen lady" is a local congregation and the "sister" is another local church and its constituents.[6]

The example of one church helping another sets a good pattern for Christians today. Christians need to help one another live the Christian life with integrity, compassion, and discipline.

John loved the members of Christ's church. He blessed them by his letter of concern and instruction. Thank God for those who mentor and coach us toward spiritual health and stability. Interdependence is a value that needs to be fostered among Christians everywhere. We must help one other learn faith and practice love. At times, self-protection is in order. Ultimately, we must develop and sustain a strong witness to those still outside of the faith.

ENDNOTES

1. Warren W. Wiersbe, *Be Real*, New Testament BE Book Series (Wheaton: Victor Books, 1972), p. 102.

2. Marvin R. Vincent, D.D., *Word Studies in the New Testament,* vol. II (Grand Rapids: William B. Eerdmans Publishing Company, 1946), p. 392.

3. Vincent, *Word Studies in the New Testament,* p. 392.

4. I. Howard Marshall, *The Epistles of John,* The New International Commentary on the New Testament (Grand Rapids: William B. Eerdmans Publishing Company, 1978), p. 64.

5. William Barclay, *The Letters of St. John and Jude* (Philadelphia: The Westminster Press, 1958), p. 163.

6. David Jackman, *The Message of John's Letters,* The Bible Speaks Series (Downers Grove: InterVarsity Press, 1988), p. 187.

OUTLINE OF 3 JOHN

It's All about Truth (3 John)

   I. **The Elder: Friend and Coach (1–2)**

  II. **Gaius: The Man in the Middle (3–8)**

 III. **Diotrephes: The Church Boss (9–10)**

 IV. **Demetrius: The Man at the Door (11–12)**

  V. **Conclusion (13–14)**

2

IT'S ALL ABOUT TRUTH

3 John 1–14

This brief letter is fascinating for anyone interested in the dynamics of a local congregation. The issue is in part about hospitality, as is the case in John's second letter, but the elder gives the opposite advice of that which he gave in the second letter. This situation involves different people who are in need of hospitality. There is also internal disagreement in the congregation, including a dominating person among them who disagrees with the apostle.

Is this third letter written to an individual in the same congregation that "the chosen lady" represents? And, might it have been written on the same day?[1] That is fairly speculative but possible. Both letters are brief, and both address the issue of hospitality. They could have been written the same day, but likely were not. John says, **I wrote to the church** (v. 9), which suggests that it was not written on the same day, but possibly to the same church. However, the problems addressed as well as the different individuals referenced imply that John was writing to two separate groups of people.

What is clear is that John had concern that the believers show discernment when it came to inviting theological enemies into their homes and gatherings. In this third letter, he encouraged the church to extend hospitality to those who were also believers, even if they were strangers.

There is a power struggle and a controversy in progress involving John, the elder; Gaius, the recipient of the letter; Diotrephes, the church boss; and Demetrius, the traveler waiting for an answer. We will use the principle persons involved as a way of organizing this study.

1. THE ELDER: FRIEND AND COACH 1-2

The author simply begins, **The elder** (v. 1). We would assume that this is the same person who penned the second letter. The title, language, and subject matter all suggest the author of the one authored the other as well, who we believe is John the apostle. He addresses Gaius as **my dear friend.** The Greek word *agapeos* could be translated as beloved or my beloved friend. The same term is used four times in this letter (vv. 1, 2, 5, 11). He adds to the warm greeting the phrase **whom I love in the truth** (v. 2). Even though the definite article is not in the original manuscripts, the phrase has the force of "the truth of God in Christ," rather than the much weaker "whom I really love." John and Gaius's bond of love was intricately tied to Christ and the gospel message.[2]

Clearly, John is serving as Gaius's mentor, coach, and encourager. He offers more than encouragement. He prays for three wonderful things in Gaius' life that are a model for us all.

He prays for his physical well-being. Specifically, he prays, **that you may enjoy good health.** Before we make "health" comments, it is worth noting that one may have good health, but fail to respect and enjoy that good health. We would be well advised to consciously appreciate the health we have, give God thanks for it, and seek to sustain it and use it for good.

 WHAT OTHERS ARE SAYING

In the early Church the Christian home was, as it should be now, the place of the open door and the loving welcome. There can be few nobler works than to give a stranger the right of entry to a Christian home. The family circle should always be wide enough to have a place for the stranger, no matter where he comes from and no matter what his colour may be.

— William Barclay

John prays for positive life circumstances. Life is complicated. It is now, and it was back then. John is showing great balance in his friendship with Gaius. He is letting him know that the church concerns are not his only concerns as they relate to Gaius. All believers need to be careful about expectations that lead to unhealthy over-commitment. The same advice is good for those in full-time ministry. We must establish balance in our lives that allows us to attend to body, mind, soul, and relationships of value, so that **all may go well with** [us].

John prays for his friend's soul. John says it in a way as to suggest that throughout life's issues, we need to determine whether our **soul is getting along well.** The term *soul* is sometimes used interchangeably with *spirit*. The Greeks had two words: *pnuema,* which is translated *spirit*, and *psuche,* which is usually translated *soul*. Basically, it seems that *soul* refers to the "aliveness" of any creature, even an animal. The *spirit* refers to a unique capacity for God. In the Church, however, the term *soul* has often been used for that part of us that is our "God connection." However one distinguishes between soul and spirit, we can say that John's concern is for the inner being of Gaius, in all of its functions related to mind, emotion, will, and faith.

2. GAIUS: THE MAN IN THE MIDDLE 3–8

John continues his comments to Gaius with more encouragement. He writes, **It gave me great joy to have some brothers come and tell about your faithfulness to the truth and how you continue to walk in the truth** (v. 3). Once again, as in the second letter, John highlights the truth in these opening lines. He is all about sound teaching and protecting the people from heresy. He lauds his friend for faithfulness in belief and faithfulness in the practice of the faith. This balance of faith and practice has been the steady theme in all three letters.

Verse 4 is such a tender and universal expression of a parent, spiritually and otherwise. John writes, **I have no greater joy than to hear that my children are walking in the truth.** The love of parents causes them to desire that their children have it better than they. They want them to excel in every way. It causes grief and pain to see their children struggle and suffer, while it brings sheer delight to see them succeed and thrive. Christian parents feel that way about the faith and spiritual health of their children. Pastors feel that way about their parishioners and those whom they have led toward Christ. Teachers often feel that way about their pupils. Coaches feel that way about those on their teams. Maybe every Christian would do well to consider a handful of "younger" Christians in the congregation as their "children" in the faith.

LIFE CHANGE

LEAVE A LEGACY

Most people want to leave something behind that allows their influence to continue. We begin to wonder what it is that will remain of our lives and efforts after we are gone. Besides whatever else we leave behind, Christians want to leave a legacy of faith and integrity, an example of how to live life in faith and love. We want others to be inspired by our lives, thereby helping them be inspired to live lives of faith and holiness in Christ. May all who come behind us find us faithful!

Verses 5–8 get to the central point of extending hospitality. Again, the warmth and respect for Gaius shows as John writes, **Dear friend, you are faithful in what you are doing for the brothers, even though they are strangers to you** (v. 5). Gaius apparently had a heart and willingness to reach out to the visiting strangers who apparently were friends of John. They were probably some of the itinerant teachers who had to rely on the support of the churches to which they ministered.

The strangers were certainly positive about Gaius. John says, **They have told the church about your love** (v. 6). He was apparently a man with a great heart and practical compassion. We cannot be sure exactly what Gaius' role was in the early Church. He may have been a leading layperson. He may have had some ecclesiastical position. We do not know for sure. Whatever Gaius' role, John gives him advice very different from that which he gave to "the chosen lady" in the second letter. He tells Gaius that he would **do well to send them on their way in a manner worthy of God.** This is a strong encouragement to treat these folks with godly kindness and grace.

This letter is the only one in the New Testament not to mention the name of Christ directly.[3] However, John says that the visiting teachers did their work **for the sake of the Name** (v. 7). To whom does "the Name" refer? The NIV is very close to the direct Greek phrase, and we find a similar usage in Acts 5:41. "The apostles left the Sanhedrin, rejoicing because they had been counted worthy of suffering disgrace for the

Name." The context of that passage is the opposition the apostles were receiving for speaking in Jesus' name. On other occasions (Acts 4:12; Phil. 2:9–10), similar use is made of "the name." The Name is Jesus.

Those traveling evangelists, teachers, and missionaries were apparently dependent only on the Church since **they went out, receiving no help from the pagans.** Since their mission was honorable, and they were men of integrity to the truth, John wanted Gaius to be sure that there

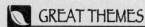

GREAT THEMES

HOSPITALITY

The Didache, the first-century Church manual to which reference was made in the introduction to the Second Epistle, shows that early Christian hospitality was sometimes abused. Instructions are given that an "apostle" may not stay beyond one day or, "in case of necessity," two. "If he stays three days, he is a false prophet" (xi. 5). On departing, he may receive enough food to last him his journey. But "if he asks for money, he is a false prophet" (xi. 6). Again, if a prophet, apparently speaking under the inspiration of the Spirit, says "give me money, or something else," he is not to be heeded unless the money is "for others in need" (xi. 12). It is recognized that true prophets have a right to stay and be supported (13), but an ordinary Christian traveler must not be entertained free for more than two or three days (xii. 2). If he wants to settle, "he must work for his living . . . If he refuses to do this, he is treading on Christ" (xii. 3–5).

would be those who would **show hospitality to such men so that they may work together for the truth** (v. 8).

3. DIOTREPHES: THE CHURCH BOSS 9–10

Now, we come to the "roadblock" to congregational hospitality. His name is Diotrephes, and he was a serious irritation to John and apparently many in the local congregation. John says that he **wrote to the church** (v. 9) apparently the one where Gaius, Diotrephes, and others were involved together. Again, we do not know if this man had any official position in the church or was simply a layperson agitated over the hospitality issue. However, John gives us a clearer picture of what he was like.

Diotrephes loved to be first. Other translations use term like "being in charge," "in control," or "being leader." In every group, there are those who are comfortable to lead if needed, those who are glad to follow, those who refuse to follow, and those who lead without being asked. Diotrephes qualified for two of those statements. There are those in our homes, places of work, places of recreation, and our churches who seem to have a need to resist otherwise respected leadership and establish themselves as a more noble authority. They are normally people of "truth" but lack grace. They are those half-done Christians who cause the rest of the folks to grow in courage and grace or to get out.

Diotrephes rejected established church leadership. John says that the man not only **loves to be first,** but he also **will have nothing to do with us.** He was overtly resisting the established leadership of the elder, John. It is unclear whether or not the whole congregation was under the thumb of Diotrephes, but at least he refused to recognize the appeals of John regarding the hospitality issue.

Diotrephes was engaged in malicious gossip. John says that if and when he came he would **call attention to what he is doing, gossiping maliciously about us** (v. 10). The Greek words for this gossip have the meaning of "babbling incoherently or verbally fluent, but empty."[4] This must have frustrated John, as it does any of us when we become aware that others are talking about us in ways that are demeaning, distorted, and disgraceful. If there are three dominant forms of temptation and sin that cripple the work of any church, they are lust, envy, and gossip. Especially when people engage in gossip, each and every one needs to be lovingly and firmly challenged by church leadership as well as their peers.

Diotrephes refused to welcome the guest missionaries. What more can be said, but that the man loved his local power base and was not about to yield it to anyone? It is even possible that this man was the ruling deacon of the congregation. Whoever he was, he alienated anyone who threatened his place of dominance among the people. In congregations like this, they rarely grow beyond a few dozen people because even outsiders can figure out the church politics fairly quickly, so they run for the next church or simply stay home.

Diotrephes put people who opposed his views out of the church. This is what makes us wonder if he had some kind of official authority. It sounds, however, as though it was a single-handed authority. We don't know a lot about him, but we do know he was an intimidator. Are we being unfair with him? Possibly. It is quite possible that his intentions were much better than it appears. And it is always good to extend grace when it comes to our reactions and responses.

The situation with Diotrephes is an excellent case for the value of accountability systems within the church and even beyond a local congregation. History has clearly demonstrated that individuals can gain a power base in a congregation and, once gained, can control that group and inevitably put severe limits on its ministry capacity. When church systems of accountability are working well, they are well worth having.

The situation with Diotrephes also serves as a warning to all of us. To some degree, most of us love attention and praise. We would rather be first than second. We would rather win than lose. So, in fact, the problems of pride, power, and preeminence can be an issue for each of us to face and address. We should each ask ourselves, "How are such flaws hindering my holiness, my relationships, and my usefulness to Christ?"

4. DEMETRIUS: THE MAN AT THE DOOR 11–14

John begins this portion with the kindly address, **Dear friend**, then makes a statement reminiscent of the first letter (1 John 3:7, 10) when he says, **do not imitate what is evil but what is good. Anyone who does what is good is from God. Anyone who does what is evil has not seen God** (v. 11). John is once again severe when it comes to walking our Christian talk. There are many arguments about the security of the Christian who continues to sin. However, nobody quotes John for such doctrine. John is clear: doing wrong violates one's connection with God. That alone is enough reason to quickly address sin with confession and the cleansing blood of Christ. Jesus came to defeat the works and the power of Satan, manifested by sin in our lives. We are called to walk in the light of God's truth and love, ceasing a lifestyle of sin.

John quotes Jesus as saying, "Those who have done good will rise to live, and those who have done evil will rise to be condemned" (John 5:29). Jesus is the just judge. He knows a person's heart and desire to obey Him or to refuse Him. Jesus admonished us not to play God by judging others (Matt. 7:1–5). God sees and knows what nobody else can. On my worst days, I would still rather face God than people when it comes to my eternal destiny. The sovereignty of God is our greatest security. His judgments are right and true (Ps. 19:9). All of that said, we must remember that John's purpose for writing is so that we "will not sin" (1 John 2:1).

So, who is this Demetrius, who **is well spoken of by everyone—and even by the truth itself** (v. 12)? Is he another leader in the congregation? Is he one of the traveling teachers or missionaries who needs a place to stay? We cannot know for sure, but it seems most likely that he is among those to whom John is urging Gaius to show hospitality. He is safe and good. John speaks **well of him** and reassures Gaius, **you know that our testimony is true.**

Many churches seem to have a Diotrephes; every church needs a Gaius; and every church needs to cultivate as many like Demetrius as possible.

Again, John, the elder, has more to say. He did also in his much longer Gospel (John 21:25). However, he would rather say it to them personally. Secondhand conversation can often become second-rate communication. He wants to personally say what is on his mind and heart. In spite of all that is happening, or because of it, he seeks to bestow **peace to** [them] (v. 13). To conclude his letter, John writes, **The friends here send their greetings. Greet the friends there by name.** What a delightful touch to ask that Gaius greet the folks, for John, by name. Everyone feels a more personal touch when they are greeted by name. Our names are important to God. May the grace of God flow through our lives to a host of people— who all have names.

ENDNOTES

1. David Jackman, *The Message of John's Letters,* The Bible Speaks Series (Downers Grove: InterVarsity Press, 1988), p. 190.

2. Ibid., p. 191.

3. Ibid., p. 192.

4. Marvin R. Vincent, D.D., *Word Studies in the New Testament,* vol. II (Grand Rapids: William B. Eerdmans Publishing Company, 1946), p. 403.

JUDE

INTRODUCTION TO JUDE

Among the exciting aspects of the book of Jude, three stand out: the person who is the likely author of this brief epistle, the blistering description of evil frauds in the Church, and the concluding doxology. Except for the well-loved and brilliant doxology, this book is largely ignored in classrooms and pulpits. However, we will soon see that there is some powerful material to relate to contemporary seekers and saints.

There are several questions concerning this book that have kept scholars in discussion and fascination, including whether or not it even belongs in the biblical canon, which Jude is the author, why it is so similar to parts of 2 Peter, why Jude quotes from non-biblical sources, what the purpose of the epistle is, who the recipients are, and the date it was written.

AUTHORSHIP AND AUTHENTICITY

There seem to be five different people mentioned in the Bible named Jude or Judas (the names are used interchangeably). It is also reasonable to believe that a person could be a divinely inspired author of some portions of the Bible without his or her name being specifically mentioned there. Of the five men named Jude who are mentioned in the Bible (Mark 14:43; Luke 6:16; John 14:22; Acts 1:13; 9:11; 15:22, 27, 32), only two have been strongly considered as the author or this letter: (1) The apostle Jude, brother or son of James (Luke 6:16; Acts 1:13); (2) Jude the half-brother of Jesus and full brother of James (Matt. 13:55; Mark 6:3).

The main objections that some scholars make to Jude, the brother of Jesus and James, are as follows: He would have likely mentioned that he was the brother of Jesus, rather than, or in addition to, James. He likely spoke Aramaic, not Greek. As a Jew, he would not have been as tuned in to the fairly Hellenistic (Greek) Gnosticism. The book should have gained immediate entrance into the biblical canon if it was well known that Jesus' brother wrote it. There are actually no strong arguments in favor of Judas the apostle (not Iscariot). And, there is no indication whatsoever that he was the brother of a James, which would have been well-known.

Why say that he was the "servant" of Jesus, not brother? Well, Jesus' own half-brother James said the same thing in his book (James 1:1). They both sensed a deep humility about their relationship to Jesus and were so much in awe of His divine identity that they chose not to encroach on it by referencing their human connection with Him.

The weight of evidence, reason, and deduction favors Jude, the brother of James and half-brother of Jesus, as the author of this potent little epistle.

Jude struggled to gain acceptance into the canon of Holy Scripture because of the following reasons: the quotations from non-canonical books, such as Enoch and the Assumption of Moses, and its non-apostolic authorship.[1] The Muratorian Canon, which dates back to about A.D. 170, includes Jude while it omits Hebrews and 1 Peter. Eusebius of Caesarea, in the fourth century, indicated that there were those who disputed Jude's apostolic authorship.[2] However, he also cites those who say that relatives of one of the brothers of the Lord, Jude by name, lived until the reign of Trajan (A.D. 98–117), giving testimony of their faith in Christ.[3]

Debate continues over whether Jude was written as early as A.D. 65 or as late as A.D. 80–100. The issue at stake is whether 2 Peter quotes from Jude or vice-versa. More than 50 percent of the content of Jude strongly resembles some of the content of 2 Peter. John Wesley indicates Jude as the later writer, saying, "St. Peter cites and confirms St. Paul's writings, and is himself cited and confirmed by St. Jude"[4] It would seem that the enemies of the church that Jude wrote about had developed their belief system and had covertly begun to enter the churches. In addition, 2 Peter speaks predicatively (2:1–2), where Jude speaks in the present and past tense (v. 4) about the false prophets. This would suggest that Jude was written sometime after A.D. 65.

Jude makes reference (v. 17) to "what the apostles of our Lord Jesus Christ foretold." It sounds as if there are some years between the apostles and his readers. This would imply that if anyone was using the other's work, Jude was making reference to the material in 2 Peter. However, similarities notwithstanding, each writer gives a unique expression to the warnings offered. And both authors are quoting the same common Old Testament sources rather than one having written all the original examples and the other copying him. In fact, most of the common material is such because they each consulted the same source.

RECIPIENTS AND THEMES

The repeated use of **dear friends** gives the letter personal warmth. It is difficult to know how large a circle of friends Jude included. Verse 1 directs the letter **to those who have been called, who are loved by God the Father and kept by Jesus Christ.** That set of descriptions covered a lot of people then and still does.

Jude's original intention was to **write to** [them] **about the salvation** [they shared], but that purpose was trumped by a sense of urgency to warn them about immoral and heretical persons who had infiltrated the church fellowship. He wants them to defend and proclaim the faith as it was given and to be aware of the infiltrators and their danger. Jude warns them about falling away from the faith and into immorality. He also describes the nature of the offenders and challenges the people to build themselves up in the faith and pray in the Spirit for wisdom, discernment, and strength. He finally encourages them to grasp the awesome power of God to protect and deliver them into divine presence, liberated and grateful.

ENDNOTES

1. R. Duane Thompson, *Commentary on Jude,* vol. VI of *The Wesleyan Bible Commentary* (Grand Rapids: William B. Eerdmans Publishing Company, 1966), p. 386.

2. *Harper Study Bible, The Holy Bible, Revised Standard Version* (New York: Harper and Row Publishers, 1964), p. 1857.

3. Gerald Bray, ed. *Ancient Christian Commentary on Scripture,* vol. XI (Downers Grove: InterVarsity Press, 2000), p. 245.

4. John Wesley, *Romans–Revelation,* vol. II of *Wesley's Notes on the New Testament* (Grand Rapids: Baker Book House, 1981), p. 345.

OUTLINE OF JUDE

I. Avoid Them Like a Plague (1–16)

    A. A Servant Writes (1–2)

    B. We Have a Problem (3–4)

    C. Sad Lessons from History (5–7)

    D. More about the Enemy (8–11)

    E. More Pictures of Pathetic Lives (12–16)

II. Keep Yourselves in God's Love (17–25)

    A. How, Then, Shall We Live? (17–23)

    B. The Incomparable Deliverer (24–25)

AVOID THEM LIKE A PLAGUE

Jude 1–16

1. A SERVANT WRITES 1–2

The identity of the author of this letter, **Jude, a servant of Jesus Christ and a brother of James** (v. 1) may be one of its great values. He calls himself a "servant" of Jesus Christ rather than His brother. Why? Reverence and humility are the probable answers. Jude realized that his relationship with Jesus transcended the fraternal bond and was now an *eternal* bond in faith and obedience. What a witness for Jesus that His siblings came to grips with His true identity!

He writes **to those who have been called, who are loved by God the Father and kept by Jesus Christ** (v. 1). Those are three powerful verbs: *called, loved,* and *kept*. The *Interlinear Greek-English New Testament* has the original order of these words as *loved, kept,* and *called.*[1]

Being **loved by God the Father** is the heart of the gospel: God is love (1 John 4:16), and God so loved us that He gave us His Son (John 3:16). **And John writes,** "This is love: not that we loved God, but that he loved us and sent his Son as an atoning sacrifice for our sins" (1 John 4:10). That is the message that begins to draw the human mind and heart to God, and opens the way for life transformation.

Jude also writes that the recipients of his letter were kept by Jesus Christ. Each of the three verb forms, *loved, kept,* and *called* are in the passive form of Greek,[2] and therefore emphasize the active grace of God in our lives, along with the commitment and discipline expected of us. Jude mentions being kept on three occasions: in the first verse, verse 21, and then at the very end in verse 24. Two different Greek verbs are used for the three occasions, however. The Greek word for *kept* in verse 1 means steadfast care and nurture of something in one's possession. In verse 21, he instructs us to keep ourselves in God's love. The second Greek verb is used in verse 24 and means "to guard something or someone from attack and destruction."[3]

So Jude offers a great balance of God's care and protection as well as our responsibility to nurture and discipline ourselves in the grace and love of God. Once again, we understand the Christian faith as a mutual, though not equal, relationship between ourselves and God.

He writes **to those who have been called**. God's call is what gives us a place and purpose in life. He calls us to himself, to reconciliation, to holiness, and to service.

Jude then offers three gifts of grace when he says, **Mercy, peace and love be yours in abundance** (v. 2). God gives us some major breaks in His mercy. The Greek

---

 LIFE CHANGE

WHAT? ME CALLED?

Many in the Wesleyan tradition think of the term *called* as relating to people God calls to ministry as a vocation, which is indeed a unique calling. However, God calls us all in many ways for many reasons. A very basic study of Scripture reveals the following about being "called":

- Jesus called His disciples to follow Him (Matt. 4:18–20).
- Jesus said to all, "Come to me all you who are weary and burdened, and I will give you rest" (Matt. 11:28–30).
- We have a call to holy living (1 Thess. 4:7; 1 Pet. 1:15).
- We are challenged to live up to our calling as Christians (Eph. 4:1).
- We must make our calling sure, or secure (2 Pet. 1:10).
- We are called to imitate God and walk in love, like Christ (Eph. 5:1–2).
- God calls us to be living sacrifices (Rom. 12:1).
- We are called to walk in His steps (1 Pet. 2:21).

Yes, each of us has a set of lofty callings from God! Let us hold our heads high, and walk in the paths He has set before us.

word *eleos* refers to mercy, compassion, and pity.[4] God overlooks so much that deserves divine wrath. He longs for us to come to our senses and repent, finding forgiveness and transformation of life in Christ.

Peace is a key term in describing the kingdom of God. Several times, the Bible refers to "the God of peace" (Rom. 15:33; 16:20; 2 Cor. 13:11; Phil. 4:9; 1 Thess. 5:23; Heb. 13:20). We are called to peace with God through our Lord Jesus Christ (Rom. 5:1). Jesus said that in Him we can have peace (John 16:33), and the world cannot take it away. Jesus blesses the peacemakers (Matt. 5:9), and one part of the fruit of the Spirit is peace (Gal. 5:22). Then, we are called to a ministry of reconciliation in bringing peace and harmony to relationships (2 Cor. 5:16–20).

2. WE HAVE A PROBLEM 3-4

Initially, Jude had wanted to write a glowing letter about the glory of **the salvation we share** (v. 3). Such a message would have likely celebrated the availability of grace to all, not only the elite who had special knowledge, as Gnosticism taught. But something has come to Jude's attention. There was a problem, a big problem: **For certain men whose condemnation was written about long ago** [had] **secretly slipped in among** [them] (v. 4). This sounds a great deal like the warning Peter gave his readers (2 Pet. 2:1–3). Because of these seducers, there is now a new priority—that he urge them **to contend for the faith that was once for all entrusted to the saints.** Not unlike the concerns John had in his letters, there were immoral and heretical infiltrators whose goal was apparently to corrupt the Church in faith and practice.

The phrase **the faith that was once for all** is loaded with meaning. It has a historical reference and future implications that are for those yet to come. The faith is an unchanging—yet unfolding—set of truths and is good for all who will give it ear, mind, and heart. No other body of truth need be given.[5] The following are important views of the faith that Christians hold.

THIS FAITH WAS REVEALED, NOT IMAGINED

Human minds did not manufacture the truths of the gospel. They were revelation before they were tradition. They are revealed by God through

Jesus Christ, the living Word of God, and they were inspired for the written Word by the Holy Spirit of God.

THIS FAITH IS TRUSTWORTHY, DURABLE, AND ENDURING

It was delivered once, for all. It deserves to be believed, lived, and passed along to others. Even more impressive is the way God's truth and Word continue to expand in their implications, guidance, and wisdom for successive generations to apply to contemporary issues.

THIS FAITH IS WORTH PROCLAIMING AND DEFENDING

The apostle Paul said as much in Philippians 1:7. There will always be obstacles *to* the faith, enemies *of* the faith, and distractions *from* the faith. It is a non-stop vigil to maintain purity of doctrine when it comes to the gospel of Jesus Christ.

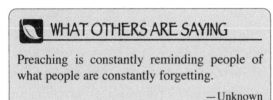

WHAT OTHERS ARE SAYING

Preaching is constantly reminding people of what people are constantly forgetting.

—Unknown

What was the nature of those described by Jude's scathing words? **They are godless men, who change the grace of our God into a license for immorality and deny Jesus Christ our only Sovereign and Lord** (v. 4). That constitutes a lot of trouble for the Church.

They were godless because of their doctrinal and moral corruption. It is very possible that they had bought into the dualism of Gnosticism (see Introduction to 1 John). In that system, material things are inherently evil and God does not inhabit them—or us. Since the body is corrupt, it makes little difference how or for what we use it. Such beliefs separated one's spiritual condition from human behavior. In other words, they sometimes endorsed immorality and presumed that God's grace would simply cover for them. Many think that way, even today. Any of us can fall prey to rationalizing our pride or lust. The capacity to compartmentalize or rationalize why we do what we do is a dangerous human gift. Misused, it leads us on a path to moral, relational, and possibly eternal destruction.

The men Jude mentions in verse 4 were godless because they denied Jesus as the Christ. Again, this was a trait of heretical teachings of the day, to rationalize away either the full deity or the humanity of Jesus Christ, and therefore minimize the meaning of His birth, life, death, resurrection, and His lordship of the Church.

3. SAD LESSONS FROM HISTORY 5–7

Jude then sensitizes his readers, and especially the seducers, to the history of unbelief and rebellion by writing, **I want to remind you that the Lord delivered his people out of Egypt, but later destroyed those who did not believe** (v. 5). God's mercy and deliverance in the past does not release us from future accountability (Num. 13, 14, 32). As John Wesley stated,"Let none therefore presume upon past mercies, as if he was now out of danger."[6] Therefore, contend for the faith.

Jude reviews several stories that were familiar to the Jews among the readers and instructive to the Gentile believers. God delivered the Israelites from slavery and the wrath of the Egyptians. It was an enormous display of God's power and protection. He provided them with a new place to live, a land with immense promise. But they were all afraid to enter the land God had provided because of the obstacles and their fear of its notorious inhabitants. Their fear overcame their faith, in the very shadow of God's miraculous deliverance from their longtime captors. Because of their unbelief, in spite of overwhelming evidence that deserved their faith, many of them died in the wilderness. Even though the people knew the story, Jude retold it. As believers, we often need to be reminded of stories like these.

WE NEED TO BE REMINDED OF TRUTH WE CONSTANTLY FORGET

That is the nature of people; we know that there is a better way to speak, think, act, and react, but how easy it is to forget and return to old attitudes and ways! That is why one of the main tasks of preaching and teaching is to constantly remind people of what people are constantly forgetting.

UNBELIEF IS DISASTROUS FOR ANY GENERATION

We are called to live by faith. John repeatedly told his readers to believe (1 John 3:23). Active faith is the primary part of our salvation at any level of spiritual development. We must be serious about teaching others to embrace the faith that was once delivered and to trust that it is still good and fresh.

THOSE BLESSED WITH GREAT PRIVILEGE HAVE GREAT RESPONSIBILITY

During His life on earth, Jesus said that to whom much was given, much would be required. The greater the opportunities, the greater the responsibility one has. Such was the case with the Israelites and their leaders. Joshua and Caleb passed the test; the others failed. Jude is probably even helping the seducers to realize that what they conceive as special and privilege comes with great accountability.

THE JUSTICE AND JUDGMENT OF GOD WILL NOT ALWAYS BE DELAYED

One of the frightening messages of this letter is that of the wrath and judgment of God. In our love of God's grace, and the grace that flows from God's love, we dare not forget that He is a God of justice, and all of us are finally accountable.

The second example Jude gives is about **the angels who did not keep their positions of authority but abandoned their own home** (v. 6). Barclay reminds us that the Jews had highly developed doctrines about angels. They even believed that every nation had its presiding angel.[7] Much is said about these views in the apocryphal book of Enoch, which Jude cites (vv. 14–15). There seem to be two storylines regarding these fallen angels.

First are the angels that fell due to their pride and rebellion. We have biblical traces of this story in Isaiah 14:12 and Luke 10:18. The second stream of teaching comes from Genesis 6:1–4. In this account, the angels were attracted to the women of earth. Female beauty drew them to come to earth, seduce the women, and sin against their purpose in life, against themselves, the women, the men, and God. The two deadly inclinations about which Jude is reminding us are pride and lust. Each of them can go from being a tendency and an inclination to a passion for rebellion against principles, people, and God. Eventually, they become our own worst enemy.

The fate of those angels, says Jude, was grim: **these he has kept in darkness, bound with everlasting chains for judgment on the great Day.** Once again, Jude's comments almost mirror those of 2 Peter 2:4.

The third example is that of Sodom and Gomorrah. These ancient cities were notorious for their sexual sins and became the object of obliteration by fire from God (Gen. 18, 19). Their sad example was fixated in the minds of the ancient Jews, for they made frequent reference to the occasion (Deut. 29:23; 32:32; Isa. 1:9; 3:9; 13:19; Jer. 23:14; 49:18; 50:40; Lam. 4:6; Ezek. 16:46, 49, 53, 55; Amos 4:11; Zeph. 2:9).

Jesus mentioned Sodom and Gomorrah in various ways (Matt. 10:15; 11:24; Luke 10:12; 17:29) along with other authors (Rom. 9:29; 2 Pet. 2:6; Rev. 11:8). Jude seems to be thinking of a particularly debasing situation when he says that **Sodom and Gomorrah and the surrounding towns gave themselves up to sexual immorality and perversion** (v. 7). The occasion likely indicated was the time the men of Sodom desired to commit homosexual rape against Lot's male visitors. Peter says of them, "With eyes full of adultery, they never stop sinning; they seduce the unstable; they are experts in greed—an accursed brood" (2 Pet. 2:14). Even today, the sin of "sodomy" is named after this infamous city.

These are dreadful examples **of those who suffer the punishment of eternal fire.** The particular Greek word for "suffering" is found only here in the New Testament. If this is an accurate description of hell, then we must beware and spare no effort to seek purity and avoid such consequences.

4. MORE ABOUT THE ENEMY 8–11

Jude is on a strong run in his description of the inside forces for evil. He calls them **these dreamers** (v. 8). The writer seems to be referring to Deuteronomy 13:1–5, which describes how to respond to "the prophet or the dreamer of dreams." These dreamers, whom he likens to the infiltrators, **pollute their own bodies, reject authority and slander celestial**

beings. There are many ways to pollute ourselves. Human nature inclines us to reject some kinds of authority, and even in casual conversation we can slander heavenly beings. It is not good enough for us to point a finger at others and say how rotten they are. We must each realize how near the edge of evil any of us could be at any given time. We must walk and talk carefully, not veering from walking in the light God gives us.

In verse 9, Jude cites an instance that is not from Scripture, but from a writing called the Assumption of Moses, an apocryphal book. This book claims that after Moses died, the archangel Michael was sent by God to claim the body. But the devil showed up and disputed Michael for the body, claiming that Moses was a murderer and that his body was evil (Gnosticism), so the devil should claim him. The angel won, but Jude's point seems to be that **even the archangel Michael, when he was disputing with the devil about the body of Moses, did not dare to bring a slanderous accusation against him, but said, "The Lord rebuke you!"** (v. 9). Apparently Jude's point is that if Michael did not even defame the devil, what right does any human have to slander an angel?

Jude then further details the behaviors of the invaders.

THEY SPEAK ABUSIVELY AGAINST WHATEVER THEY DO NOT UNDERSTAND

Once again, before we wag our finger at them, think about how easy it is for any of us to do the same thing—and many of us have. Almost anything will do: an idea, a style, research results, variations of theology or ritual, people of other races or cultures, even those from different experiential backgrounds from our own. All of these things are sometimes a mystery to us. And, what we do not understand, or are not comfortable with, we tend to criticize and prejudice ourselves against. May God help us be done with such attitudes and behaviors.

It is an amazing thing that Jesus was incredibly compassionate, candid, and forgiving to all manner of sinners. He got the most fired up and angry at the "holiness" folks of His day. He was upset because they had a form of religion and loved to show it off, but their heart for others was light years away from the heart of God. What can the Christians and the churches of today learn from this?

THEY FOLLOW THEIR INSTINCTS TO THEIR DESTRUCTION

Before we shake our heads once more about their degradation, consider your own human instincts that create problems for you, especially in relationships. Jude's words could refer to what we call addictions or base passions gone wild, or undisciplined. Self-discipline is heavily under-rated as a means toward spiritual health and wholeness.

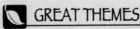

GREAT THEMES

LIFE IS OUT OF CONTROL

Control is a big issue in life. In most situations that involve conflict, whether in kindergarten, in war, or in the Church, the issue is *control*. Then, there are lives out of control. Self-discipline is a myth; self-centeredness is king. Jude gives us a rare and rugged insight into the real issues that many people deal with today. They have become imbedded in immorality, irreverence, and insubordination.

In the end, they have cultivated lives of immorality, irreverence, and insubordination.

Jude then cites a series of biblical characters whose lives were tragic examples of wayward living. We will study them in the order Jude mentions them.

THEY HAVE TAKEN THE WAY OF CAIN (GEN. 4:1–15)

Cain is mentioned in Scripture as the firstborn of Adam and Eve. One of the often-quoted lines from Cain is, "Am I my brother's keeper?" He asked that of God, shortly after murdering his brother over a worship issue.

The Genesis account indicates that something about Cain's behavior and his offerings to God were flawed, so God's favor was on Abel, but not Cain. The reaction by Cain was anger and resentment. God even warned Cain (Gen. 4:7) that sin was crouching nearby, ready to conquer him, and that he needed to deal with some issues. Cain ignored God's counsel and then continued in his way of disobedience, defiance, envy, anger, resentment, and then murder. Cain is the prototype and example of human nature unchecked. His self-absorption became more dominant a force in him than his fear of God or inclination to repent, even when conviction was brought about directly by God. May it never be said about us that we **have taken the way of Cain** (v. 11).

THEY HAVE RUSHED FOR PROFIT INTO BALAAM'S ERROR (NUM. 22–24; REV. 2:14)

Balaam was a prophet of Moab and apparently a true servant of God. He was approached by Balak, the king of Moab, for a favor. Numbers 22:6 would give us the impression that Balaam had been known as a powerful man of God with capacity to evoke blessing or curse on a people. He had a lofty spiritual profile, accentuated by his capacity to hear directly from God (Num. 22:8).

Balak, the king of Moab, saw that the hordes of Israelites had moved into his territory, and he was terrified that they would devour his kingdom. So he requested that Balaam pronounce a curse on the Israelites. Balaam was warned by God not to curse those whom He had blessed, so Balaam refused Balak's request. However, his mistake was to listen to subsequent and lucrative offers by Balak. Eventually, Baalam coached Balak how his people might seduce the Israelites to perform spiritual sacrilege and sexual immorality, therefore corrupting them and neutralizing them as a political threat.

One of the devastating lines uttered by Balak to Balaam is, "The LORD has kept you from being rewarded" (Num 24:11). This thought has likely been the seed planted in many minds, causing a person to wonder if God's will is what holds them back and hinders them rather than helping them. The truth is that what God wants for us is always what is best for us. His will is positive and liberating for us. His will leads to the continually expanded life, not the shrunken one. Balaam's error offers us warning that it is a deadly path to allow ourselves to keep entertaining temptation once God has empowered us to turn it down. Doing so is like trying to hug a coiled snake; we will get bit, and the poison may kill us. Beware not to rush **for profit into Balaam's error** (v. 11).

THEY HAVE BEEN DESTROYED IN KORAH'S REBELLION (NUM. 16:1–35)

Korah is the man who led a major rebellion of 250 high-level Israelite leaders against Moses and Aaron. The Lord was going to destroy the whole group of them, but Moses interceded for their lives. It would appear that Korah's intent was to overthrow Moses and become the new leader of Israel. The rebellion met, however, with a dramatic judgment. God told Moses to warn the people to put some space between themselves and the tents of the three primary rebels and their families. In an awesome display of vindication of Moses and Aaron—and judgment of Korah and all of his followers—the earth opened up and swallowed them all alive (Num. 16:31–34).

THERE ARE LESSONS TO BE LEARNED

These stories reveal the value God places on sacrificial worship by His people, the sanctity of the witness of His people, and the supporting of the work of His leaders. In each of the three cases just discussed, the transformational value of repentance was overlooked or ignored by Cain, Balaam, or Korah. Each had opportunity to review what they had done or were considering, make a change of mind and heart, and then move in a godly direction. None of them did. The lesson to us is the importance of being willing to exercise the grace of repentance as often as we need in order to allow God to continue to transform us into His likeness.

5. MORE PICTURES OF PATHETIC LIVES 12–16

Next Jude warns his readers by describing the polluting influence of the "certain men" (v. 4) on the Church's holy feasts, their self-serving nature, their empty promises, their hypocritical lives, their shameful lifestyle, and most importantly, their dire destiny. The consequential descriptions of all of these are **twice dead** (v. 12) and **for whom blackest darkness has been reserved forever** (v. 13). It seems that Jude is maxing out the "fear-threat" approach to reach the infiltrators—and anyone who is even remotely impressed or persuaded by them.

Again, Jude takes a quote from Enoch: **See, the Lord is coming with thousands upon thousands of his holy ones to judge everyone** (v. 14). He predicts that God will **convict all the ungodly of all the ungodly acts they have done in the ungodly way, and of all the harsh words ungodly sinners have spoken against him** (v. 15). It literally can wear you out to try to comprehend the nature of the problem.

After the horrifying judgment to be brought on these poor souls, it is alarming to read the next set of descriptions about them: **These men are grumblers and faultfinders; they follow their own evil desires; they boast about themselves and flatter others for their own advantage** (v. 16).

Read the list again. It is easy to join Jude in animosity toward these rascals; yet it is stunning to see this list and realize that if this describes the enemy, the enemy may sometimes be us. It is not that hard for the average Christian to identify struggles we have with some of those very temptations. In all of my years of reading this "smoking" letter, I have never allowed myself to realize how culpable I really was to some of the sins that Jude lists. But that is human nature; we project a lot of things on others when we are guilty of the very things for which we criticize and condemn them. May God help us to have the capacity that Jesus mentioned—to see the beam in our own eye (Matt. 7:1–5).

ENDNOTES

1. I. Howard Marshall, *The Epistles of John,* The New International Commentary on the New Testament (Grand Rapids: William B. Eerdmans Publishing Company, 1978), p. 951.

2. R. Duane Thompson, *Commentary on Jude*, vol. VI of *The Wesleyan Bible Commentary* (Grand Rapids: William B. Eerdmans Publishing Company, 1966), p. 389.

3. William F. Arndt, and F. William Gingrich, *A Greek-English Lexicon of the New Testament* (Chicago: The University of Chicago Press, 1957), p. 875.

4. Ibid., p. 249.

5. Marvin R. Vincent, D.D. *Word Studies in the New Testament,* vol. I (Grand Rapids: William B. Eerdmans Publishing Company, 1969), p. 712.

6. John Wesley, *Romans–Revelation*, vol. II of *Wesley's Notes on the New Testament* (Grand Rapids: Baker Book House, 1981), p. 59.

7. William Barclay, *Gospel of John,* vol. I (Philadelphia: The Westminster Press, 1956), p. 215.

2

KEEP YOURSELVES IN GOD'S LOVE

Jude 17–25

1. HOW, THEN, SHALL WE LIVE? 17–23

Jude gives one final warning about those who would influence his readers adversely. It is difficult to know who or what he is quoting when he says, **In the last times there will be scoffers who will follow their own ungodly desires** (v. 18). These warnings sound very similar to 1 Timothy 4:1–3 or 2 Peter 3:3. Since Jude has been writing about concepts that closely

reflect 2 Peter 2, perhaps Peter is his source for this prophecy as well. In the more than two thousand years since Jude penned his words, there continue to be numerous examples of such scoffers and **men who divide** [the Church], **who follow mere natural instincts and do not have the Spirit** (v. 19). Every generation of Christians seems to think that such a revelation is unique to

 GREAT THEMES

So You Want Justice?

Many of us wonder how God can stay in the background while so many people suffer the evil and carnage that is brought on by wicked people. This apparent lack of active engagement is what causes many to lose faith, or it keeps them from coming to faith in a good and powerful God. We tend to want justice, and it does not always help to say, "Payday someday." But, just think for a moment: What if God displayed justice on us each time we deserved it? Who would be left standing among us? We can be thankful, personally, for His grace, mercy, and patience. In time, justice will be served. In the meantime, grace is available.

their times. The implication may be that we have been in the last times for quite a while, and that the patience, grace, and mercy of God continue to favor us with opportunities to repent and walk in the light.

Jude strikes a contrast by mentioning some lifestyle disciplines of the believer who hopes to live with God forever. Please note the phrase *lifestyle disciplines*. The typical phrase among us is *spiritual disciplines*. We tend to limit those to prayer, reading Scripture, and fasting. Jude helps us expand the list. Notice that the first four he lists are about our relationship to the faith and the Father, Son, and Holy Spirit. The essence of the Holy Trinity is mentioned in these brief phrases. They give us insight into how we relate to all of God. The last three are about our actions toward other people, especially those who are struggling and in need. The following are seven disciplines of healthy Christians.

BUILD YOURSELVES UP IN YOUR MOST HOLY FAITH (V. 20)

A Christian's life is built on the truth of God and the truth from God. It is holy because it is a faith based on God's revelation to us, focused on Jesus Christ, God's Son, our Savior and Lord. We mature by studying the faith, learning to apply the faith, and by sharing the faith with others. It is also a holy faith because its goal is the transformation of those who believe (Matt. 5:48; Rom. 12:1–3; 2 Cor. 3:17–18; Eph. 3:14–21; Phil. 1:9–11; 1 Pet. 1:15; 2 Pet. 1:3–9; 3:18).

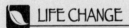 LIFE CHANGE

WHEN GOD PRAYS FOR US

The most amazing times of prayer are when we cannot say a thing, but the Holy Spirit says it for us! Read and rejoice over this truth from Romans 8:26–27: "In the same way, the Spirit helps us in our weakness. We do not know what we ought to pray for, but the Spirit himself intercedes for us with groans that words cannot express. And he who searches our hearts knows the mind of the Spirit, because the Spirit intercedes for the saints in accordance with God's will." Imagine it: God's Spirit praying for us when we cannot! What an awesome God!

PRAY IN THE HOLY SPIRIT (V. 20)

Jude is not interested in a person simply logging "prayer mileage." He wants us to pray with the help of the Holy

Spirit. To pray in the Spirit means that our prayers need to reflect more of the Holy Spirit than the human spirit, which tends to be self-serving. When we pray in the Spirit, we must be concerned about the things of the Spirit, such as we find mentioned in John 16:13–15, Romans 8:12–16, and Galatians 5:22–23.

KEEP YOURSELVES IN GOD'S LOVE (V. 21)

What Jude may be thinking about here is the old covenant relationship between God and His people as we read it in Exodus 24:1–8.[1] God's covenant had conditions, which mainly involved obedience to His will. John indicates that obeying God's commands to believe in Jesus the Christ and to love one another (1 John 3:23–24) shows that we love God. There is the discipline of keeping ourselves in God's love by walking in the light He has given us.

WAIT FOR THE MERCY OF OUR LORD JESUS CHRIST TO BRING YOU TO ETERNAL LIFE (V. 21)

It is possible that this point is a modifier of the discipline of keeping ourselves in God's love that the previous point discussed. However, patience is not only a virtue; it is more often a discipline with great value. God will fulfill His justice toward sin and His salvation will be completed for the saints. We must "occupy until he comes" (Luke 19:13). That does not just mean that we are just filling time and space. It implies danger, death, sacrifice, and discipline. It can involve fear and faith; it requires praying to God and networking and negotiating with people. To occupy can be a dangerous and exhausting task, wherever it is being done.

BE MERCIFUL TO THOSE WHO DOUBT (V. 22)

It is very easy to get impatient and cynical with doubters. After all, can't they just get with the program and start believing? Some can, but some cannot. Many complicating factors lead a person to doubt. The honest doubter deserves our patient mercy, as well as someone to reveal Christ to them in words and works.

SNATCH OTHERS FROM THE FIRE AND SAVE THEM (V. 23)

John Wesley was a young child when there was a consuming fire that struck the parsonage where his entire family lived. John called for help from the second floor. After heroic efforts, John was rescued and from that point on considered himself "a brand plucked from the burning" (Zech. 3:2). This event gave him a sense of God's providence in his life and produced a deep passion and sense of purpose. His personal deliverance from the flames led to a passion for others and their salvation.

When we help others come to faith in Christ, in a sense, we are snatching them from the fires of hell that would have been their eternal destiny.

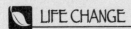 **LIFE CHANGE**

SEEING GOD

While a friend was traveling by train across the country at a particularly difficult time in his life, he made acquaintance with a custodian at a train station. During the conversation that ensued about life and its complications, the custodian offered a four-word piece of counsel, priceless in its wisdom and truth: "See God in everything." He was not suggesting that God causes everything, but that He can be found, ready to sustain and help, no matter what we're dealing with.

TO OTHERS SHOW MERCY, MIXED WITH FEAR (V. 23)

Mercy is intended to be an incentive to wake up and address the problem for which we are receiving mercy. That is why fear is appropriately mixed with mercy. We never want to take God's mercy for granted. It was on the basis of God's amazing mercies that Paul built his case for each of us to offer our bodies as living sacrifices (Rom. 12:1). Mercy emerges from grace, but it needs to result in repentance and transformation.

2. THE INCOMPARABLE DELIVERER 24–25

These two verses are probably the most often read and recognized in this book. Many people know little else about Jude. They are a truly magnificent pair of verses, among the most dynamically eloquent portrayals of God's nature and activity in the life of a believer.

He is the God **who is able** (v. 24). There are at least two other New Testament comments about God's ability to help us. Romans 16:25 says that God is able to establish us by the gospel and the proclamation of Jesus Christ. Ephesians 3:20–21 reminds us that God is able to do immeasurably more than we can ask or imagine, according to His power that is at work within us. And, here in Jude, He is the God who is able to **keep** [us] **from falling and to present** [us] **before his glorious presence without fault and with great joy**. These are all amazing statements. What do they tell us about God and His work within us?

HE IS THE GOD WHO CAN KEEP US STANDING

The phrase **keep you from falling** is graphic. It can refer to many kinds of falls: into sin, into despair, back into our old life, into pride, into self-deception, or into a sense of hopelessness. God knows when we need Him to keep us from falling. It helps, however, to be living close to Him in the first place. Such promises of deliverance are not given to those who are far away in faith. Only a sentence or two before verse 24, Jude says, "Keep yourselves in God's love as you wait for the mercy of our Lord Jesus Christ . . ."

HE IS THE GOD OF TRANSFORMING GRACE AND POWER

Here we see what Wesley saw, namely, the "optimism of grace." Rather than a God who is austere and has predetermined all things totally beyond our influence, we see a God who is able to work in our lives and make real changes. He who calls us to be holy is able to help us become holy.

HE IS THE GOD WHO DELIVERS US

He gives us real protection, real transformation, and real deliverance. That is because we serve an awesome God who has great affection for His creation and especially for His children on this earth. He is the only **God our Savior** (v. 25). The deliverance is **without fault and with great joy.** One can think of a lot of reasons why appearing before the presence of God, our final Judge, could leave us feeling great shame, guilt, fear, regret, sadness, or even hopelessness. But Jude indicates that it will be more like a celestial party. Possibly that great joy will be commingled with an immense sense of fulfillment, affirmation, and completion. We can only imagine.

Normally, the term "Savior" is reserved for Jesus Christ, at least from the New Testament perspective. However, this is not the only use of the phrase referring to God as Savior. In Luke 1:46–47, Mary, the mother of Jesus is worshiping, saying, "My soul glorifies the Lord, and my spirit rejoices in God my Savior . . ." The apostle Paul introduces his first letter to Timothy with "Paul, an apostle of Christ Jesus by the command of God our Savior and of Christ Jesus our hope." Twice more, in the same letter, Paul uses the phrase (2:3; 4:10). Again, the phrase is used three times in Paul's epistle to Titus (1:3; 2:10; 3:4).

What are we to make of this phrase? Is it not a phrase we deem reserved for Christ? Before the incarnation of God in Christ, God the Father was the repeated Deliverer and Savior of the Israelites. God has always been a Savior. He is our Savior in the being of Jesus the Christ, and our eternal salvation will also be at His command and because of His grace, mercy, and love.

Lift up your head and your heart, Christian. You faithfulness to Christ will gain you the ultimate deliverance by the ultimate Deliverer.

 GREAT THEMES

THREE GREAT BENEDICTIONS

Romans 16:25–27—Now to him who is able to establish you by my gospel and the proclamation of Jesus Christ, according to the revelation of the mystery hidden for long ages past, but now revealed and made known through the prophetic writings by the command of the eternal God, so that all nations might believe and obey him—to the only wise God be glory forever through Jesus Christ! Amen.

Ephesians 3:20–21—Now to him who is able to do immeasurably more than all we ask or imagine, according to his power that is at work within us, to him be glory in the church and in Christ Jesus throughout all generations, for ever and ever! Amen.

Jude 24–25—To him who is able to keep you from falling and to present you before his glorious presence without fault and with great joy—to the only God our Savior be glory, majesty, power and authority, through Jesus Christ our Lord, before all ages, now and forevermore! Amen.

Verse 25 continues its exaltation of the God who deserves to be celebrated and reverenced for His **glory, majesty, power and authority,** and it is all to be recognized **through Jesus Christ our Lord**, who bore the shame and was broken for our sins, and who became the perfect offering of sacrifice for our sins: yours, mine, and the whole world. May His name be praised.

We close the comments on Jude with a paraphrase of this glorious pair of verses, as a benediction:

From a people who are inclined to slip and fall, we offer praise and glory to God, who is able to keep us on our feet. From a people who experience pain and failure and the shame of sin, we exalt God who will deliver us innocent and with exceeding great joy. From a people who desperately need deliverance, we honor and worship the God who redeems and protects, empowers us and makes us ultimate winners, through Jesus Christ our Lord—from every yesterday, even today, and every tomorrow into eternity. Oh, Yes.

ENDNOTES

1. William Barclay, *The Letters of St. John and Jude* (Philadelphia: The Westminster Press, 1958), p. 241.

SELECT BIBLIOGRAPHY
For 1–3 John, Jude

Arndt, William F. and Gingrich, F. William. *A Greek-English Lexicon of the New Testament*. Chicago: The University of Chicago Press, 1957.

Barclay, William. *A New Testament Wordbook*. New York: Harper and Brothers Publishing, 195–.

Barclay, William. *Gospel of John*. Vol. I. Philadelphia: The Westminster Press, 1956.

Barclay, William. *The Letters of St. John and Jude,* Philadelphia: The Westminster Press, 1958.

Bray, Gerald, ed. *Ancient Christian Commentary on Scripture*. Vol. XI. Downers Grove: InterVarsity Press, 2000.

Brooke, A. E., B.D. *Johannine Epistles*. International Critical Commentary. New York: Charles Scribner's Sons, 1912.

Bryant, Al. *The John Wesley Reader.* Waco: Word Books, 1983.

Bultmann, Rudolf. *The Johannine Epistles,* English Translation. Philadelphia: Fortress Press, 1973.

Cox, Leo G. *The Wesleyan Bible Commentary*. Vol. 6. Grand Rapids: William B. Eerdmans Publishing Company, 1966.

Dodd, C. H. *The Johannine Epistles*. New York: Harper and Brothers, 1946.

Dunning, H. Ray and Greathouse, William M. *An Introduction to Wesleyan Theology*. Kansas City: Beacon Hill Press, 1982.

Grider, J. Kenneth. *A Wesleyan Holiness Theology*. Kansas City: Beacon Hill Press, 1994.

Harper, Steve. *John Wesley's Message for Today*. Grand Rapids: Zondervan Publishing House, 1983.

Harper Study Bible. The Holy Bible, Revised Standard Version. Harper and Row Publishers, New York: 1964.

Houlden, James Leslie. *The Johannine Epistles*. Harper's New Testament Commentaries. New York, Evanston, San Francisco, London: Harper and Row Publishers, 1973.

Jackman, David. *The Message of John's Letters*. The Bible Speaks Series. Downers Grove: InterVarsity Press, 1988.

Lee, Luther, D.D. *Wesleyan Manual: A Defense of the Organization of the Wesleyan Methodist Connection*. Syracuse: Samuel Lee, Publisher, 1862.

Kohlenberger, John R. III, Gen. Ed., *The Contemporary Parallel New Testament*. Oxford: Oxford University Press, 1997.

Kyser, Robert. *I, II, II John*. Augsburg Commentary on the New Testament. Minneapolis: Augsburg Publishing House, 1986.

Marshall, Alfred. *The New International Version Interlinear Greek-English New Testament*. Grand Rapids: Zondervan Publishing House, 1976.

Marshall, I. Howard. *The Epistles of John*. The New International Commentary on the New Testament. Grand Rapids: William B. Eerdmans Publishing Company, 1978.

Martin, Dr. Ted E. *Beacon Bible Expositions*. Vol. 12. Kansas City: Beacon Hill Press, 1983.

Purkiser, W. T., *Exploring Christian Holiness*. Vol. 1. Kansas City: Beacon Hill Press, 1983.

Stott, J. R. W., M.A. *The Epistles of John*. Tyndale New Testament Commentaries Series. Grand Rapids: William B. Eerdmans Publishing Company, 1964.

The Hymnal for Worship and Celebration. Waco: Word Music, 1986.

Thompson, R. Duane. *Commentary on Jude*. Vol. VI of *The Wesleyan Bible Commentary*. Grand Rapids: William B. Eerdmans Publishing Company, 1966.

Turner, George Allen and Montey, Julius R. *The Gospel of John*. Grand Rapids: William B. Eerdmans Publishing Company, 1964

Vincent, Marvin R., D.D. *Word Studies in the New Testament*. Vol. I. Grand Rapids: William B. Eerdmans Publishing Company, 1969.

Vincent, Marvin R., D.D. *Word Studies in the New Testament.* Vol. II. Grand Rapids: William B. Eerdmans Publishing Company, 1946.

Wesley, John. *Romans–Revelation.* Vol. II of *Wesley's Notes on the New Testament.* Grand Rapids: Baker Book House, 1981.

Westcott, Brooks Foss, D.D. D.C.L. *The Epistles of St. John.* Tyndale New Testament Commentaries Series. Grand Rapids: William B. Eerdmans Publishing Company, 1950.

Wiersbe, Warren W. *Be Real.* New Testament BE Book Series. Wheaton: Victor Books, 1972.

Wiersbe, Warren W. *Be Alert.* New Testament BE Book Series. Wheaton: Victor Books, 1984.

Wiley, H. Orton and Culbertson, Paul T. *Introduction to Christian Theology.* Kansas City: Beacon Hill Press, 1963.

Wiliams, R. R. *The Cambridge Bible Commentary on the New English Bible.* Cambridge: Cambridge University Press, 1965.

Wynkoop, Mildred Bangs. *A Theology of Love.* Kansas City: Beacon Hill Press, 1961.